B

Law

Ann Doughty BA,
Ann Holmes BA, M Phil, Grad Dip
and David Kelly BA

Charles Letts & Co Ltd
London, Edinburgh and New York

First published 1989
by Charles Letts & Co Ltd
Diary House, Borough Road, London SE1 1DW

Text: © Ann Doughty, Ann Holmes and David Kelly 1989
Illustrations: © Charles Letts & Co Ltd 1989

British Library Cataloguing in Publication Data

Doughty, Anne.
  Business law.
  1. Great Britain. Commercial law.
  I. Title.   II. Holmes, Anne.   III. Kelly, David.
  344.106'7

ISBN 0 85097 851 3

Ann Doughty, Ann Holmes and David Kelly are all Senior Lecturers in Law at Staffordshire Polytechnic.

Ann Doughty has written numerous publications, some of which are based on her comparative studies of law and crime in England and Italy. She is a member of the Higher National Validating Body in Business Studies, and of the Higher National Review Body, of B/TEC.

Ann Holmes was previously one of Her Majesty's Inspectors of Factories, and her professional activities have included being a moderator for the ACCA and for the RSA.

David Kelly has been a Senior Lecturer for four years, prior to which he was engaged in research at Kent University. Together with Ann Doughty, he is Chief Examiner in Law for the Midland Examining Group.

© Acknowledgements
The authors and publisher are grateful to the following bodies for permission to use copyright material: Business and Technician Education Council (BTEC); Chartered Association of Certified Accountants (ACCA); Chartered Institute of Management Accountants (CIMA); Institute of Chartered Secretaries and Administrators (CIS); Institute of Legal Executives (ILE); Institute of Purchasing and Supply (IPS); Staffordshire Polytechnic.

Printed and bound in Great Britain by
Charles Letts (Scotland) Ltd

Contents

Introduction

This book has been written to assist undergraduates with the law components on Business Studies degree courses, and indeed any other undergraduates who study the law relating to business. It can be used by students on IPS, AAT, ACCA, CIMA and CIS courses, and it could be used as a resource for BTEC higher students. Nevertheless, we would advise students on any course to check the contents of the course syllabus against the contents of the book before using it.

The purpose of the book is to offer a useful aid to revision, but it could also be used as an introduction to topics supplemented by reading of specialist texts as indicated in this book. A student could use the book to summarize topics in a way that has been popular with students for generations, and in doing so could avoid the worrying and time consuming part of the process (i.e. making decisions about what it is important to note and to learn).

At the end of each chapter are given a number of questions of a type commonly experienced on the courses outlined. Most of these questions are taken from actual examination papers or courses. Outline answers are given to the questions, which should be expanded to fill out the details. These answers should not be considered definitive, but can be very helpful when preparing for examinations.

This text uses only round brackets to indicate dates associated with cases. The convention of using square brackets in particular circumstances was felt to be inappropriate for this book.

The authors regret the sexist overtones in the use of the pronoun 'he' throughout the text, rather than 'he or she'. The latter expression was rejected in order to make the text shorter and easier to read, but the authors would not like the reader to imply any disrespect to the female sex.

In certain cases, chapters are grouped together because they concern the same subject (e.g. chapters 4, 5 and 6 on contract law). Not all chapters in these groupings will have questions or lists of recommended reading, therefore; these will appear in one of the other chapters in the grouping.

The authors wish to express their thanks to the people who have helped compile this book. Thanks to Ann Cooper for typing the manuscript and to Jackie Pate for her assistance. It is also important to thank the staff of Charles Letts and their advisers for their invaluable comments, and our young but vociferous critics, Michael, James and Kate, who gave us encouragement.

Thanks are also due to the following bodies for their permission to reproduce examination questions:

The Chartered Association of Certified Accountants, the Institute of Legal Executives, the Chartered Institute of Management Accountants and Staffordshire Polytechnic. In addition, we would like to thank the Business and Technical Education Council, the Institute of Purchasing and the Institute of Marketing for permission to indicate their style of questions.

1 How to study and pass exams

1.1 How to use this book

There is no doubt that anyone who studies law as a major subject, or as part of a multidisciplinary course, needs to summarize the key points accumulated from lectures and text-books. The enormous amount of information available on each topic needs to be condensed to a manageable collection of points. The students of today frequently pose the question 'What do I have to learn?'. The answer to this will vary according to the course which is being studied, and the nature of the assessment. This book has been written as an appropriate summary, and points have been selected, primarily for the student of Business Studies courses, but also for students on professional or vocational courses. Because it is comprehensive in its coverage, it cannot deal with each topic in as much depth as a specialist text. In order to enable students to take advantage of such further reading, specialist texts are recommended at the end of each chapter.

Sample questions are provided at the end of each chapter. These are followed by summarized standard answers, so that the use of the information is clearly demonstrated in a variety of contexts. Students are strongly advised to attempt these questions, even briefly, or in full according to time available, before turning to the answers.

Brief summary points can be identified in the headings used for each topic. Business students on degree or professional courses may use these points as a checklist for revision for each topic, and a guide to points for consideration in problem questions. BTEC students too can use such headings as a reminder of issues to be considered in tackling a practical problem on such topics.

1.2 Method of working

Each legal topic is normally introduced to students by lecture or research materials. The student is expected to read further material, and solve problems in relation to the topic. At the end of this process, it is important to identify the key points of interest, and understand them in essence.

Normally, it is advisable for a student to spend a certain amount of time each week assimilating and summarizing the current topic. You may find it helpful to keep a card index summarizing or listing appropriate cases for a topic, or checklists of useful summary points. This book can provide such a checklist if time is short, but it is better to identify key points, and then compare and adjust the summary with this text to improve understanding.

There is no point in denying that students have passed examinations using just the summary process without reference to original cases, statutes, journals or research materials such as Hansard (Parliamentary reports) and White Papers. It is equally true, however, that such students would have improved their understanding of the topic and increased their grades if they had spent some time looking over source materials, especially on assignment topics and examination topics.

1.2.1 Looking at cases

Each legal case in a textbook is accompanied by a reference, which helps you to find the original case report, e.g. *Donoghue* v. *Stevenson* (1932), AC 562. Lawyers always read the 'v.' or 'versus' as 'against' or 'and'. Thus they would read the reference as 'Donoghue against Stevenson' or 'Donoghue and Stevenson', etc. The reference contains the year of the report, in this case 1932, the type of report, in this case AC means Appeal Court case, and the actual page number of the case, which here is 562.

Case Reports: most common abbreviations

Initials	Case reports
App. Cas.	Appeal Cases
AC	Appeal Cases
TLR	*Times* Law Reports
LT	*Law Times* Reports
WLR	Weekly Law Reports
All ER	All England Law Reports
Cr. App. R.	Criminal Appeal Reports
QB	Queen's Bench Division
KB	King's Bench Division

It is not necessary to read every case in the course, but it can be beneficial to look at a few important cases.

1.2.2 Dealing with cases

Many students find that legal cases are a worrying aspect of the study of law. All of us feel overwhelmed from time to time by the number and diversity of cases involved. There are far too many cases in a common law system for the human mind to digest. However, many of the cases have interesting stories to tell as well as significant points of law. It has already been suggested that card files can be used to summarize the material facts and important points of judgment. These can be used for recollection and revision at a later date.

It is sometimes useful to remember the approximate date of a case to put cases in sequence, or note a recent decision, but students are not asked to quote dates or case references from memory.

1.2.3 Use of journals

There are several journals containing useful, up-to-date articles on particular legal topics. Some of the most helpful publications for students are the *New Law Journal*, the *Law Society Gazette*, the *Law Quarterly Review*, and the *Modern Law Review*.

1.2.4 Reference to statutes

Original statutes are available in law libraries, to check the wording or context of a piece of legislation. Such statutes are quite commonly used in examinations. It is wise to check at an early stage whether statutes will be used in the examination room. If statutes are made available in the examination, you should spend more time and effort familiarizing yourself with the layout and content of the statute concerned, so that you can use it with speed. Key statutes are identified within the appropriate appendix of this book.

1.2.5 Difficult topics

It is not wise to 'jump over' or try to avoid difficult topics. The nature of problem questions means that you cannot be sure what areas may arise in your investigations. At each point of study it is not possible to predict what other points in the course may depend on this particular principle or method of argument e.g. contract law can be seen as a basis for sale of goods, agency, insurance etc. It is therefore advisable to tackle problems of understanding as they arise, to avoid the risk of storing up trouble.

1.3 Coping with examination questions

Examination questions on law papers are traditionally of two basic types: essay questions and problem questions. It is rare to find multiple choice questions at this level, but another type of question gaining in popularity, especially in BTEC courses is the 'case study' type of question, which is, in many ways analogous to the problem question.

An essay question in law is best tackled in the traditional way with an introduction, a middle and conclusion. A useful basic guideline is always to make strong and pointed references to the question which has been asked. It is possible that not all the points in your original summary of the topic will be relevant to the particular question. Repeated references to the question will ensure that you stick to what is relevant, and do not just regurgitate automatically everything that you know about the topic.

There may well be a 'house style' for the quotation of cases and statutes in an answer in your course or college, so it is wise to enquire about this before handing in work. If there is no 'house style', cases are normally quoted as one party 'v.' another and underlined, e.g. <u>Donoghue</u> v. <u>Stevenson</u>. Statutes must have dates appended e.g. Sale of Goods Act, 1979, and important section numbers should be quoted.

1.3.1   Problem questions

In tutorials and examinations, there will be a number of problem questions, in the form of a situation in which legal issues are raised, and you are asked to give advice to one party or another, or comment on the situation in general.

It is important to read the problem carefully and express an opinion on all the facts stated; even if you consider a fact immaterial, state your reasons for your conclusions. Examples at the end of various chapters in this book will illustrate this method.

Such problems are often modelled on legal situations as they occur in real life, but a useful tip is that the problem, as stated for the student, will contain very little information that is not absolutely relevant. In actual situations involving legal problems, it is important to select the facts which the law considers material, out of a mass of related and unrelated facts.

The facts stated in the problem case as offered are conclusive, that is, if the facts state that 'Arthur defrauded the company', then this must be assumed. It is not wise to consider how that fraud was proved, or the possibility that Arthur did not defraud the company.

If in doubt, whether a fact is worthy of consideration, use your common sense and knowledge of law to determine whether it is important, for example, if a consumer purchases a red saloon car with a faulty engine, the fact that the car is red is hardly likely to be important unless the question indicates some particular problem about the colour of the car.

It may be a good thing to note the absence of an important fact, e.g. whether a car, in a purchase, was sold when it was faulty, or became faulty some time after the sale. If no indication is given, then all possibilties should be discussed.

If it seems necessary to infer facts in the problem (e.g. that since there was an accident in the problem and damages are being claimed, the implication is that persons or property must have been injured) then always state clearly what you have inferred from the facts stated.

In traditional law problems, the answer should be an impersonal, objective opinion on the facts, no matter which party you are asked to advise. In case study, or role-play situations, however, it may be necessary to emphasize one particular role. The points used in this latter situation will be the same as in the traditional problem but they will need to be emphasized appropriately with respect to the particular role, e.g. whether such points might be an advantage or disadvantage in arguing a particular case.

Always tackle a problem right from the start of your answer. Do not write a summary of the appropriate law or area of law. As you answer the question, you must support your answer with legal rules and cases, and you can elaborate on the requirements of law in those circumstances.

When using a legal case, cite the name of the case and state the appropriate legal conclusion involved. If you cannot recall the name, then a sentence about the facts of the case will suffice.

The problem may not be covered by a single authority – in these circumstances, the closest relevant authorities will suffice.

Some questions enquire about the possibility of one party 'being able to sue' another. Such a phrase means 'sue successfully'. It is not appropriate to write, for example, 'X can sue Y, but he may not be successful'.

1.4   Planning

No matter what the assignment or examination, it is worth some forward planning, both before the piece of work is undertaken, and at the time of execution (a reference to the work and not to the examination!).

It is a good idea to plan each topic, and check your plan by tackling a few sample past questions. The chapter headings in this book will assist you with your plan, which can be used flexibly according to the particular questions posed. When some headings are established under each topic, then check that you can fill out each one with some detail, and illustrate them with relevant cases, examples, or statutes as necessary (see later chapters of this book for appropriate illustrations).

In this preparation for examinations, an excellent method is to tackle past question papers, and plan answers for the questions set. It is also important to organize notes on various topic areas, with headings, key statutes and key cases.

Your planning may involve card index files, or a separate notebook, but many students have successfully guided their studies by highlighting and annotating the textbook itself. This can save valuable time.

Once in the examination, a short plan, drafted at the start of an answer, will often prevent you from missing out some basic element of the topic, when you are being enthusiastically carried away by some other points of interest.

Law is a rewarding subject, and the time you have spent in preparation and organization will not be wasted.

2 The nature and sources of law

2.1 The nature of law

Law is a formal method of social control, which exhibits many fascinating characteristics. A body of law can be defined by its function, or by the abstract ideals behind it. The tasks of law are so varied that it may seem to exhibit conflicting characteristics, e.g. it may be seen as a force for the prevention of ills, or for the perpetuation of power and status; it may be seen as preventing discrimination or as a worrying source of discrimination in itself. Law reflects the policies of government, and the predominant forces in our society. Thus it is an interesting reflection of prevailing priorities and values.

This chapter examines some characteristics of the nature of law, then the sources of law, and concludes by looking at various types of law by describing some general overall categories used by lawyers, e.g. criminal and civil law.

Questions relating to the information in this chapter often revolve around the nature of law in terms of its characteristics, the origins or sources of law, or on some courses, shorter questions asking for a description of some particular section of the chapter such as 'civil law'.

2.1.1 Custom

It is sometimes stated that law arises out of custom and tradition. This may be true in some areas of law – certainly, it would be very hard for the law to maintain credibility if it defied the traditions and customs of a society. However, it is rarely acknowledged in the formal sense that custom is a source of law. Law is based on statutes and cases, although occasionally a passing reference to custom may have some influence on a minor point. There are two instances in which this occurs:

1 acknowledgement of a local custom;

2 acknowledgement of a commercial custom.

Local custom: there are limitations on the circumstances in which a local custom will be taken into consideration by Courts. The party wishing to use a local custom in an argument must prove:

1 that the custom has existed from 'time immemorial'. (NB For the lawyer this is the year 1189, the year of accession of Richard I, which is considered to be the beginning of legal history.) In practice, this means proving that the custom has existed for as long as people can remember;

2 that it has been continuously exercised;

3 that it has been exercised as of right and openly, so that people did not have to ask permission, for example, to practice the custom;

4 that it is reasonable;

5 that it is certain;

6 that it is consistent with other customs and statutes.

Commercial customs: these are essentially business practices that may influence the judge's understanding of a commercial situation. In these cases, the practice must be certain, reasonable and generally accepted in the trade. It may well be of fairly recent origin.

2.1.2 Law as a body of rules

Law **can** be described as a body of rules, but if so, it must be distinguished from rules of etiquette or morals, or even from habitual behaviour. The discussion on this debate can be summarized by stating that the rules which comprise the law are formally created, and frequently involve sanctions and enforcement procedures. Criminal law is a good example of law with sanctions, but some civil law remedies, such as damages for breach of contract might be seen as penalties to encourage a particular sort of behaviour.

2.1.3 Sanctions

A legal system involves the use of sanctions, in order to punish in criminal law, and enforce good behaviour in other areas of law. Not all legislation involves sanctions, however. A great deal of modern welfare legislation, for example, is created to enable people to claim benefits, rather than to enforce particular behaviour patterns. Nevertheless the association of law with the implementation of sanctions is strong and universal.

2.1.4 Changes of law and developments in society

The law must be flexible, because it is working within the context of a society which is constantly changing. Thus, in fashions, morals, technological developments, for example, the law loses credibility if it refuses to acknowledge current situations. It cannot, however, respond to temporary changes of a volatile nature, because the law cannot be uncertain. Hence the law tends to acquire the reputation of being old-fashioned and unresponsive.

2.1.5 Economic and social problems

Law is often created in response to particular problems. It is often created to smooth over economic problems, for example land ownership, multiple ownership (e.g. company and partnership) and succession to title of property. It may also be linked with social problems, e.g. unemployment, or rights of parents and children.

2.1.6 Historical development

Most countries in the world use codes and statutes as the basis of their legal systems. In Europe these codes are still considerably influenced by the codes of Justinian, from the days of the Roman Empire. Roman law has had relatively little effect on English law, which has, since early times, allowed principles of law to be developed and laid down by the Courts, in the 'common law'. Statutes were not regarded as being of basic importance in the English legal system until the 13th century. The most important period of development in statutes has been the 19th and 20th centuries, when a large amount of the legislation in use today was developed.

The common law was first developed nationally after the Norman conquest, to establish and preserve the rights of Norman landowners. Thus 'property' is a basic part of the common law, and other matters, such as trespass and recovery of debt were drawn in as it developed. The rules of the common law became so rigid in time that they were in some respects considered inflexible. Historically, petitions for relief from the injustice of the common law were heard by the Chancellor, who then created rules of 'equity' in cases of moral injustice.

Equity and the common law were brought together by the Judicature Acts of 1873–5. It is largely since this time that the large and complex body of case law (around 33 000 cases) that makes up the common law today, has developed.

2.2 Sources of law

There are four sources of law in the English legal system:

1 statute or legislation;
2 judicial precedent, or case law;
3 EEC;
4 custom.

2.2.1 Statute

Statutes are of prime importance, and represent the major vehicle for the implementation of government policy. They are the most effective vehicle for law reform, since law can be changed immediately, from the date of commencement of the statute. In contrast, the development of law in the Courts may take years, over a series of cases. Statutes are efficient because they involve expert lawyers to draft them, and can have inputs from committees, where interested parties may be represented and the statutes can be reviewed by technical experts. An examination of a variety of statutes will reveal that statutes often reflect the politics and the government of the day.

Statutes are used variously for the revision of law, its consolidation or for overall codification of a whole area of law.

Parliament is sovereign, and can create any law that it sees fit. There are some limits on this sovereignty, such as geographical extent. Statutes can be enforced in the UK, but often only in England and Wales, as both Scotland and Northern Ireland have certain separate legislative provisions. A statute will only be effective outside the country if it specifically states this, e.g. as for the crime of murder. The Courts occasionally can decide to extend the power of a statute, e.g. cases relating to custody of children where parent or parents live abroad.

Another limitation on the power of Parliament to enact legislation, is that it cannot legally bind its successors. However, Parliament can, and does bind the Courts of law. They must follow statutes, no matter what their inclination. In relation to the Courts, Parliament is supreme.

Most pieces of legislation are initiated by the Government. The government department concerned draws up the statement of what it wishes to enact, and this is presented to the Parliamentary draftsmen. After the Bill is drafted to the satisfaction of the Minister, it proceeds to a first and second reading. It then goes through the Parliamentary committee stage, and after amendments it has its third and final reading. This process is repeated in both Houses of Parliament. It must then be submitted for Royal Assent, and after this it becomes an Act of Parliament.

Although Parliament is supreme in the creation of statutes, their interpretation and implementation is left largely to the Courts, which have devised a series of guidelines for the interpretation of statutes.

The English law Courts adopt a literal interpretation of statutes, and place great emphasis on the words and content of the particular statute. Unlike Courts in many other countries, they will not refer to extra-legislative materials, or preliminary debate. It is argued by the Courts, that such extra-legislative materials may not be representative of Parliament's intention as a whole. Thus it is safer to ignore them. Various rules and assumptions have been accepted, however. For example, unless stated to the contrary:

1 a statute is not retrospective;

2 a statute will be construed or interpreted narrowly if it restricts the liberty of a citizen;

3 it does not conflict with existing law;

4 it was drawn up with full knowledge of existing law.

The Courts are now seeking to implement law according to the intention of Parliament. Various rules have been developed for this purpose. Some examples of these are:

1 The grammatical or literal rule
This is the rule that words in statutes should be given their ordinary grammatical or dictionary meaning, and interpreted in the same way throughout the statute.

2 The Golden Rule
The statute should be interpreted to avoid absurdity. In *Re Sigsworth* (1935)* the Golden Rule was applied to prevent the murderer of a testator inheriting under the testator's will.

3 The Mischief Rule
The statute will be interpreted to remedy the mischief it was designed to prevent. An example of this is that in one case, prostitutes, who were tapping on a window from inside a house in order to attract potential clients, were held guilty of soliciting 'in the street'.

---

* 'Re' at the beginning of a case simply means 'In the matter of . . .', e.g. as above 'In the case of Sigsworth'.

4 *Expressio unius est exclusio alterius*

This Latin phrase, which literally means, 'if I mention one I exclude others' means that, if a statute expresses something about one class of things, or more than one, then it has, by implication, excluded all other things not mentioned.

5 The rule of context

The meaning of a word should be understood in the context of that particular statute.

Delegated legislation The complexity and volume of modern legislation is such that it would not be possible for Parliament to pass all the legislation necessary to run a modern society. Hence, if legislation needs technical expertise or flexibility of implementation, it may delegate its powers to Ministers to produce **statutory instruments,** or to local authorities to produce bye-laws. Statutory instruments and bye-laws are, in effect, statements which have the force of law, and have been authorized by legitimate means, but which have not been through the Houses of Parliament etc. in the normal statutory process. They supplement statutes, because of the vast amount of legislation that Parliament has to deal with. These are always subject to review by Parliament. In practice this means that Parliamentary committees have the opportunity for overall review, and Parliament can disallow any rules created.

The Courts may challenge a statutory instrument if it appears to be *ultra vires* (which means that it has been created outside the powers granted by Parliament).

Much concern is expressed about this type of legislation, on the grounds that Parliament is losing control over the law-making process. It is argued, in reply, that such legislation is necessary, and since it is subject to review by the Courts and Parliament, it is under control constitutionally. There is some debate about whether the controls actually exercised are sufficient.

2.2.2 Cases

The English legal system is different from that of other European countries because it is a common law system. This means that the law can be developed through cases in the Courts.

The Courts operate in a hierarchical system. The lowest Courts are the magistrates' Courts, the Crown Courts (criminal) and the County Courts (civil). These Courts do not create or develop law at all, but they must follow the higher Courts in their decisions (see next chapter for description of Courts).

If a case progresses through the Courts, the decisions are increasingly important, up to a decision in the House of Lords, which is the strongest arbiter of all. Since 1966, the House of Lords itself has been able, exceptionally, to depart from its own decisions. Decisions of the Court of Appeal are also considered very important, but they can be overruled by the House of Lords, should the case go higher. The House of Lords itself can now be overruled in cases which come within the ambit of the Treaty of Rome – as in these cases, there can be an appeal to the European Court.

A case only climbs up the Court 'ladder' if there are grounds for appeal against a decision. There are grounds for appeal against a decision on points of law, or occasionally on a question of fact. At the higher level, Court proceedings may cost hundreds of thousands of pounds, so a decision to allow an appeal is not taken lightly. Few cases that reach the elevated heights of the higher courts can be privately funded. Such cases are normally financed by bodies such as companies, trade unions or insurance firms.

Ratio decidendi

The *ratio decidendi* is that part of the judgment which is followed by later Courts. It is made up of the essential principles of law that were used to deal with that particular set of facts, i.e. the material facts of that case. The law which is to be followed by other Courts consists of those principles applied in those particular circumstances, and clearly no judge will be bound to apply those principles if the particular circumstances do not occur again. The circumstances are considered in general terms. For example, if Fred drinks a glass of lemonade in which there is a decomposed mouse, suffers ill-health as a result and subsequently loses his job, the general circumstances of this case might be that a person is injured by the negligence of others which causes foreseeable damage. These general circumstances must apply in another case, for a court to follow precedent.

Obiter dicta

Any additional statements that the judge makes about the law in a case, which are not based directly on the facts of that case, are called *obiter dicta*. These statements can be used as persuasive authority in future cases, but they are not wholly binding.

Distinguishing

If a judge sees that a case is very similar to the one he is considering currently, but that there is a difference, in some important respect, he may distinguish the case. He does this by drawing attention to the difference in facts between the two cases, and pointing out why this means that he will reach a different conclusion.

It is clearly important for a barrister in argument or 'pleadings' to encourage the judge to distinguish cases that are not favourable to the client's case.

The court may also decide not to follow a decision if it is *per incuriam*, which means that it does not take into account some basic point from a previous case, or it has been overruled by a statute or some other judgment.

There are many arguments about the advantages and disadvantages of judicial law-making. Some of them read as follows:

Advantages of judicial precedent system:

1 There is flexibility from one case to the next, since no two cases are exactly the same.

2 It avoids rigidity in the law.

3 It allows the law to respond to current conditions in society.

4 It allows the law to reflect public policy (standards of society, or of the dominant political forces in society).

Disadvantages of judicial precedent system:

1 The unpredictability of decisions, which can appear to lack consistency.

2 The judges are creating law, in effect, through undemocratic means.

3 The law is not always clear, so it is sometimes quite difficult to identify the *ratio decidendi*.

4 It is an unwieldy system, involving such a vast number of cases.

2.2.3 Custom

Custom is a source of law, but it is less important than other major sources of law in this section. For details of custom as a source of law, see section 2.2.1 earlier in this chapter.

2.2.4 The EEC

Since Britain became a member of the EEC, through the European Communities Act, 1972, it has had to submit to European legislative bodies on European matters. The major institutions of the EEC are the Council of Ministers, the Commission of European Communities and the European Parliament. The most important legislative bodies are the Council and the Commission.

The Council and the Commission can issue regulations, directives and decisions. Regulations are binding on member states without any further processes, whereas directives must be implemented through the State's own legislative procedure. Decisions are only binding on the particular parties concerned which could be a state, a company or even a person.

If a case in the House of Lords concerns a European treaty, then it must be sent, under Article 177 of the Treaty of Rome, to the European Court. The European Court declares the 'correct' interpretation of the treaty and the House of Lords must follow that interpretation. The influence of the European institutions is bound to increase, and will be commented upon in relation to particular areas of law in appropriate chapters throughout this book.

2.2.5 Other sources of law

It is important to note that the phrase 'sources of law' has several meanings.

1 Legal sources – consisting of statute, common law, custom and EEC as mentioned above.

2 Historical sources – consisting of factors that may influence or lead up to the creation of law, e.g. reports of a Royal Commission, customs and traditions, moral or religious beliefs.

3 Literary sources – consisting of recorded statements of law. These sources do not create law but simply record what is the existing law, e.g. text-books, law reports.

4 Formal sources – consisting of the political powers which give force to the rules of law, e.g. Parliament in the English legal system, which gives force and validity to the law.

2.3 Civil and criminal law

Civil law exists to enable citizens of the state to enforce their rights. The idea developed to allow people to gain relief or compensation, if their person or property is abused. Criminal law exists to suppress anti-social behaviour, and provide protection for society against threatening behaviour. It also exists to penalize the offenders involved in such behaviour.

2.3.1 Civil law

Civil law is private law, concerned with the demands of citizens who seek legal remedies for their problems. (It must be noted that there is another meaning of 'civil law' as used to denote European civil law systems, in contrast to our common law system.) Civil law includes such areas of law as contract, tort, family law and succession. The plaintiff (complaining party) sues the defending party to claim redress, to obtain damages for deprivation suffered or obtain an equitable remedy such as an injunction (an order to stop or prevent some behaviour) or specific performance of a contract to force a party to behave in a particular way.

2.3.2 Criminal law

Criminal law is necessarily public law. Although private prosecutions may take place, where public interest allows access to the law, the nature of crime is such that it is defined as a threat to the harmony of that society. (For instance, if a person drinks to excess and drives a vehicle, he is behaving in a way which is a threat to the stability of our society, since he threatens the lives of members of that society, and society wishes to reject that form of behaviour.) Thus, in criminal law the cases are usually recited as 'the State against . . . (the offender)' and written *R* v. (*Offender*). '*R*' means 'Regina', and represents the public person of the Crown, and so we can see the case as 'the Crown against the potential criminal'. Criminal cases provide penalties for behaviour, and sentence people who have been prosecuted for offences.

2.4 Common law and equity

2.4.1 The common law

The common law of England has been variously described as the law of the common people, or the law of the judges. It rather depends on whether the judiciary are seen as representing the interests of the ordinary person, or they are seen as being deliberately or unknowingly impervious to those interests. Undoubtedly there are examples of both styles of judicial behaviour!

In medieval times, itinerant justices travelled from county to county to sit at Assize Courts (NB assizes comes from the French verb *asseoir*, 'to sit'). These Courts were finally abolished in 1971. They used a declaratory style of law, which gradually developed a series of rigid principles, e.g. that the only remedies available were monetary. The Judicature Acts 1873–5 improved this system by forcing it to work alongside the law of equity (i.e. in the same courts). See section 2.1.6.

2.4.2 Equity

The Court of Chancery was empowered originally to hear appeals from the common law. The appeals were morally based claims, 'He who comes to Equity, must come with clean hands'. In the early days, it was difficult to pick out consistent principles, and critics said that Equity varied with 'the length of the Chancellor's foot', because there was great variation between the Chancellors. However, by the 19th century, equitable principles were emerging as a separate body of law developed in chancery and Equity brought a new dimension to the common law in several respects:

1 new rights, e.g. between the trustee and beneficiary;

2 new remedies, e.g. injunctions;

3 new procedures, e.g. allowing different kinds of cases to proceed.

Judges now have the discretion to use equitable principles in all areas of the common law and equity is no longer a separate type of law. Some of these principles have even been encompassed in statute e.g. the deserted wife's equity in the Matrimonial Homes Act 1967, which ensures that the deserted wife has a financial claim on the assets of the property.

Sample questions

1 What are the sources of law in England?

Suggested answer

The following points should be considered:
The discussion concerns the **legal** sources of law.
Statutes are a basic source of law and often revise or consolidate existing rules. Statutes are subject to interpretation by the Courts, according to certain standard rules of statutory interpretation. Examples of these rules can be given, such as the mischief rule (that the statute will be interpreted according to the mischief that it was trying to remedy).

Law is also created by the judicial precedent, which emerges through the hierarchical system of courts, e.g. *Donoghue* v. *Stevenson*, used as a basis for law of negligence. Such cases are instances of judicial law-making in the House of Lords, and Court of Appeal. Custom is another source of law, both local custom and commercial custom, which embodies trade practices where appropriate.

The EEC can make law on matters concerning the Treaty of Rome, e.g. competition law. Another most important source of law is delegated legislation created by Ministers or local authorities with statutory powers.

The most fundamental sources are, however, statutes and the cases in the Courts.

2 How is law formed?

Suggested answer

The following points should be considered:
Most law is formed in Parliament, by the Courts or by delegated legislation. There is no written constitution in Britain.

Most statutes start in the Government. The relevant department will consider the idea, and then the Bill has its first and second reading and gets to committee stage. It then has a final reading in both Houses of Parliament and if passed acquires the Royal Assent.

Law made in the Courts must be in a case, which must go through the hierarchy of Courts, although there is now a leapfrogging procedure to the House of Lords for cases of special importance. In 1966 the House of Lords decided that it would not always be bound by its own decisions.

Describe the system of *stare decisis, ratio decidendi* and the process of distinguishing. Make brief mention of custom, EEC law and delegated legislation.

3 Is law a body of rules?

Suggested answer

The following points should be considered:
It seems a reasonable description of law, but how can you distinguish law from a game?

This description does not incorporate the special ways in which laws are formed, nor the fact that they are enforced and sometimes have sanctions attached to them.

There are limited sources of law, Parliament, the Courts, the EEC and custom. Judicial precedent does try to incorporate some of the rules or standards of society, but at the same time equity has lead to a break away from the common law, but only for those who come with 'clean hands'!

Customs are incorporated in a very particular way. There are fundamentally different types of law in criminal and civil law.

Describing law as a 'body of rules' is an oversimplification. It plays a complex role in a changing society.

Further reading

Farrar, J. *Introduction to Legal Method* (Sweet and Maxwell)
Harris, Phil *An Introduction to Law* (Weidenfield and Nicholson)

3 The Courts

The Courts provide the formal setting for the resolution of legal disputes, and are usually the last resort for parties with unresolved differences. The parties to an action can be private individuals, or companies, local authorities or even the State itself. The Courts traditionally resolve most problems put before them. However, settlements are made out of Court fairly frequently. The Courts are organized in a hierarchical structure, and each Court has its own functions and responsibilities. Most Courts are linked in the hierarchy to other Courts, by a system of appeals to or from the other Courts in the system (see Fig. 3.1).

There have been several recent Acts of Parliament defining the Court structure, notably the Administration of Justice Act, 1970, the Courts Act, 1971 and the Supreme Court Act, 1981.

Distinctions can be drawn between civil and criminal Courts, and original or appellate jurisdiction, i.e. whether the case is first heard (at first instance) or it is on appeal to that Court.

Questions on the Courts are not common, and you would be advised to look at past examination papers to check their frequency before revising 'Courts' as a separate subject. Where questions on the Courts do arise, they are likely to be about the hierarchy of the Courts or about legal personnel, in particular solicitors and barristers.

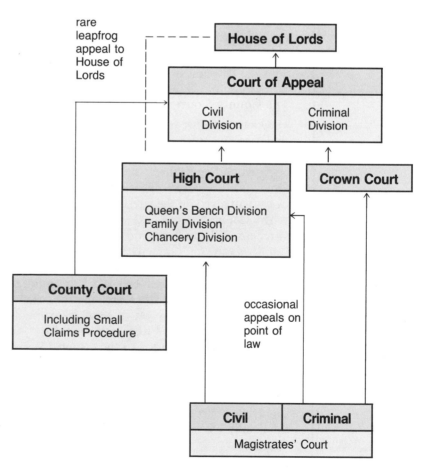

Fig. 3.1 The hierarchy of Courts

3.1 Civil and Criminal Courts

Civil cases are about private interests, and one legal person (an individual, a company or a local authority) **sues** another for a certain reason, e.g. in the hope of getting damages for physical injury or financial loss. Such a case does not normally involve the police, unless a crime has also been committed. Trespass is a civil matter; a famous case was the intrusion of Michael Fagan into the Queen's bedroom. The only **criminal** offence he committed was the theft of some wine which he discovered and drank.

Some Courts deal with criminal and civil cases, but, on the whole, the distinctions are well drawn. Criminal Courts are concerned with cases in which behaviour is anti-social, and the person concerned is **prosecuted** for his behaviour. This prosecution is normally brought by the State, but it is possible to bring a private prosecution.

3.1.1 Magistrates' Courts

Magistrates' Courts are the lowest Courts in the official hierarchy, and hear the most cases. They have criminal and civil jurisdiction. The magistrates themselves are laypersons, with the exception of some professional lawyers, called stipendiary magistrates. The stipendiary magistrate normally sits alone, whereas there must be at least two lay magistrates, and there may be as many as seven. The lay magistrates are advised on legal points by a qualified lawyer acting as clerk to the Court.

The main function of the Magistrates' Court is to give summary justice to people involved in less serious crimes. The maximum penalties such Courts can give are six months' imprisonment, and/or a fine of up to £1000.

Minor offences account for the majority of cases before these Courts, but magistrates can also commit people on more serious charges for trial in the Crown Court, which can dispense greater penalties. They can also grant bail, or decide to remand someone in prison to await trial. There are also special juvenile Courts composed of selected magistrates who deal with child offenders.

The civil law responsibilities undertaken by magistrates vary from issuing drink licences and betting licences, to family matters of maintenance and domestic violence.

3.1.2 Civil Courts

The Magistrates' Courts, as previously described, carry out a small and varied amount of civil work. Other civil Courts are the County Court, the High Court and the Civil Division of the Court of Appeal.

The County Court

The County Court is administered by a Registrar, and has power to deal with minor civil cases in contract and tort up to £5000. In some other matters, however, this sum is increased so that the County Court can deal with the affairs of a company which is being wound up to the value of £120 000. All these figures are reviewed from time to time, and it is wise to check their value in any particular year. Your local County Court will give you the latest information if you cannot obtain it from other sources.

The County Courts deal with a great variety of matters such as bankruptcy, hire purchase and landlord and tenant disputes. An appeal against a decision of the County Court goes directly to the Civil Division of the Court of Appeal.

The County Court incorporates a 'small claims' facility which is known as the **Small Claims Procedure**. This is a very important development, to help people with claims of less than £1000 arising from such events as sales of goods, negligent treatment in the provision of services. It involves a less formal, relatively low cost procedure whereby the Registrar hears cases, often without formal legal representation and sits in arbitration of the dispute. Any appeal from this procedure goes direct to the circuit judge sitting in the County Court.

The High Court

The High Court is split into three divisions (see Fig. 3.1), the Queen's Bench Division, the Family Division and the Chancery Division. Each of these divisions has separate functions:

Queen's Bench Division: This is the responsibility of the Lord Chief Justice and his **puisne** judges ('puny' or lesser judges) who hear the majority of cases based on contract and tort. It is the main civil Court for disputes involving more than £5000. This is the Court that deals with such cases as actions for damages from motor accidents or factory accidents. It is also the division containing the 'Admiralty Court', dealing with accidents or loss at sea. It tends to pick up cases not falling into strict categories for the other two divisions, and it has a supervisory function over the lower Courts and tribunals. It is the Queen's Bench Division that can issue the writ of *habeas corpus* (literally translated as 'have the body') to secure the release of a person who has been unlawfully detained.

Family Division: This division deals with domestic disputes, such as divorce, access to children, and adoption. It is overseen by the President of the Family Division, and usually sits with three puisne judges.

Chancery Division: The Chancery Division deals with important financial areas of law such as tax, wills, trusts and property. It can also deal with some appeals from the County Courts. It is nominally headed by the Lord Chancellor and Master of the Rolls but it is actually run by the Vice-Chancellor with the assistance of puisne judges.

The High Court is bound by the decisions of the House of Lords and the Court of Appeal, and also usually by its own decisions in the same division.

Court of Appeal (Civil Division)

This Court deals almost entirely with appeals from the High Court, the County Court, the Restrictive Practices Court and tribunals. It hears appeals on questions of law (i.e. whether the law was interpreted and applied correctly) and questions of fact (i.e. whether the facts were all before the Court and handled correctly).

If the appeal succeeds, or in legal terminology, the appeal 'is allowed', the Court of Appeal may reverse the decision of a lower Court, or amend it, or order a retrial. It can also hear appeals about the exercise of discretion in such matters as costs.

The Master of the Rolls heads the Civil Division of the Court of Appeal, and he is assisted by the Lords Justices of Appeal. The Court of Appeal is bound by the decisions of the House of Lords, and by its own earlier decisions, except if there are conflicting decisions, or a decision was given *per incuriam* (with inaccuracy through an oversight).

House of Lords

This is the ultimate Court of appeal for criminal and civil cases. It sits separately from the parliamentary body, using peers holding high judicial office, called Lords of Appeal in Ordinary.

The House of Lords hears appeals on civil cases from Northern Ireland and Scotland as well as from the English Court of Appeal. Its decisions are binding on all other Courts. Since 1966, the House of Lords itself has on occasion departed from its own previous decisions 'where it appears right to do so'.

3.1.3 Criminal Courts

The Magistrates' Court has been identified as the lowest level of criminal Court, which also hears the majority of cases. The other criminal Courts are the Crown Court, occasionally the Divisional Court (part of the Queen's Bench Division), the Criminal Division of the Court of Appeal and the House of Lords.

Crown Courts

The Crown Court is now part of the Supreme Court (defined as the Court of Appeal, the High Court of Justice, and the Crown Court). It consists of three tiers to deal with varying levels of offence. The top tier deals with class 1 offences – the most serious crimes, e.g. murder. These are dealt with by a High Court judge. Class 2 offences include manslaughter, infanticide and rape, and must also normally go before a High Court judge. Class 3 and Class 4 offences are normally less serious, and include cases which could be heard in Magistrates' Courts, but where the defendant has elected trial before a jury.

Court of Appeal (Criminal Division)

This is an appeal Court only, and it hears appeals from persons convicted on indictment (an offence which is tried by a jury at Crown Court level is an indictable offence). The Court has powers to dismiss the appeal, quash the conviction or order a new trial. It can also substitute an alternative verdict or sentence. The Court is normally bound by its previous decisions, as well as by those of the House of Lords, but it may depart from an earlier decision of its own, in the interests of justice.

House of Lords

In criminal cases there are appeals to the House of Lords from England and Northern Ireland, and from the Courts-Martial Appeal Court. The Court delivers its decisions, known as 'opinions', and they are handed down to the Court of Appeal to deal with the actual parties to the case. The House of Lords reaches a decision on the principle of law, and leaves the delivery of the judgment for the parties concerned to the Court of Appeal.

3.2 Special Courts

Other important Courts are the Judicial Committee of the Privy Council, the Restrictive Practices Court and the European Courts. It is not usual to require a great deal of detail about these, and an awareness of their role and general responsibilities will suffice.

3.2.1 Judicial Committee of the Privy Council

This Court consists of the Lord President of the Council, Lord Chancellor, ex-Lord Chancellors, and Lords of Appeal in Ordinary. Their decisions have only persuasive authority in the English Courts. The Court deals with matters on appeal from various other countries, or from the Isle of Man, Channel Islands, or from British territories, such as Hong Kong, and special Courts such as ecclesiastical Courts and medical tribunals.

Some Commonwealth countries have chosen to retain this system of appeal voluntarily, e.g. Singapore and New Zealand.

3.2.2 Restrictive Practices Court

This Court deals with restrictive trade practices in cases that are referred to it by the Director General of Fair Trading. The Office of Fair Trading led by the Director General was set up under the Fair Trading Act 1973. Restrictive trade practices are agreements relating to trade which have been described as contrary to public interest, e.g. price restrictions or restrictive arrangements between producers or suppliers of certain goods which limit public choice for no justifiable reason.

This Court has equal status to a High Court. A judge and two lay-members sit in the Court, and appeals are taken directly to the Court of Appeal.

Various firms have sought to register restrictive practices under the legislation, but very few of the practices have been considered to be 'in the public interest' by the Court.

3.2.3 The European Courts

The European Court of Justice has authority to ensure correct interpretation and application of the Treaty of Rome (which binds us to the European community). Its decisions on the interpretation of the community law are final, and superior even to the House of Lords in that particular sphere. The relevant points of law are settled by the European Court and then referred back to the national court for judgment on the particular case.

Another European Court is the European Court of Human Rights, which deals with violations of the European Convention on Human Rights. This Court has made certain rulings against the British Government concerning prisoners, mental patients and immigrants.

3.3 Administrative procedures for settling disputes

There are various procedures for settling disputes outside the courts, which ought to be considered alongside the Court system. Three such procedures are tribunals, public enquiries and arbitration.

3.3.1 Tribunals

These have grown up primarily to deal with problems surrounding the vast amount of social legislation that has built up since the Second World War. They can adjudicate in matters not normally dealt with by the Courts, and it is not necessary for people to have legal representation. People can be represented by accountants, for example, trade union representatives or social workers. Tribunals can use specialists in the area of concern, and do not have to abide by formal rules of evidence.

There is a Council on Tribunals, set up by the Tribunals and Inquiries Act 1971, which acts as an advisory body, and reviews the workings of the various tribunals. Some leading tribunals are the National Insurance Tribunal, the Lands Tribunal and the Industrial Tribunal. There are over 60 tribunals in total. They differ in membership and rules of procedure. Legal aid is not available for hearings at tribunals.

The advantage of the tribunal procedure is that it is cheaper and faster than going to the Courts, and the tribunal can use specialists and practitioners in particular fields of concern.

3.3.2 Public inquiries

Public inquiries are held to give individuals a chance to contribute their own views when the decision of a government department affects their lives and their interests. They are particularly associated with the issue of use of land, and they often debate this issue, e.g. in relation to the siting of airports, power stations and motorways.

Public inquiries come under the jurisdiction of the Council of Tribunals. Their recommendations are put to the relevant Minister, but he is not bound to follow those recommendations. The inquiries are normally conducted by a civil servant appointed by the Minister.

3.3.3 Arbitration

On some occasions, parties to a contract agree to settle any disputes by arbitration. The arbitrator can be chosen by the parties themselves as a specialist in the area of concern. This is cheaper than going to Court, and has the advantage of offering a private hearing. This means that it is not subject to public scrutiny, which could damage business interests.

The parties make an agreement that the arbitrator's decision shall be final and binding. The arbitrator does not have to be named in the agreement, but there must be some agreed means of selection. Another advantage is that disputes can be settled outside working hours. Arbitrations are not bound by precedent and each case is considered on its own merits. This occasionally leads to several different cases about the same incident, which can seem wasteful of resources. Parties to an arbitration have a right to appeal to a Court, except where they have all signed an agreement not to do so. There have been various pieces of legislation associated with arbitrations, and it is emphasized that awards given in these proceedings must be enforced by the Courts.

Arbitrations are often used for international trade because the process avoids disputes about legal jurisdiction.

Although it may frequently be a method which the parties to a contract select, it can be ordered by the Court, or laid down as a procedure in a statute. Arbitration is used, as well, in disputes covered by Codes of Practice, e.g. the ABTA code for travel agents. Arbitration also takes place under the small claims procedure in the County Court.

3.4 Personnel of the law

The personnel involved in litigation are solicitors, barristers and the judiciary, but these people have other functions apart from Court work. The other personnel in the Courts are magistrates and jurors, who give particular contributions as lay-people. Lay magistrates are people who are appointed by the Lord Chancellor on the advice of various selection committees. Jurors are selected from the electoral register from people in the age range 18 to 65.

3.4.1 Solicitors

Solicitors are the branch of the legal profession with which the general public are most likely to be familiar. They conduct a great deal of the day-to-day legal work on matters such as home conveyances, wills and matrimonial problems.

The profession has its own Solicitors' Disciplinary Tribunal, to which clients can take claims if they feel they have been mistreated. The Tribunal is presided over by two practising solicitors and a layman, and may impose fines, strike solicitors off the roll, or order payment of costs.

For purposes of litigation, solicitors have access to the lower Courts, the Magistrates' Court, the County Court and occasionally the Crown Court. Otherwise, in higher Courts, they must instruct a barrister to represent the client, and historically they have inherited a deferential role towards barristers, whereby barristers act as consultants.

3.4.2 Barristers

The practising barristers are much fewer in number than solicitors (currently about 5500, compared with 45 000), and they specialize in court work for the higher Courts. Some barristers work for industry, and do not practise, while others are employed in different situations – drafting legal documents for example.

Barristers do not meet their clients directly to be instructed on a client's case, but are instructed by solicitors and usually only meet the client fairly late in the proceedings. They work in chambers, administered by a chambers' clerk. They are all members of one of the four Inns of Court, i.e. Gray's Inn, Lincoln's Inn, Inner Temple and Middle Temple. They have to work on the 'taxi-rank' principle of accepting any case that they are offered in their own field of work, provided that the client can pay. In practice, since work is referred to barristers by solicitors, this can act as an unofficial screening process, because the solicitor can select suitable types of client for particular barristers. Complaints against barristers are investigated by a committee of the Bar Council, which may refer matters to a higher Disciplinary Tribunal.

3.4.3 Unification of the legal profession

There has been much debate over the question of whether the two professions of solicitor and barrister should unite. The advantages and disadvantages of such a step are constantly argued, and can be summarized as follows:

Advantages

1 It is assumed that the cost of litigation would decrease, because of the need to instruct only one lawyer rather than two.

2 It would avoid communication problems between both solicitor and barrister, and client and barrister, and would shorten the process by avoiding duplication of work and effort.

3 It would be less confusing for the client.

Disadvantages

1 It would not allow one profession to specialize in litigation.

2 It would not ensure that the best legal brains in litigation are available to all clients, because if they were one profession, the best would probably be working for top business consortiums, and would not be available to the public.

3.4.4 Judges

The judges of the higher Courts are drawn from the ranks of practising barristers, usually those of 10 years' standing, and for the higher courts, of 15 years' standing. The judge is traditionally independent of influence from the Government, and he is largely protected because he cannot be sued for his work in the court. In order to preserve impartiality and freedom from political influence it has been made extremely hard to dismiss a judge; it would take a vote from both Houses of Parliament to remove one.

Judges undergo no special training for their work apart from experience as a barrister, and they frequently specialize only in their particular field of work, after they have been appointed to the bench.

3.4.5 Other legal personnel

Recently there has been a move to establish another branch of lawyers, called Licensed Conveyancers, whose basic job is to convey property. The first licenses were issued by the Director General of Fair Trading in May 1987. The Council for Licensed Conveyancers has an examination system, but the qualifying process is not as long or as involved as that of a solicitor or barrister.

There are also legal executives, who work in solicitors' offices and have their own training programme. Legal executives carry out much of the routine work in solicitors' offices.

On a national level, two important legal offices are those of the Attorney-General and the Solicitor-General. Both of these are political appointments, held by practising barristers. The Attorney-General represents the Crown in Court, and advises the Crown on legal matters. He is assisted by the Solicitor-General. Other national appointments have been mentioned in other parts of this book, such as the Lord Chief Justice, Lord Chancellor (another political appointment) and the various Presidents of the Court.

Sample questions

1 Give an account of the Courts within the English legal system that have jurisdiction to hear cases on the law of contract and commercial law.

BA, Business Studies

Suggested answer

The following points should be considered:

A general introduction about the English Court system would be appropriate, with its hierarchy of Courts, and the creation and development of law by the higher Courts. It should be mentioned that there are separate criminal and civil systems.

The particular Courts concerned are most likely to be the Queen's Bench Division of the High Court, and the County Court. Appeals will go to the Court of Appeal (Civil Division) and the House of Lords. If the case is affected by the Treaty of Rome a case may be considered by the European Court of Justice.

The Queen's Bench Division deals with contract and tort and has miscellaneous responsibilities. The County Court deals with cases up to £5000, or can be used as a small claims court if dealing with lower amounts. The Queen's Bench division has two specialized Courts, the Admiralty Court and the Commercial Court, and it is clearly the latter that will hear the cases identified in the question.

Many cases may be resolved by arbitration, and there is even some provision within the Court system, in the form of the small claims procedure in the County Court.

If a point of law arises, the case may go as high as the Court of Appeal of the House of Lords. The House of Lords will normally only consider the point of law, and hand the case back down for judgment.

2 What advantages to businessmen might arbitration be thought to have over litigation?

IPS

Suggested answer

The following points should be considered:

Introduce the fact that it is possible to provide for arbitration in a contract, provided the procedure is sufficiently described e.g. an arbitrator is chosen, or there is an agreed means of selection of an arbitrator.

The advantages may be seen to be as follows:

Cost: because it will probably be cheaper than the Courts.

Privacy: it will not be a public hearing that could besmirch the name of a business.

Convenience: it can be settled outside working hours, so that valuable working time is not lost.

Arbitration proceedings are not bound by precedent. The awards are enforced, however, by the Courts. International negotiations benefit from this form of procedure, since there is no dispute about legal jurisdiction.

The disadvantage of this procedure is possibly that the same incident may give rise to many cases, which may cause inconsistency, and waste of resources.

3 Examine the nature and function of both the County Court and the Magistrates' Court.

Suggested answer

The following points should be considered:

Introduction: give a brief explanation of our hierarchy of Courts. These particular Courts are at the lower end of the system and therefore handle a great many of the cases.

The County Court is a civil Court, but the Magistrates' Court does both civil and criminal work.

The personnel of both Courts can be described, the circuit judge and registrar for the County Court and the lay magistrates and stipendiary magistrates. The County Court has jurisdiction up to £5000, and in addition has the small claims procedure with jurisdiction up to £1000.

The Magistrates' Court deals with criminal cases up to £1000 fine or six months' imprisonment. It is reasonable to give some examples of the kind of cases dealt with e.g. hire-purchase in the County Court and matrimonial case decisions about custody etc. or petty crime in the Magistrates' Court.

Further reading

Harris, Phil *An Introduction to Law* (Weidenfield and Nicolson)
Marsh and Soulsby *Business Law* (McGraw-Hill)

4 The nature and function of contract law

In our society, commercial activity takes the form of an exchange of commodities. This short chapter introduces contract law, the method by which such commercial exchanges are regulated, and hence is of the utmost importance. The general law of contract is essentially the product of the Common Law, although there have been statutory inroads made into this field, particularly in the area of consumer protection. One notable piece of legislation of this type, that will demand close scrutiny, is the Unfair Contract Terms Act, 1977.

4.1 Definition

The simplest possible description of a contract is, 'a legally binding agreement'.

It should be noted that although all contracts are the outcome of agreements, not all agreements are contracts, i.e. not all agreements are legally enforceable. It is in order to decide which agreements will be enforced by the Courts that one requires an understanding of the rules and principles of contract law.

The emphasis placed on agreement highlights the consensual nature of contracts. It is sometimes said that a contract is based on *consensus ad idem*, a meeting of minds. This is slightly misleading, however, because English contract law applies an objective test in determining whether a contract exists or not. It is not concerned with what the parties actually had in mind, but with what their behaviour would lead others to conclude.

4.2 Formalities

There is no general requirement that contracts be made in writing. They can be created by word of mouth, or by action, as well as in writing. Contracts made in this way are known as parol or simple contracts, whereas those made under seal are known as specialty contracts. It is usually left to the parties to decide the form, but in the circumstances listed below, formalities are required.

1 Contracts which must be made under seal. Essentially this requirement applies to leases of property extending for more than three years.

2 Contracts which must be in writing. Amongst this group are included:

(a) bills of exchange, cheques and promissory notes (Bills of Exchange Act, 1882);

(b) consumer credit agreements, such as hire purchase contracts (Consumer Credit Act, 1974);

(c) contracts of marine insurance (Marine Insurance Act, 1906).

3 Contracts which must be evidenced in writing. There are two contracts of this type:

(a) contracts of guarantee (Section 4 of the Statute of Frauds, 1677);

(b) contracts for the sale or other disposition of land (Section 40 of the Law of Property Act, 1925).

4.3 Special agreements

At the outset it is necessary to distinguish the legal effect of particular agreements, as follows:

1 Valid contracts. These are agreements which the law recognizes as binding. The

Court will enforce the contract by either insisting on performance or awarding damages for breach.

2 Void contracts. This is actually a contradiction in terms, for this type of agreement does not constitute a contract: it has no legal effect. Agreements may be void for a number of reasons, including mistake, illegality, public policy, or the lack of a necessary requirement, such as consideration. The ownership of property exchanged under a void contract does not pass and remains with the original owner.

3 Voidable contracts. These are agreements which may be avoided, i.e. set aside, by one of the parties. If, however, no steps are taken to avoid the agreement, then a valid contract ensues. Examples of contracts which may be voidable are those which have been entered into on the basis of fraud, misrepresentation or duress. Goods which are exchanged under a voidable contract can be sold to an innocent third party, who will receive good title.

4 Unenforceable contracts. These are agreements which, although legal, cannot be sued upon for some reason. An example would be where the time limit for enforcing the contract has lapsed.

The following three chapters will deal with the major substantive rules relating to contracts, but first a warning in relation to examinations:

Contract forms the major component in most syllabuses. It is not possible to select particular areas as more important than others and, therefore, more likely to be examined. Unfortunately any aspect of Contract may be asked about, and therefore the student must be familiar with most, if not all, aspects of the subject. For example, it may be legitimate to expect a question on the vitiating factors in relation to contracts. (See chapter 7.) It is not possible, however, to predict which particular vitiating factor will be selected. To restrict one's knowledge would be extremely hazardous. The student may well know Mistake and Misrepresentation very well, but that will be to no avail if the question happens to be on Duress, as it might well be.

Questions on the subject of Contract are set out at the ends of chapters 5 and 6.

Further reading

Cheshire, Fifoot and Furniston *Law of Contract* (Butterworths)
Davies, F. R. *Contract* (Sweet and Maxwell)

5 The formation of a contract

Not every agreement, let alone every promise, will be enforced by the law. But what distinguishes the enforceable promise from the unenforceable one? The essential elements of a binding agreement are as follows:

1 offer;

2 acceptance;

3 consideration;

4 capacity;

5 intention to create legal relations;

6 there must be no vitiating factors present.

Elements 1 to 5 must be present, and element 6 must be absent, in order for there to be a contract. This chapter will deal with the first five elements in turn. The vitiating factors will be considered separately in chapter 7.

5.1 Offer

An offer is a promise, which is capable of acceptance, to be bound on particular terms. The person who makes the offer is the offeror; the person who receives the offer is the offeree. The offer must not be vague.

> *Scammel* v. *Ouston* (1941)
>
> Ouston ordered a van from Scammel on the understanding that the balance of the purchase price could be paid on 'hire-purchase terms over two years'. Scammel used a variety of hire-purchase terms, and the actual terms of Ouston's agreement were never settled. When Scammel failed to deliver the van, Ouston sued for breach of contract.
>
> **Held:** The action failed. No contract could be established, because of the uncertainty of the terms.

5.1.1 Distinguishing factors of an offer

An offer must be distinguished from the following:

1 A mere statement of intention

> *Re Fickus* (1900)
>
> A father informed his prospective son-in-law that his daughter would inherit under his will.
>
> **Held:** The father's words were simply a statement of intention. They were not an offer, and therefore he could not be bound by them.

2 A mere supply of information

> *Harvey* v. *Facey* (1893)
>
> The plaintiff telegraphed the defendants as follows: 'Will you sell us Bumper Hall Pen? Telegraph lowest cash price'. The defendant answered: 'Lowest price for Bumper Hall Pen £900'. The plaintiff then telegraphed: 'We agree to buy Bumper Hall Pen for £900'. The plaintiff sued for specific performance.
>
> **Held:** The defendant's telegram was not an offer capable of being accepted by the plaintiff. It was simply a statement of information.

3 An invitation to treat, which is merely an invitation to others to make offers. The person making the invitation to treat is not bound to accept any offers made to him.

The following are examples of common situations involving invitations to treat:

(a) **The display of goods in a shop window**

> *Fisher v. Bell* (1961)
>
> A shopkeeper was prosecuted for offering offensive weapons for sale, by having flick-knives in his window.
>
> **Held:** The shopkeeper was not guilty as the display in the shop window was not an offer for sale but only an invitation to treat.

(b) **The display of goods on the shelves of a self-service shop**

> *Pharmaceutical Society of GB v. Boots Cash Chemists* (1953)
>
> The defendants had particular drugs on open display in their self-service store. They were charged with breaking a law which provided that drugs could only be sold under the supervision of a qualified pharmacist. Although a qualified person was stationed at the cash desk it was maintained that the contract of sale had been formed when the customer removed the goods from the shelf.
>
> **Held:** Boots were not guilty. The display of goods on the shelf was only an invitation to treat. The customer's offer to buy them could be accepted or refused at the cash desk where the pharmacist was situated.

(c) **An advertisement in a publication**

> *Partridge v. Crittenden* (1968)
>
> Partridge was charged with offering a wild bird for sale, contrary to the Protection of Birds Act, 1954, after he placed an advertisement in a magazine.
>
> **Held:** He was not guilty of the offence because the advertisement was not an offer, but merely an invitation to treat.
>
> Similarly an advertisement to hold an auction is not an offer to hold it and no one can sue if it is not in fact held.
>
> *Harris v. Nickerson* (1873)
>
> A prospectus issued by a company in order to induce people to buy shares is another example of an invitation to treat.

5.1.2 Offers to particular people

An offer may be made to a particular person or to a group of people, or to the world at large. If the offer is restricted, then only the people to whom it is addressed can accept it; but if the offer is made to the public at large, it can be accepted by anyone.

> *Carlill v. Carbolic Smoke Ball Co* (1893)
>
> The company advertised that they would pay £100 to anyone who caught influenza after using their smoke ball as directed. Carlill used the smoke ball, but still caught influenza and claimed £100. Amongst a number of defences argued for the company, it was suggested that the advert could not be an offer as it was not addressed to Carlill.
>
> **Held:** It was an offer to the whole world, which Mrs Carlill had accepted by her conduct. There was therefore a valid contract.

5.1.3 Acceptance of offers

A person cannot accept an offer which they do not know about. If a person offers a reward for the return of a lost watch, and someone returns it without knowing about the offer, they cannot claim the reward.

Motive for accepting is not important, as long as the person knows of the offer (*Williams v. Carwadwine* (1833)).

5.1.4 Rejection of offers

Rejection, where the offeree expressly rejects an offer, terminates the offer. The offeree cannot later accept the original offer. A counter-offer, where the offeree tries to change the terms of the offer has the same effect.

> *Hyde* v. *Wrench* (1840)
>
> Wrench offered to sell his farm for £1000. Hyde offered £950, which Wrench rejected. Hyde then informed Wrench that he accepted the original offer.
>
> **Held:** There was no contract, as Hyde's counter-offer had effectively ended the original offer.

A counter-offer must not be confused with a request for information. This does not end the offer, which can still be accepted (*Stevenson* v. *McLean* (1880)).

5.1.5 Revocation of offer

Revocation (cancellation) occurs when the offerer withdraws his offer.

1 An offer may be revoked at any time before acceptance.

> *Routledge* v. *Grant* (1828)
>
> Grant offered to buy Routledge's house, and gave six weeks for Routledge to accept. Within that period, however, he withdrew his offer.
>
> **Held:** Grant was entitled to withdraw his offer at any time before acceptance.

In certain cases involving unilateral offers, revocation is not permitted once the offeree has started performing the task requested.

> *Errington* v. *Errington* (1952)
>
> A father promised his son and daughter-in-law that he would convey a house to them when they had paid off the outstanding mortgage. After the father's death his widow sought to revoke the promise.
>
> **Held:** The promise could not be withdrawn as long as the mortgage payments continued to be met.

2 Revocation is not effective until it is actually received by the offeree.

> *Byrne* v. *Van Tienhoven* (1880)
>
> The defendant offerors carried out their business in Cardiff, the plaintiff offerees in New York.
> On 1 October an offer was made by post.
> On 8 October a letter of revocation was posted, seeking to withdraw the offer.
> On 11 October plaintiffs accepted the offer.
> On 20 October the letter of revocation arrived.
>
> **Held:** The revocation did not take effect until it arrived, and the defendants were bound by the contract which had been formed by the plaintiff's acceptance.

3 Communication of revocation may be made through a reliable third party.

> *Dickinson* v. *Dodds* (1876)
>
> Dodds offered to sell property to Dickinson and told him that the offer would be left open until Friday. On the Thursday the plaintiff was informed by a reliable third party, who was acting as an intermediary, that Dodds intended selling the property to someone else. Dickinson still tried to accept the offer on the Friday, by which time the property had already been sold.
>
> **Held:** The sale of the property amounted to revocation, which had been effectively communicated by the reliable third party.

4 A promise to keep an offer open is only binding where there is a separate contract to that effect. This is known as an option contract, and the promisee must provide consideration for the promise to keep the offer open.

5.1.6 Lapsing of offers

An offer will lapse in the following circumstances:

1 Where there is a stated time limit for acceptance, on the expiry of that period of time.

2 Where no time limit is stated, on the expiry of a reasonable time.

3 Where the offeree dies.

4 Where the offeror dies and the contract was one of a personal nature (*Bradbury* v. *Morgan* (1862)).

5.2 Acceptance

Acceptance is necessary for the formation of a contract. Once the offeree has accepted the offer a contract comes into effect. Both parties are bound. The offeror can no longer withdraw his offer, nor can the offeree withdraw his acceptance.

5.2.1 Form of acceptance

In order to form a binding agreement the acceptance must correspond with the terms of the offer. The offeree must not introduce new terms.

> *Neale* v. *Merritt* (1830)
>
> One party offered to sell property for £280. The other purported to accept the offer by sending £80 and promising to pay the remainder by monthly instalments.
>
> **Held:** There was no contract, as the plaintiff had not accepted the original offer as stated.

As has been seen in *Hyde* v. *Wrench*, a counter-offer does not constitute acceptance.

Conditional acceptance does not create a contract. Thus an agreement 'subject to contract' is not binding (*Winn* v. *Bull* (1877)).

Acceptance may be in the form of express words, either oral or written; or it may be implied from conduct.

> *Brogden* v. *Metropolitan Railway Co* (1877)
>
> The plaintiff, having supplied the company with coal for a number of years, suggested that they should enter into a written contract. The company agreed and sent Brogden a draft contract. He altered some points, and returned it marked 'approved'. The company did nothing further about the document, but Brogden continued to deliver coal on the terms included in the draft. When a dispute arose Brogden denied the existence of any contract.
>
> **Held:** The draft contract had become a contract when both parties acted on it.

5.2.2 Communication of acceptance

Acceptance must be communicated by the offeree to the offeror. Silence cannot amount to acceptance.

> *Felthouse* v. *Bindley* (1863)
>
> An uncle had been negotiating the purchase of his nephew's horse. He eventually wrote offering to buy the horse for £30 and 15 shillings, stating, 'If I hear no more about him, I shall consider the horse mine at this price.' When the horse was later mistakenly sold by an auctioneer, the uncle sued the auctioneer in conversion.
>
> **Held:** The uncle had no cause for action as the horse did not belong to him. Acceptance could not be imposed on the offeree on the basis of his silence.

The following are exceptions to the general rule that acceptance must be communicated.

1 Where the offeror has waived his right to receive communication. In unilateral contracts, such as *Carlill* v. *Carbolic Smoke Ball Co*, acceptance occurs when the offeree performs the required act. There is no need to inform the offeror of this acceptance.

2 Where acceptance is through the postal service, it is complete as soon as the letter, properly addressed and stamped, is posted. The contract is concluded even if the letter does not reach the offeror.

> *Adams* v. *Lindsell* (1818)
>
> On 2 September, the defendant made an offer to the plaintiff. Due to misdirection the letter was delayed. It arrived on 5 September and Adams immediately posted an acceptance. On 8 September Lindsell sold the merchandise to a third party. On 9 September the letter of acceptance from Adams arrived.
>
> **Held:** There was valid acceptance when Adams posted the letter and Lindsell was therefore liable for breach of contract.

As has already been seen in *Byrne* v. *Van Tienhoven*, the postal rule applies equally to telegrams. It does not apply, however, when means of instantaneous communications are used (*Entores* v. *Miles Far East Corp* (1955)). So when acceptance is made by means of telephone or telex, the offeror must actually receive the acceptance.

5.2.3 Avoidance of postal rule

In order to avoid the effect of the postal rule, the offeror can make acceptance effective only on actual receipt (*Holwell Securities* v. *Hughes* (1974)). The offeror can also require that acceptance be communicated in a particular manner. Where he does not insist that acceptance can only be made in the stated manner, then acceptance is effective if it is communicated in a way no less advantageous to the offeror.

> *Yates Building Co* v. *R. J. Pulleyn and Sons* (1975)
>
> An option to purchase land was stated to be exercisable by registered or recorded delivery letter. The offeree actually accepted by ordinary post.
>
> **Held:** The method of acceptance stated was not mandatory and the offeror had suffered no inconvenience through the method actually used.

5.2.4 Invitation of tenders

In the case of tenders the person who invites a tender is simply making an invitation to treat. The person who submits a tender is the offeror, and the other party is at liberty to accept or reject the offer as he pleases.

The effect of acceptance depends on the wording of the invitation to tender. If the invitation states that the potential purchaser will require to be supplied with a certain quantity of goods, then his acceptance constitutes a contract and he will be in breach if he fails to order any goods from the tenderer.

If, on the other hand, the invitation states only that the potential purchaser may require goods, acceptance gives rise only to a standing offer. There is no compulsion on the purchaser to take any goods, but he must not deal with another supplier. Each order given forms a separate contract and the supplier must deliver any goods required within the limit stated in the tender. He can revoke his standing offer, but he must supply any goods already ordered.

> *Great Northern Railway* v. *Witham* (1873)
>
> The defendant successfully tendered to supply the company with 'such quantities as the company may order from time to time'. After fulfilling some orders, Witham refused to supply any more goods.
>
> **Held:** Witham was in breach of contract in respect of the goods already ordered, but once those were supplied he was at liberty to revoke his standing offer.

5.3 Consideration

5.3.1 The nature of consideration

English law does not enforce gratuitous, or bare, promises, unless they are made under seal. Consideration can be understood as the price paid for a promise. The element of bargain implicit in the idea of consideration is evident in the following definition by Sir Frederick Pollock, adopted by the House of Lords in *Dunlop* v. *Selfridge* (1915) as:

> An act or forbearance of one party, or the promise thereof, is the price for which the promise of the other is bought, and the promise thus given for value is enforceable.

It is sometimes said that consideration consists of 'some benefit to the promisor, **or** detriment to the promisee'. It should be noted that it does not have to be both, although it usually is. If the promisee acts to his own detriment, it is immaterial that the action does not directly benefit the promisor.

Forbearance involves not acting, or giving up some right. An example is forbearance to sue. If two parties, A and B, believe that A has a cause of action against B, then if B promises to pay a sum of money to A if he will give up his action, there is a valid contract: A has provided consideration by giving up his recourse to law. It would not constitute consideration, however, if A knew his claim was hopeless or invalid.

5.3.2   Types of consideration

Consideration can be divided into the following categories:

1 Executory consideration. This is the promise to perform an action at some future time. A contract can be made on the basis of an exchange of promises. This is known as an executory contract.

2 Executed consideration. In the case of unilateral contracts, where the offeror promises something in return for the offeror's doing something, the promise only becomes enforceable once the offeree has actually performed the required act. If A offers a reward for the return of his lost watch, the reward only becomes enforceable once it has been found and returned to him.

3 Past consideration, which, in spite of its title, is not a valid form of consideration. In this case the promise is given after the action which is supposed to be the consideration for it. It is not sufficient to support a promise, as consideration cannot consist of an action already wholly performed before the promise was made.

> *Re McArdle* (1951)
> A number of children were entitled to a house on the death of their mother. Whilst the mother was still alive, a son and his wife lived with her, and the wife made various improvements to the house. The children later promised to repay the wife £488 for the work done.
> **Held:** The work was completed when the promise was given. It was therefore past consideration, and the promise could not be enforced.

There are exceptions to the rule that past consideration will not support a valid contract:

(a) under Section 27 of the Bills of Exchange Act, 1882, past consideration can create liability on a bill of exchange;

(b) under Section 29 of the Limitation Act, 1980, a time barred debt becomes enforceable again if it is acknowledged in writing;

(c) where the plaintiff performed the action at the request of the defendant and payment was expected, then any subsequent promise to pay will be enforceable.

> *Re Casey's Patents* (1892)
> The joint owners of patent rights asked Casey to find licensees to work the patents. When he had done so they promised to reward him.
> **Held:** The promise made to Casey was enforceable. There had been an implied promise to reward him before he performed his action. The later payment only fixed the extent of that reward.

5.3.3 Rules relating to consideration

That consideration must not be past is only one of the rules relating to consideration. The others are as follows:

1 The performance must be legal. The Court would not enforce a promise to pay for a criminal act.

2 The performance must be possible. A promise to do something that is impossible cannot form the basis of a contract.

3 Consideration must move from the promisee. If A promises B £1000 if B gives his car to C, then normally C cannot enforce B's promise, because he has provided no consideration.

> *Tweddle* v. *Atkinson* (1861)
>
> On the occasion of the marriage of A and B, their respective fathers entered into a contract to pay money to A. When one of the parents died without having made the payment, A tried to enforce the contract against his estate.
>
> **Held:** A could not enforce the contract as he had not provided any consideration for the father's promise.

4 Consideration need not be adequte. It is up to the parties themselves to decide the terms of their contract. The court will not intervene to require equality in the value exchanged, as long as the agreement has been freely entered into. In *Chappell and Co* v. *Nestlé Co* (1959) it was held that a used chocolate wrapper was consideration, although of no value to Nestlé.

> *Thomas* v. *Thomas* (1842)
>
> The executors of a man's will promised to let his widow live in his house in return for rent of £1 per year.
>
> **Held:** The £1 was sufficient consideration to validate the contract, although it did not represent an adequate rent.

5 Consideration must be sufficient. The performance of an existing duty does not usually provide valid consideration. The rules governing existing duty are as follows:

(a) The mere discharge of a public duty cannot be consideration.

> *Collins* v. *Godefroy* (1831)
>
> The plaintiff was subpoenaed to give evidence for the defendant, who also promised to pay him.
>
> **Held:** The defendant did not have to pay, as Collins had provided no consideration by merely performing his public duty.

If the promisee does more than his duty, however, he is entitled to claim on the promise, as in *Glassbrook* v. *Glamorgan C.C.* (1925), where the police supplied more protection than their public duty required.

(b) The mere performance of a contractual duty already owed to the promisor cannot be consideration for a new promise.

> *Stilk* v. *Myrick* (1809)
>
> When two members of his crew deserted, a ship's captain promised the remaining members of the crew that they would share the deserters' wages if they completed the voyage.
>
> **Held:** The promise was not enforceable, as the sailors only did what they were already obliged to do by their contracts of employment.

Again, in this case performance of more than the existing duty will be valid consideration. In *Hartley* v. *Ponsonby* (1857) the facts were somewhat similar to those in *Stilk* v. *Myrick*, but the crew did more than they had agreed previously to do, because the number of deserters had been so great as to render the return of the ship unusually hazardous.

(c) The performance of a contractual duty owed to one person **can** be valid consideration for a promise made by another person.

> *Shadwell* v. *Shadwell* (1860)
>
> The plaintiff had entered into a contract to marry. His uncle promised that if he married his fiancée, the uncle would pay him £150 per year, until the earnings reached 600 guineas. When the uncle died owing several years' payments, the nephew sued his executors to recover the outstanding money.
>
> **Held:** The plaintiff should succeed, as his going through with the marriage was sufficient consideration for his uncle's promise, even though he was already contractually bound to his fiancée.

In *Tweddle* v. *Atkinson* (1861), the promise was not enforceable because it was not made to the groom.

5.3.4 Consideration in regard to the waiver of existing rights

At common law, if A owes B £10, but B agrees to accept £5 in full settlement of the debt, B's promise to give up his existing right must be supported by consideration. In *Pinnel's Case* (1602) it was stated that a payment of a lesser sum on the due date in satisfaction of a greater sum cannot be any satisfaction for the whole. This view was approved in:

> *Foakes* v. *Beer* (1884)
>
> Mrs Beer had obtained a judgment against Dr Foakes in debt for £2091. She had agreed in writing to accept payment of this amount in instalments. When payment was finished she claimed a further £360 as interest due on the judgment debt.
>
> **Held:** Mrs Beer was entitled to the interest. Her promise to accept the bare debt was not supported by any consideration from Dr Foakes.

There are exceptions to this rule:

1 Payment in kind will discharge the debt. Again, the payment does not have to be adequate. Thus A can discharge a £10 debt by giving B £5 and a sweet.

It should be noted that payment by cheque is no longer treated as substitute payment (*D. & C. Builders Ltd* v. *Rees* (1966)).

2 Payment of a lesser sum before the due date of payment, or at a different place will discharge the debt fully (*Pinnel's Case*).

3 A composition arrangement with creditors, that they will accept part-payment of their debts in full settlement will effectively discharge the debt (*Good* v. *Cheesman* (1831)).

4 Payment of a smaller sum by a third party will discharge a larger debt (*Welby* v. *Drake* (1825)).

5.3.5 Promissory estoppel

This equitable doctrine operates to prevent promisors from going back on their promises. It first appeared in *Hughes* v. *Metropolitan Railway Co* (1877), and was revived by Lord Denning in the *High Trees* case.

> *Central London Property Trust Ltd* v. *High Trees House Ltd* (1947)
>
> In 1937 the plaintiffs let a block of flats to the defendants at a fixed rent. Due to the war it was difficult to let the flats and the parties entered into a second agreement whereby the rent was halved. No consideration was given for this promise and although it was reduced to writing, it was not sealed. By 1945 all the flats were let and the plaintiffs claimed the full rent both as to the future and for part of the previous period.
>
> **Held:** The plaintiffs were entitled to the full rent in the future but were estopped from claiming the full rent for the period from 1941 until 1945.

Promissory estoppel may be used as a defence in an action to recover a debt which the plaintiff has previously promised to forgo. Unfortunately the precise scope of the doctrine of promissory estoppel is far from certain. There are a number of conflicting judgments on the point, some judges adopting a wide understanding of the doctrine with others preferring to keep it narrowly constrained. The following rules may be stated, however:

1 It arises from a promise made with the intention that it be acted upon, and it is acted on. It was once thought that the promisee had to act to his detriment, but now it is considered that he only has to have acted on the promise (*W. J. Alan and Co.* v. *El Nasr Export and Import Co* (1972)).

2 It operates to suspend rights and the promisor can, with reasonable notice, retract his promise. Rights are only extinguished when the parties cannot resume their original positions.

3 It relates only to the variation or discharge of rights within a contract. It does not relate to the formation of a contract, and does not obviate the need for consideration to establish a contract. This point is sometimes made by stating that promissory estoppel is 'a shield not a sword' (*Combe* v. *Combe* (1951)).

4 It only applies where the promise is given voluntarily.

> *D. & C. Builders* v. *Rees* (1966)
>
> The defendants owed the plaintiffs £482, but would only pay £300. As the builders were in financial difficulties they accepted the £300 in full settlement of the account. The plaintiffs later claimed the balance.
>
> **Held:** The debt had to be paid in full. The defendants had been forced to accept the lesser sum; and as estoppel could not be claimed in such circumstances, the case had to be decided in line with the rule in *Pinnel's Case*.

5.4 Privity of contract

There is some debate as to whether privity is a principle in its own right, or whether it is simply a conclusion from the more general rules relating to consideration. In any case it is a general rule that a contract can only impose rights or obligations on persons who are parties to it. This is the doctrine of privity.

> *Dunlop* v. *Selfridge* (1915)
>
> Dunlop sold tyres to a distributor, Dew & Co, on terms that the distributor would not sell them at less than the manufacturer's list price, and that they would extract a similar undertaking from anyone they supplied with tyres. Dew & Co, resold tyres to Selfridge who agreed to abide by the restrictions and to pay Dunlop £5 for each tyre they sold in breach of them. When Selfridge sold tyres at below the list price, Dunlop sought to recover the promised £5 per tyre.
>
> **Held:** Dunlop could not recover damages on the basis of a contract between Dew and Selfridge, to which they were not a party.

The strict rule of privity can be avoided through a number of devices:

1 The beneficiary may be able to enforce the promise by suing in some other capacity.

> *Beswick* v. *Beswick* (1967)
>
> A coal merchant sold his business to his nephew, in return for a consultancy fee of £6.10s per week during his lifetime, and thereafter an annuity of £5 per week payable to his widow. After the uncle died the nephew stopped paying his widow. When she became administratrix of her husband's estate she sued the nephew for specific performance of the agreement in that capacity and also in her personal capacity.
>
> **Held:** Although the widow was not a party to the contract, and she could not have been granted specific performance in her private capacity, her action, in the capacity of administratrix, was successful and specific performance was ordered.

2 A collateral contract may be effective to enforce promises.

> *Shanklin Pier Ltd* v. *Detel Products Ltd* (1951)
> The plaintiffs contracted to have their pier repainted. On the basis of promises as to quality, the defendants persuaded the pier company to insist that a particular paint produced by Detel was used. The painters used the paint but it proved unsatisfactory. The plaintiffs sued for breach of the original promise. The defendants countered that the only contract was between them and the painters to whom they had sold the paint, and the pier company were not a party to that contract.
> **Held:** The pier company were successful. In addition to the contract for the sale of paint, there was a second collateral contract between the plaintiffs and the defendants by which Detel guaranteed the suitability of the paint in return for the pier company specifying that the painters used it.

3 A party can transfer the benefit of a contract to a third party through the formal process of assignment. The assignment must be in writing, and the assignor receives no better rights under the contract than the assignor possessed. The burden of a contract cannot be assigned without the consent of the other party.

4 The other main exception to the privity rule is agency, where the agent brings about contractual relations between two other parties.

5.5 Capacity

5.5.1 Definition

Capacity refers to a person's ability to enter into a contract. In general, all adults of sound mind have full capacity. The capacity of certain individuals, however, is limited.

5.5.2 Minors

A minor is a person under the age of 18. The law tries to protect such persons, by restricting their contractual capacity. The rules which apply are a mixture of common law and statute, and depend on when the contract was made. Contracts entered into prior to 9th June 1987 are governed by the Infants Relief Act, 1874, contracts entered into after that date are subject to the Minors' Contracts Act, 1987.

Valid contracts

1 A minor is bound to pay for necessaries, i.e. things necessary to maintain him, that have been supplied to him. Necessaries are defined, in the Sale of Goods Act, Section 3, as goods suitable to the condition in life of the minor and to his actual requirements at the time of sale.

> *Nash* v. *Inman* (1908)
> A tailor sued a minor to whom he had supplied clothes, including 11 fancy waistcoats. The minor was an undergraduate at Cambridge University.
> **Held:** Although the clothes were suitable according to the minor's station in life, they were not necessary as he already had sufficient clothing.

A minor is only required to pay a reasonable price for any necessaries purchased.

2 A minor is bound by a contract of apprenticeship or employment as long as it is, on the whole, for his benefit.

> *Doyle* v. *White City Stadium* (1935)
> Doyle, as a minor, obtained a professional boxer's licence, which was treated as contract of apprenticeship. The licence provided that he would be bound by the rules of the Boxing Board of Control, who had power to retain any prize money if he was ever disqualified. He claimed that the licence was void, as it was not for his benefit.
> **Held:** The conditions in the licence were enforceable. In spite of the penal clause it was held to be beneficial to him, taken as a whole.

There has to be an element of education or training in the contract and ordinary trading contracts will not be enforced.

> *Mercantile Union Guarantee Corp* v. *Ball* (1937)
> A minor who operated a haulage business entered into a hire-purchase agreement in respect of a lorry.
> **Held:** The minor could not be held liable to pay the hire-purchase instalments.

Voidable contracts

Voidable contracts are binding on the minor, unless he repudiates them during the period of his minority or within a reasonable time after reaching the age of majority. These are generally transactions in which the minor acquires an interest of a permanent nature with continuing obligations – examples are contracts for shares, or leases of property, or partnership agreements.

If the minor has made payments prior to his repudiation of the contract, he cannot recover it unless there has been a total failure of consideration, and he has received no benefit whatsoever.

> *Steinberg* v. *Scala* (*Leeds*) (1923)
> Miss Steinberg, while still a minor, applied for and was allotted shares in the defendant company. After paying some money on the shares she defaulted and repudiated the contract. The company agreed that her name be removed from its register of members, but refused to return her money.
> **Held:** Steinberg's claim failed. As she had received membership rights there had not been a total failure of consideration.

Void contracts

Under the Infants Relief Act, 1874, the following contracts were stated to be absolutely void;

1 Contracts for the repayment of loans.

2 Contracts for goods supplied other than necessities.

3 All accounts stated, i.e. admissions of money owed.

In addition, no action could be brought on the basis of the ratification, made after the attainment of full age, of an otherwise void contract.

Although the Act stated that such contracts were absolutely void, in effect this simply meant that they could not be enforced against the minor. The other party could not normally recover goods or money transferred to the minor. Where, however, the goods had been obtained by the minor by fraud, and they were still in his possession, the other party could rely on the doctrine of restitution to reclaim them.

The minor could enforce the agreement against the other party, although specific performance would not be available.

The major effect of the Minors' Contracts Act, 1987 is that the contracts mentioned in the Infants Relief Act are no longer absolutely void, but are to be evaluated in line with common law rules stated previously; i.e. they will be either valid or voidable.

The repeal of the Infants Relief Act also permits for the ratification of unenforceable, or voidable, contracts after the attainment of majority (Section 1).

The Minors' Contracts Act also makes any guarantee of a minor's contractual obligation enforceable against the guarantor, even though the actual contract may not be enforceable against the minor for want of capacity (Section 2).

The Court also is given wider powers to order the restoration of property acquired by a minor. Now it can order restitution where it thinks it is 'just and equitable' to do so, and is no longer restricted to cases where the minor has acquired the property through fraud (Section 3).

The law does not permit the other party to enforce a contract indirectly by substituting an action in tort, or quasi-contract, for an action in contract.

> *Leslie* v. *Shiell* (1914)
>
> Shiell, whilst a minor, obtained a loan from Leslie by lying about his age. Leslie sued to recover the money as damages in an action for the tort of deceit.
>
> **Held:** The action must fail, as it was simply an indirect way of enforcing the void contract.

5.5.3 Persons who are of unsound mind or who are drunk

A contract by a person who is of unsound mind or under the influence of drink or drugs is *prima facie* valid. In order to avoid a contract, such a person must show:

1 that his mind was so affected at the time that he was incapable of understanding the nature of his actions;

2 that the other party either knew or ought to have known of his disability.

The disabled person must, however, pay a reasonable price for necessaries sold and delivered to him. This situation is governed by the same rules as apply to minors.

5.5.4 Corporations

The capacity of corporations to enter into contracts, and the doctrine of *ultra vires*, will be dealt with in a later chapter.

5.6 Intention to create legal relations

All of the aspects considered previously may well be present, and yet there still may not be a contract. The courts will only enforce those agreements which the parties intended to have legal effect. Although expressed in terms of the parties' intentions, the test for the presence of such intentions is once again an objective, rather than a subjective, one. For the purposes of this topic agreements can be divided into two categories, in which different presumptions apply:

5.6.1 Domestic and social agreements

In this type of agreement there is a presumption that the parties did not intend legal relations to arise.

> *Balfour* v. *Balfour* (1919)
>
> When a husband returned to Ceylon to take up his employment he promised his wife, who could not return with him due to health problems, that he would pay her £30 per month as maintenance. When the marriage later ended in divorce, the wife sued for the promised maintenance.
>
> **Held:** There was no intention that legal relations be created between the couple, and therefore the promise was not legally enforceable.

The presumption against married couples intending to create legal relations may be rebutted.

> *Merritt* v. *Merritt* (1970)
>
> After a husband had left the matrimonial home, he met his wife and promised to pay her £40 per month, from which she undertook to pay the outstanding mortgage on their house. The husband, at the wife's insistance, signed a note agreeing to transfer the house into the wife's sole name when the mortgage was paid off. The wife paid off the mortgage, but the husband refused to transfer the house.
>
> **Held:** The agreement was enforceable, as in the circumstances the parties had clearly intended to create legal relations.

5.6.2 Commercial agreements

Here the strong presumption is that the parties intended legal relations to arise from their dealings.

The presumption is, however, rebuttable.

> *Edwards* v. *Skyways* (1964)
>
> Employers undertook to make an *ex-gratia* payment to an employee they had made redundant.
>
> **Held:** The use of the term *'ex-gratia'* was not enough to rebut the presumption that legal relations had been intended, and the employee was entitled to the payment.

It is possible to rebut the presumption, as in the following cases, where the parties expressly provide that no legal relations are to arise:

> *Jones* v. *Vernon's Pools Ltd* (1938)
>
> The plaintiff claimed to have submitted a correct forecast. The defendants denied receiving it and relied on a clause on the coupon which stated that the transaction was 'binding in honour only'.
>
> **Held:** The clause showed that no legal relations were intended. The plaintiff, therefore, had no cause for action.

In *Rose & Frank Co* v. *Crompton & Bros Ltd* (1925) it was held that an express clause stating that no legal relations were to be created by a business transaction was effective.

5.6.3 Collective agreements between trade unions and employers

In *Ford Motor Co* v. *AUEFW* (1969) it was decided that such agreements are presumed not to give rise to legal relations, and Ford could not take an action against a union which ignored an agreement with them.

Once again the presumption can be rebutted, if the circumstances of the particular case make it clear that the parties intend legal relations to be created.

Sample questions

1 (a) Explain the legal effect in the law of contract of:

(i) an invitation to treat;

(ii) a tender;

(iii) a counter-offer.

(b) H advertised in a variety of journals that an auction of paintings would take place on 30th March. J travelled 100 miles to the auction on 30th March and found a notice outside saying 'Auction cancelled today: will be held 30th April'. J attended the auction on 30th April and bid £1000 for a painting. He changed his mind and called out, 'Bid withdrawn'. The auctioneer did not hear him and banged his hammer for the third time. Advise H.

ACCA

Suggested answer

(a) (i) The important point here is to distinguish an invitation to treat from an offer.

The most important cases relating to invitations to treat, at least one of which should be mentioned are:

Fisher v. *Bell.*

Partridge v. *Crittenden.*

Pharmaceutical Society of GB v. *Boots Cash Chemists.*

(ii) The parties involved in the tender must be distinguished in terms of who is the offeror and who is the offeree. Distinction should be made between the effect of tenders for specific goods, and those for goods 'as and when required'. Reference should be made to *Great Northern Railway* v. *Witham*.

(iii) The fact that a counter offer destroys the original offer must be stated – *Hyde* v. *Wrench.*

It should be distinguished from a request for more information – *Stevenson* v. *McLean.*

(b) There are three points to consider in this question:

(i) The advertisement of the auction is only an invitation to treat. It can be withdrawn and J has no right to sue – *Harrison* v. *Nickerson.*

(ii) J's bid is an offer which may be accepted by the auctioneer's hammer falling for the third time. (Section 57 of the Sale of Goods Act, 1979).

(iii) J's offer can be revoked at any time before acceptance, but it must be communicated to the auctioneer. The auctioneer did not hear J's revocation, so it has not been communicated (*Byrne* v. *Van Tienhoven*). J is therefore liable to pay H £1000.

2 Advise C whether she may enforce the promises in the following situations:

(a) C, who was driving to Manchester, was asked by D to buy a suitcase for D from a department store there. D paid C for the suitcase. On C's return with the suitcase D promised to pay her for her petrol.

(b) On her wedding day E went to C, her hairdresser, and promised to buy C some expensive perfume if she styled E's hair exceptionally well.

(c) F, C's brother, promised to sell her his BMW car, which is worth £12 000, for £1200.

ILE

Suggested answer

(a) This question essentially relates to past consideration. D only promises to pay for the petrol after C has performed the act for which it is supposed to be consideration (*Re McArdle*). The question then is whether it comes within the exceptions to the past consideration rule, as stated in *Re Casey's Patents*.

(b) Can the hairdresser hold C to her promise, as she will be under an existing contractual duty to style C's hair? (*Stilk* v. *Myrick*). It would seem likely as she promises to provide extra consideration by styling the hair 'exceptionally well', thus doing more than she would normally (*Ward* v. *Byham*).

(c) This involves a consideration of intention to create legal relations. In family situations there is a presumption that there is no intention to create legal relations (*Balfour* v. *Balfour*). This presumption can be rebutted, however (*Merritt* v. *Merritt*.) In this situation it is unlikely that C will be able to rebut the presumption.

3 Consider the following:

(a) Carol owes David £700. David agrees that if Carol's boyfriend Edward paints his house (the work is worth £400) he will regard Carol's debt as discharged. Edward does the work. David now sues for the balance.

(b) Fred owes £50 to Graham, £100 to Helen and £250 to Ian. He writes to each of his creditors explaining that he can only pay 20 per cent of his debt and asks each of them to accept such payment in full and final settlement of his debt. All his creditors agree in writing to this arrangement. However, Ian, who is in financial difficulty, now wishes to sue for the whole sum owed to him.

Discuss. Would your answer differ if the above arrangement had been made at a meeting where all the parties concerned were present?

ILE

Suggested answer

(a) Normally the payment of a lesser sum cannot discharge a debt (see *Pinnel's Case*). However, although David was owed £700 by Carol, and only received value to the extent of £400, he will be unable to recover any money from her for two reasons;

(i) the debt was discharged by payment in kind rather than money, and this is effective to discharge the debt (*Pinnel's Case*).

(ii) the debt was discharged by a third party, and this also effectively discharges the debt (*Hirachand Punamchand* v. *Temple* (1911)).

(b) This involves a third exception to the general rule in *Pinnel's Case*. Where a debtor enters into a composition agreement with his creditors, they are all bound by their agreement to accept a proportionate payment of their debt as full satisfaction.

Unfortunately, in this case Fred has not entered into such an agreement but has merely entered into individual arrangements with his creditors. In this instance, the rule in *Pinnel's Case* applies—Ian can go back on his promise, and sue to recover the outstanding part of the debt. If all the creditors met and agreed to accept part payment, there would be a composition agreement.

4 (a) Discuss the capacity of a minor to make a contract.

(b) Consider the effect of the following agreements entered into by P who is 17 years of age:

(i) a lease of a flat for five years;

(ii) an order for a new suit of clothes;

(iii) an agreement with Q that Q will train him to be a motor mechanic.

ACCA

Suggested answer

(a) This requires an examination of the factors considered in section 5.6.2. It will be noticed that at the time this question was set the Infants Relief Act would have been in force. From now on any answer would be required to deal with the consequences of the repeal of that Act by the Minors' Contract Act 1987. Examples of valid and voidable contracts should be given, together with examples of contracts which were previously void under the Infants Relief Act.

(b) This part looks for application of the general law to particular situations.

(i) This is a voidable contract, involving the minor in an interest of a continuing nature. P can repudiate the contract immediately, or within a reasonable time of his achieving his majority. He will not be able to recover payments made during his minority unless there was a total failure of consideration, which is unlikely.

(ii) This is apparently a contract involving necessaries. P will be bound by the agreement, but will only have to pay a reasonable price for the clothes (*Nash* v. *Inman*).

(iii) This is also a valid contract, and will be enforceable as long as it is, on the whole, for P's benefit (*Doyle* v. *White City Stadium*).

Further reading

For further reading on the topics covered in this chapter, see chapter 4.

6 Contents of a contract

The previous chapter dealt with how a binding contractual agreement comes to be formed; this chapter will consider what the parties have actually agreed to do.

6.1 Contract terms and mere representations

As the parties will normally be bound to perform any promise that they have contracted to undertake, it is important to decide precisely what promises are included in the contract. Some statements do not form part of a contract, even though they might have induced the other party to enter into the contract. These pre-contractual statements are called representations. The consequences of such representations being false will be considered in chapter 7, but for the moment it is sufficient to distinguish them from contractual terms, which are statements which **do** form part of the contract. There are four tests for distinguishing a contractual term from a mere representation:

1 Where the statement is of such major importance that the promisee would not have entered into the agreement without it, then it will be construed as a term.

> *Bannerman* v. *White* (1861)
>
> As the defendant wanted to buy hops for brewing purposes, he asked the plaintiff if they had been treated with sulphur. On the basis of the plaintiff's false statement that they had not been so treated, he agreed to buy the hops. When he discovered later that they had been treated with sulphur, he refused to accept them.
>
> **Held:** The plaintiff's statement about the sulphur was a fundamental term of the contract, and as it was not true, the defendant was entitled to repudiate the contract.

2 Where there is a time gap between the statement and the making of the contract, then the statement will most likely be treated as a representation.

> *Routledge* v. *McKay* (1954)
>
> On 23 October the defendant told the plaintiff that a motorcycle was a 1942 model. On 30 October a written contract for the sale of the bike was made, without reference to its age. The bike was actually a 1930 model.
>
> **Held:** The statement about the date was a pre-contractual representation, and the plaintiff could not sue for damages for breach of contract.

This rule is not a hard and fast one. In *Schawell* v. *Reade* (1913), the court held that a statement made three months before the final agreement was part of the contract.

3 Where the statement is oral, and the agreement is subsequently drawn up in written form, then exclusion from the written document will suggest that the statement was not meant to be a contractual term (see *Routledge* v. *McKay*).

4 Where one of the parties to an agreement has special knowledge or skill, then statements made **by** them will be terms, but statements made **to** them will not.

> *Dick Bentley Productions Ltd* v. *Harold Smith (Motors) Ltd* (1965)
>
> The plaintiff bought a Bentley car from the defendant after being assured that it had only travelled 20 000 miles since its engine and gearbox had been replaced. When this statement turned out to be untrue the plaintiff sued for breach of contract.
>
> **Held:** The statement was a term of the contract and the plaintiff was entitled to damages.

> *Oscar Chess Ltd* v. *Williams* (1957)
>
> Williams traded in one car when buying another from the plaintiffs. He told them that his trade-in was a 1948 model; whereas it was actually a 1939 model. The company sued for breach of contract.
>
> **Held:** The plaintiffs could not sue for breach of contract. The statement as to the age of the car was merely a representation, and the right to sue for misrepresentation had been lost due to delay.

6.2 Conditions, warranties, and innominate terms

Once it is decided that a statement is a term, rather than merely a pre-contractual representation, it is necessary to determine which type of term it is, in order to determine what remedies are available for its breach.

Terms can be classified as one of three types.

6.2.1 Conditions

A condition is a fundamental part of the agreement – it is something which goes to the root of the contract. Breach of a condition gives the innocent party the right **either** to terminate the contract and refuse to perform his part of it, **or** to go through with the agreement and sue for damages.

6.2.2 Warranties

A warranty is a subsidiary obligation which is not vital to the overall agreement, and does not totally destroy its efficacy. Breach of a warranty does not give the right to terminate the agreement. The innocent party has to complete his part of the agreement, and can only sue for damages.

The difference between the two types of term can be seen in the following cases:

> *Poussard* v. *Spiers & Pond* (1876)
>
> The plaintiff (Mme Poussard) had contracted with the defendants to sing in an opera they were producing. Due to illness she was unable to appear on the first night, or for some nights thereafter. When Mme Poussard recovered, the defendants refused her services as they had hired a replacement for the whole run of the opera.
>
> **Held:** Her failure to appear on the opening night had been a breach of a condition, and the defendants were at liberty to treat the contract as discharged.

> *Bettini* v. *Gye* (1876)
>
> The plaintiff had contracted with the defendants to complete a number of engagements. He had also agreed to be in London for rehearsals six days before his opening performance. Due to illness, he only arrived three days before the opening night, and the defendants refused his services.
>
> **Held:** On this occasion there was only a breach of warranty. The defendants were entitled to damages, but could not treat the contract as discharged.

The distinction between the effects of a breach of condition as against the effects of a breach of warranty were enshrined in Section 11 of the Sale of Goods Act 1893 (now SGA, 1979). For some time it was thought that these were the only two types of term possible, the nature of the remedy available being prescribed by the particular type of term concerned. This simple classification has subsequently been rejected by the courts as too restrictive, and a third type of term has developed: the innominate term.

6.2.3 Innominate terms

In this case, the remedy is not prescribed in advance simply by whether the term breached is a condition or a warranty, but depends on the consequence of the breach.

If the breach deprives the innocent party of 'substantially the whole benefit of the contract', then the right to repudiate will be permitted; even if the term might otherwise appear to be a mere warranty.

If, however, the innocent party does not lose 'substantially the whole benefit of the contract', then he will not be permitted to repudiate but must settle for damages, even if the term might otherwise appear to be a condition.

> *Cehave v. Bremer (The Hansa Nord)* (1976)
> A contract for the sale of a cargo of citrus pulp pellets, to be used as animal feed, provided that they were to be delivered in good condition. On delivery, the buyers rejected the cargo as not complying with this provision, and claimed back the price paid from the sellers. The buyers eventually obtained the pellets when the cargo was sold off, and used them for their original purpose.
> **Held:** Since the breach had not been serious, the buyers had not been free to reject the cargo, and the sellers had been correct to keep the money paid.

6.3 Express and implied terms

So far, all the cases considered have involved express terms: statements actually made by one of the parties, either by word of mouth or in writing. Implied terms are not actually stated, but are introduced into the contract by implication.

Implied terms can be divided into three types:

6.3.1 Terms implied by statute

For example, under the Sale of Goods Act, 1979, terms relating to description, merchantable quality, and fitness for purpose are all implied into sale of goods contracts.

6.3.2 Terms implied by custom

An agreement may be subject to customary terms, not actually specified by the parties. For example, in *Hutton* v. *Warren* (1836) it was held that customary usage permitted a farm tenant to claim an allowance for seed and labour on quitting his tenancy. It should be noted, however, that custom cannot override the express terms of an agreement (*Les Affreteurs* v. *Walford* (1919)).

6.3.3 Terms implied by the Courts

Generally it is a matter for the parties concerned to decide the terms of a contract, but on occasion the Court will presume that the parties intended to include a term which is not expressly stated. They will do so where it is necessary, to give business efficacy to the contract. Whether a term may be implied can be decided on the basis of 'the officious bystander' test. Imagine two parties, A and B, negotiating a contract. A third party, C, interrupts to suggest a particular provision. A and B reply that that particular term is understood. Thus will the Court decide that a term should be implied into a contract.

> *The Moorcock* (1889)
> The appellants, owners of a wharf, contracted with the respondents to permit them to discharge their ship at the wharf. It was apparent to both parties that when the tide was out the ship would rest on the river bed. When the tide was out the ship sustained damage by settling on a ridge.
> **Held:** There was an implied warranty in the contract that the place of anchorage should be safe for the ship. The shipowner was entitled to damages for breach of that term.

6.4 The parol evidence rule

If all the terms of a contract are in writing, then there is a strong presumption that no evidence supporting a different oral agreement will be permitted to vary those terms.

> *Hutton* v. *Watling* (1948)
>
> On the sale of a business together with its goodwill, a written agreement was drawn up and signed by the vendor. In an action to enforce one of the clauses in the agreement the vendor claimed that it did not represent the whole contract.
>
> **Held:** The vendor was not entitled to introduce evidence on this point as the written document represented a true record of the contract.

The presumption can be rebutted, however, where it is shown that the document was not intended to set out all of the terms agreed on by the parties.

> *Re SS Ardennes* (1951)
>
> A ship's bill of lading stated that it might proceed 'by any route ... directly or indirectly ...'. The defendants promised that the ship would procede directly to London from Spain with its cargo of tangerines. However, the ship called at Antwerp before heading for London, and as a result the tangerines had to be sold at a reduced price. The shippers sued for damages.
>
> **Held:** They should succeed, as the bill of lading did not constitute the contract between the parties, but merely evidenced their intentions. The verbal promise was part of the final contract.

6.5 Exemption or exclusion clauses

In a sense, an exemption clause is no different from any other clause, in that it seeks to define the rights and obligations of the parties to a contract. An exemption clause is a term in a contract which tries to exempt, or limit, the liability of a party in breach of the agreement. Exclusion clauses give rise to most concern when they are included in 'standard form' contracts, in which one party, in a position of commercial dominance, imposes his terms on the other party, who has no choice (other than to take it or leave it) as far as the terms of the contract go. Such standard form contracts are contrary to the ideas of consensus and negotiation which underpin contract law; for this reason they have received particular attention from both the judiciary and the legislature, in an endeavour to counteract their perceived unfairness.

The actual law relating to exclusion clauses is complicated by the interplay of the common law, the Unfair Contract Terms Act, 1977, and the various Acts which imply certain terms into particular contracts.

The following points should be observed, with regard to exclusion clauses:

1 Has the exclusion clause been incorporated into the contract?

2 Does the exclusion clause effectively cover the breach?

3 What effect does the Unfair Contract Terms Act have on the exclusion clause?

6.5.1 Has the exclusion clause been incorporated into the contract?

An exclusion clause cannot be effective unless it is actually a term of a contract. There are three ways in which such a term may be inserted into a contract: by signature, notice, or custom.

6.5.1.1 Signature

If a person signs a contractual document, then he is bound by its terms, even if he did not read it.

> *L'Estrange* v. *Graucob* (1934)
>
> A café owner bought a vending machine, signing a contract without reading it, which took away all her rights under the Sale of Goods Act, 1893. When the machine proved faulty she sought to take action against the vendors.
>
> **Held:** She had no cause of action as she had signified her consent to the terms of the contract by signing it.

The rule in *L'Estrange* v. *Graucob* may be avoided where the party seeking to rely on the exclusion clause misled the other party into signing the contract (*Curtis* v. *Chemical Cleaning & Dyeing Co* (1951)).

6.5.1.2   Notice

Apart from the above, an exclusion clause will not be incorporated into a contract unless the party affected actually knew of it, or was given sufficient notice of it. In order for notice to be adequate, the document bearing the exclusion clause must be an integral part of the contract, and given at the time the contract is made.

> *Chapleton* v. *Barry UDC* (1940)
>
> The plaintiff hired a deck-chair and received a ticket which stated on the back that the council would not be responsible for any injuries arising from the hire of the chairs. After he was injured because his chair collapsed, Chapleton sued the council.
>
> **Held:** The plaintiff was successful. The ticket was merely a receipt, and could not be used effectively to communicate the exclusion clause.

> *Olley* v. *Marlborough Court Ltd* (1949)
>
> A couple arrived at a hotel and paid for a room in advance. On reaching their room they found a notice purporting to exclude the hotel's liability in regard to thefts of goods not handed in to the manager. A thief later stole the wife's furs.
>
> **Held:** The hotel could not escape liability, as the disclaimer had only been made after the contract had been formed.

Whether the degree of notice given has been sufficient is a matter of fact, but in *Thornton* v. *Shoe Lane Parking Ltd* (1971) it was stated that the greater the exemption, the greater the degree of notice required.

6.5.1.3   Custom

Where the parties have had previous dealings on the basis of an exclusion clause, that clause may be included in later contracts (*Spurling* v. *Bradshaw* (1956)), but it has to be shown that the party affected had actual knowledge of the exclusion clause.

> *Hollier* v. *Rambler Motors* (1972)
>
> On each of the previous occasions when the plaintiff had had his car repaired at the defendant's garage he had signed a form containing an exclusion clause. On the last occasion he had not signed such a form. When the car was damaged by fire through negligence the defendants sought to rely on the exclusion clause.
>
> **Held:** There was no evidence that Hollier had been aware of the clause to which he had been agreeing and, therefore, it could not be considered a part of his last contract.

6.5.2   Does the exclusion clause effectively cover the breach?

As a consequence of the disfavour with which the judiciary have looked on exclusion clauses, they have developed a number of rules of construction which operate to restrict the effectiveness of exclusion clauses.

1 The *contra proferentum* rule

This requires that any uncertainties or ambiguities in the exclusion clause be interpreted against the meaning claimed for it by the person seeking to rely on it.

> *Andrews* v. *Singer* (1934)
>
> The plaintiffs contracted to buy some 'new Singer cars' from the defendant. A clause excluded 'all conditions, warranties and liabilities implied by statute, common law, or otherwise'. One car supplied was not new.
>
> **Held:** The requirement that the cars be new was an express condition of the contract and therefore was not covered by the exclusion clause.

In *Hollier* v. *Rambler* it was stated that as the exclusion clause could be interpreted as applying only to non-negligent accidental damage, or to include damage caused by negligence; it should be restricted to the former, narrower, interpretation. As a consequence, the plaintiff could recover for damages caused to his car by the defendant's negligence.

2 The doctrine of fundamental breach

In a series of complicated and conflicting cases, ending with the House of Lords decision in *Photo Production* v. *Securicor*, some Courts attempted to develop a rule that it was impossible to exclude liability for breach of contract if a fundamental breach of the contract had occurred; i.e. the party in breach had failed altogether to perform the contract.

> *Photo Production v. Securicor Transport* (1980)
>
> The defendants had entered into a contract with the plaintiffs to guard their factory. An exclusion clause exempted Securicor from liability even if one of their employees caused damage to the factory. One of the guards later deliberately set fire to the factory. Securicor claimed the protection of the exclusion clause.
>
> **Held:** Whether an exclusion clause could operate after a fundamental breach was a matter of construction. There was no absolute rule that total failure of performance rendered such clauses inoperative. The exclusion clause in this particular case was wide enough to cover the events that took place.

6.5.3 What effect does the Unfair Contract Terms Act, 1977 have on the exclusion clause?

This act represents the statutory attempt to control exclusion clauses. In spite of its title, it is really aimed at unfair exemption clauses, rather than contract terms generally. It also covers non-contractual notices which purport to exclude liability under the Occupiers' Liability Act, 1957. The controls under the Act relate to two areas:

1 Negligence

There is an absolute prohibition on exemption clauses in relation to liability in negligence resulting in death or injury (Sections 2 and 5). Exemption clauses relating to liability for other damage caused by negligence will only be enforced to the extent that they satisfy the 'requirement of reasonableness' (Section 2).

2 Contract

These provisions apply in consumer transactions. They also apply in non-consumer transactions, where one party deals on the other's standard terms. Any exclusion clause which seeks to avoid liability for breach of contract is only valid to the extent that it complies with the 'requirement of reasonableness' (Section 3). This test also applies where a clause seeks to permit a party to avoid performing the contract completely, or to permit performance less than reasonably expected.

The implied term relating to title, under Section 12 of the Sale of Goods Act, cannot be excluded in any contract (Section 6(1)).

The other implied terms as to description, fitness, merchantable quality, and sample, cannot be excluded in a consumer contract (Section 6(2)); and in a non-consumer transaction any restriction is subject to the 'requirement of reasonableness' (Section 6(3)).

A person deals as a consumer if he does not make the contract in the course of business, nor holds himself out as so doing, and the other party does make the contract in the course of business, the goods being supplied normally for private consumption (Section 12).

The requirement of reasonableness means 'fair and reasonable . . . having regard to the circumstances . . .' (Section 11). The second schedule of the Act provides guidelines for the application of the reasonableness test in regard to non-consumer transactions, but it is likely that similar considerations will be taken into account by the courts in consumer transactions. Amongst these considerations are:

(a) the relative strength of the parties' bargaining power;
(b) whether any inducement was offered in return for the limitation on liability;
(c) whether the customer knew, or ought to have known, about the existence or extent of the exclusion;

(d) whether the goods were manufactured or adapted to the special order of the customer.

> *George Mitchell (Chesterhall) Ltd* v. *Finney Lock Seeds Ltd* (1983)
>
> The respondents planted 63 acres with cabbage seed supplied by the appellants. The crop failed, due partly to the fact that the wrong type of seed had been supplied, and partly to the fact that the seed supplied was of inferior quality. When the respondents claimed damages, the sellers relied on the protection of a clause in their standard conditions of sale limiting their liability to replacing the seeds supplied or refunding payment.
>
> **Held:** The respondents were entitled to compensation for the loss of the crop. The House of Lords decided that although the exemption clause was sufficiently clear and unambiguous to be effective at common law, it failed the test of reasonableness under the Unfair Contract Terms Act.

It is likely that many of the situations in the cases considered under the common law prior to the UCTA would now be decided under the Act. It is still important, however, to understand the common law principles for the very good reason that the UCTA does not apply in many important situations. Amongst these are transactions relating to insurance, interests in land, patents and other intellectual property, the transfer of securities, and the formation of companies or partnerships.

Exemption clauses and UCTA – the questions to ask

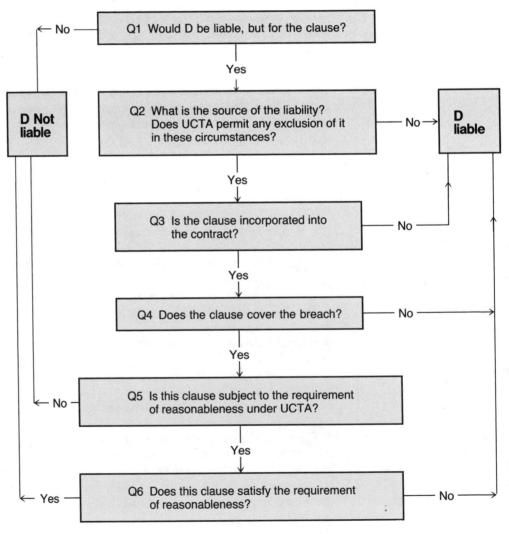

Note: this flow chart does not always work with Section 4, Section 3(2)(b) and non-contractual notices under Section 2(2)).

Sample questions

1 Distinguish between conditions, warranties, and innominate terms, and consider, in particular, whether the recognition of innominate terms necessarily leads to increased uncertainty.

LLB, Staffordshire Polytechnic

Suggested answer

This requires an explanation of the meaning of the three concepts, and the consequences of breaching of them (see Section 6.2). In addition, it raises the potential difficulty in regard to innominate terms, that the effect of the breach is not known beforehand, but only after its consequences have been determined. This may be thought to lead to uncertainty; on the other hand, the certainty that flows from restricting terms to the two mutually exclusive categories of condition and warranty is sometimes more apparent than real. The reason for this is that the parties cannot know with total certainty whether the courts will consider a particular term to be a condition or a warranty.

2 In what ways did the Unfair Contract Terms Act, 1977 change the law in relation to exclusion or limiting clauses?

ILE

Suggested answer

This requires a consideration of the nature of exclusion clauses, the common law treatment of them before the UCTA, 1977, and the way in which that statute has altered the situation.

The major common law principles were the *contra proferentum* rule and the doctrine of fundamental breach. The main part of any answer must, however, concentrate on the UCTA, and the following points should be mentioned:

1 The prohibition on exclusion clauses in relation to death or injury caused by negligence.

2 The fact that, in consumer contracts, any exclusion clause must pass the test of reasonableness.

3 The fact that the same requirement as to reasonableness applies in non-consumer transactions where the contract is made on the basis of one party's standard terms.

What is actually understood by reasonableness should also be considered.

3 Under what circumstances will terms be implied into a contract?

LLB, Staffordshire Polytechnic

Suggested answer

Implied terms should be distinguished from express terms, and mention should be made of the three ways in which implied terms may be introduced into a contract: by statute, by custom and by the Court. Appropriate examples of each type should be given. The most contentious type is the third of these, and most attention should be given to a consideration of when the Courts will take upon themselves the burden of introducing a term into a contract. An explanation of what is meant by giving a contract business efficacy should be provided, and *The Moorcock* case cited as an example.

Further reading

For further reading on the topics covered in this chapter, see chapter 4.

7 Vitiating factors

In this chapter it is intended to consider the vitiating factors – those elements which will render any agreement either void, or voidable, depending on which vitiating factor is present. Those considered will be:

1 mistake;

2 misrepresentation;

3 duress;

4 undue influence;

5 contracts void or illegal for reasons of public policy.

7.1 Mistake

Generally speaking, the parties to a contract will not be relieved from the burden on their agreement simply because they have made a mistake. If one party makes a bad bargain, that is no reason for setting the contract aside. Very few mistakes will affect the validity of a contract at common law, but where a mistake is operative, it will render the contract void. It is usual to divide mistakes into the following three categories:

1 common mistake;

2 mutual mistake;

3 unilateral mistake.

7.1.1 Common mistake

This is where both parties to an agreement share the same mistake about the circumstances surrounding the transaction. In order for the mistake to be operative, it must be of a fundamental nature.

> *Bell* v. *Lever Bros Ltd* (1932)
>
> Bell had been employed as chairman of a company controlled by Lever Bros. When he became redundant they paid off the remaining part of his service contract. Only then did they discover that Bell had been guilty of offences which would have permitted them to dismiss him without compensation. They claimed to have the payment set aside on the basis of the common mistake that neither party had considered the possibility of Bell's dismissal for breach of duty.
>
> **Held:** The action must fail. The mistake was only as to quality and was not sufficiently fundamental to render the contract void.

The cases suggest that a mistake as to quality can never render an agreement void for mistake, and that the doctrine of common mistake is restricted to the following two specific areas:

1 *Res extincta*
In this case, the mistake is as to the existence of the subject matter of the contract.

> *Couturier* v. *Hastie* (1856)
>
> A contract was made in London for the sale of corn being shipped from Salonica. Unknown to the parties, however, the corn had already been sold.
>
> **Held:** The London contract was void, as the subject matter of the contract was no longer in existence.

2 *Res sua*

In this case, the mistake is that one of the parties to the contract already owns what he is contracting to receive.

> *Cooper* v. *Phibbs* (1867)
>
> Cooper agreed to lease a fishery from Phibbs. It later transpired that he actually owned the fishery.
>
> **Held:** At common law the lease had to be set aside. In equity, however, Phibbs was given a lien over the fishery in respect of the money he had spent on improving it, permitting him to hold the property against payment.

Cooper v. *Phibbs* is an example of one possible way in which equity may intervene in regard to common mistake, namely setting an agreement aside on terms. Alternatively the agreement may even be set aside completely in equity.

> *Magee* v. *Pennine Insurance Co Ltd* (1969)
>
> A proposal form for car insurance had been improperly filled in by the plaintiff. When the car was subsequently written off, the insurance company offered Magee £375 as a compromise on his claim. After he had accepted this offer, the defendants discovered the error in the proposal form, and sought to repudiate their agreement.
>
> **Held:** Although not void at common law, the agreement could be set aside in equity.

7.1.2 Mutual mistake

This occurs where the parties are at cross purposes. They have different views of the facts of the situation, but they do not realize it.

An agreement will not necessarily be void simply because the parties to it are at cross purposes. In order for mutual mistake to be operative, i.e. to make the contract void, it must comply with an objective test. The Court will try to decide which of the competing views of the situation a reasonable person would support, and the contract will be enforceable on such terms.

> *Smith* v. *Hughes* (1871)
>
> The plaintiff offered to sell oats to the defendant. Hughes wrongly believed that the oats were old, and on discovering that they were new oats, he refused to complete the contract.
>
> **Held:** The defendant's mistake as to the age of the oats did not make the contract void.

> *Scriven Bros* v. *Hindley & Co* (1913)
>
> At an auction, the defendants bid for two lots believing both to be hemp. In fact one of them was tow, an inferior and cheaper substance.
> Although the auctioneer had not induced the mistake, it was not normal practice to sell hemp and tow together.
>
> **Held:** In the circumstances, where one party thought he was buying hemp while the other thought he was selling tow, the contract was not enforceable.

If the Court is unable to decide the outcome of the 'reasonable person test', then the contract will be void.

> *Raffles* v. *Wichelhaus* (1864)
>
> The defendants agreed to buy cotton from the plaintiffs. The cotton was to arrive 'ex *Peerless* from Bombay'. There were, however, two ships called *Peerless* sailing from Bombay; the first in October, the second in December. Wichelhaus thought he was buying from the first, Raffles thought he was selling from the second.
>
> **Held:** The agreement would be void for mutual mistake. Under the exceptional circumstances it would have been impossible for the Court to decide which party's view was the correct one.

In respect of mutual mistake, equity follows the common law.

> *Tamplin* v. *James* (1880)
>
> James purchased a public house at auction. He had believed wrongly that the property for sale included a field which the previous publican had used. The sale particulars stated the property for sale correctly, but James did not refer to them. When he discovered his mistake James refused to complete the transaction.
>
> **Held:** In spite of his mistake an order of specific performance would be granted against James.

7.1.3 Unilateral mistake

This occurs where only one of the parties to the agreement is mistaken as to the circumstances of the contract, and the other party is aware of that fact. Most cases of unilateral mistake also involve misrepresentation, although this need not necessarily be so.

It is important to distinguish between these two elements – whereas unilateral mistake makes a contract void, and thus prevents the passing of title in any property acquired under it, misrepresentation merely makes a contract voidable, and good title can be passed before the contract is avoided. This distinction will be seen in *Ingram* v. *Little* and *Phillips* v. *Brooks*.

The cases involving unilateral mistake mainly relate to mistakes as to identity. A contract will only be void for mistake where the seller intended to contract with a different person from whom he actually did contract.

> *Cundy* v. *Lindsay* (1878)
>
> A crook named Blenkarn ordered linen handkerchiefs from Cundy. His order from 37 Wood Street was signed so as to look as if it were from Blenkiron & Co, a reputable firm, known to Cundy, who carried on business at 123 Wood Street. The goods were sent to Blenkarn, who sold them to Lindsay. Cundy sued Lindsay in conversion.
>
> **Held:** Cundy succeeded. He only intended to deal with Blenkiron & Co. As there was no contract with Blenkarn, title could not be passed on to Lindsay.

Where the parties enter into a contract face to face, it is generally presumed that the seller intends to deal with the person before him, and therefore he cannot rely on unilateral mistake to avoid the contract.

> *Phillips* v. *Brooks* (1919)
>
> A crook selected a number of items in the plaintiff's jewellery shop, and proposed to pay by cheque. On being informed that the goods would have to be retained until the cheque was cleared, he told the jeweller that he was Sir George Bullough of St James's Square. On checking in a directory that such a person did indeed live at that address, the jeweller permitted him to take away a valuable ring. The crook later pawned the ring to the defendant. Phillips then sued the defendant in conversion.
>
> **Held:** The contract between Phillips and the crook was not void for mistake. There had not been a mistake as to identity, but only as to the creditworthiness of the buyer. The contract had been voidable for misrepresentation, but the crook had passed title before Phillips took steps to avoid the contract.

A similar decision was reached by the Court of Appeal in *Lewis* v. *Avery* (1971), in which a crook obtained possession of a car by misrepresenting who he was to the seller. The Court declined to follow its earlier decision in *Ingram* v. *Little* (1960), a very similar case. It is generally accepted that *Lewis* v. *Avery* represents the more accurate statement of the law.

Here again equity follows the common law, and considers contracts tainted by unilateral contracts to be void.

7.1.4 Mistake in respect of documents

1 *Non est factum*

When someone signs a document under a misapprehension as to its true nature, the law may permit him to claim *non est factum*, i.e. that the document is not his deed. The mistake relied on must relate to the type of document signed, and not just to its contents.

> *Foster* v. *Mackinnon* (1869)
>
> Mackinnon, an elderly man of feeble sight, was asked to sign a guarantee, as he had done in the past. The document put before him was in fact a bill of exchange, which was later endorsed to the plaintiff.
>
> **Held:** Under the circumstances, Mackinnon's plea of *non est factum* was successful.

The person signing the document must not have been careless in regard to its contents.

> *Saunders* v. *Anglia Building Society* (1970)
>
> Mrs Gallie, a 78-year-old widow, signed a document without reading it, whilst her glasses were broken. She had been told, by a person named Lee, that it was a deed of gift to her nephew, but in fact it was a deed of gift to Lee. Lee later mortgaged the property to the respondent building society. Mrs Gallie sought to repudiate the deed of gift on the basis of *non est factum*.
>
> **Held:** Her action failed. The document was of the type Mrs Gallie expected to sign, and her failure to read it amounted to carelessness.

2 Rectification

Where the written document fails to state the actual intentions of the parties, it may be altered under the equitable doctrine of rectification.

> *Joscelyne* v. *Nissen* (1970)
>
> The plaintiff agreed to transfer his car-hire business to his daughter in return for her agreeing to pay certain household expenses, although this was not stated in a later written contract.
>
> **Held:** The father was entitled to have the agreement rectified to include the terms agreed.

7.2 Misrepresentation

As has been stated previously, a statement which induces a person to enter into a contract, but which does not become a term of the contract, is a representation. A false statement of this kind is a misrepresentation, and renders the contract voidable. The innocent party may rescind the contract, or in some circumstances claim damages. See Fig. 7.1.

Misrepresentation can be defined as a false statement of fact, made by one party before or at the time of the contract, which induces the other party to enter into the contract. The following points follow from this definition:

1 There must be a statement. There is no general duty to disclose information, and silence does not generally amount to a representation. There are exceptions to this rule:

(a) Where the statement is a half-truth. It may be true, but misleading none the less.

> *Notts Patent Brick & Tile Co* v. *Butler* (1886)
>
> The buyer of land asked the seller's solicitor whether the land was subject to any restrictive covenants. The solicitor said that there were none that he knew of, but did not mention that he had not read the documents to find out.
>
> **Held:** The solicitor's statement was a misrepresentation, and the buyer could rescind the contract.

(b) Where the statement was true when made, but has subsequently become false before the contract is concluded.

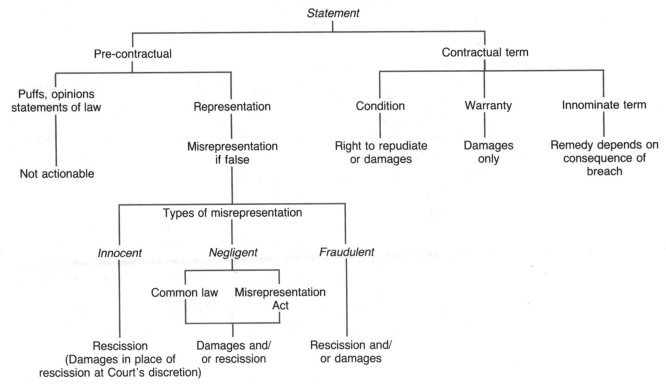

Fig. 7.1 Forms of misrepresentation

> *With* v. *O'Flanagan* (1936)
> In January the seller of a doctor's practice told the prospective buyer that it was worth £2000 per annum. By the time the contract was concluded, its value had dropped substantially, to only £5 per week.
> **Held:** The representation was of a continuing nature, and as it was false when it induced the contract, the buyer was entitled to rescind.

(c) Where the contract is *uberrimae fidei*; i.e. it is based on utmost good faith. In contracts of this nature, such as those involving insurance, there is a duty to disclose all material facts.

2 The following statements will not amount to representation:

(a) Mere sales puffs: the statement must have some meaningful content. Thus in *Dimmock* v. *Hallett* (1866), it was held that a statement that land was 'fertile and improvable' was not actionable as a misrepresentation.

(b) Statements of law. Everyone is presumed to know the law, and therefore, in theory, no one can be misled as to what the law is.

(c) Statements of opinion. These are not actionable, because they are not statements of fact.

> *Bisset* v. *Wilkinson* (1927)
> The vendor of previously ungrazed land in New Zealand stated that it would be able to support 2000 sheep. This turned out to be untrue.
> **Held:** The statement was only an expression of opinion and as such was not actionable.

If the person does not actually believe the truth of the opinion he expresses, then an action for misrepresentation will be possible (*Edgington* v. *Fitzmaurice* (1884)).

3 The statement must actually induce the contract. This means that:

(a) The statement must have been addressed to the person claiming to have been misled.

(b) The person claiming to have been misled must have been aware of the statement.

(c) The person claiming to have been misled must have relied on the statement.

> *Horsfall* v. *Thomas* (1962)
>
> Horsfall made and sold a gun to Thomas. He concealed a fault in it by means of a metal plug, but Thomas never even examined the gun. After short usage, the gun blew apart. Thomas claimed that he had been misled, by the plug, into buying the gun.
>
> **Held:** The plug could not have misled him as he had not examined the gun at the time of purchase.

(d) The statement must be material. It must have been such as would have induced a reasonable person to enter into the contract.

7.2.1 Types of misrepresentations

Misrepresentation can be divided into three types:

1 Fraudulent misrepresentation

The false representation is made, knowing it to be false, or believing it to be false, or recklessly careless whether it is true or false. The difficulty with this type of misrepresentation is proving the necessary mental element; it is notoriously difficult to show the required *mens rea* of fraud.

> *Derry* v. *Peek* (1889)
>
> The Directors of a company issued a prospectus, inviting the public to subscribe for shares. The prospectus stated that the company had the power to run trams by steam power, but in fact it only had power to operate horse-drawn trams; it required the permission of the Board of Trade to run steam trams. The Directors assumed that permission would be granted, but in fact it was refused. When the company was wound up, the Directors were sued for fraud.
>
> **Held:** There was no fraud, as the Directors had honestly believed the statement in the prospectus.

2 Negligent misrepresentation

The false representation is made in the belief that it is true, but without reasonable grounds for that belief. (It follows that the directors in *Derry* v. *Peek* would now be liable for negligent misrepresentation.) There are two categories of negligent misrepresentation:

(a) At common law. Prior to 1963, the law recognized no such concept as negligent misrepresentation. The possibility of liability for such misstatements arose from *Hedley Byrne & Co* v. *Heller* (1964) (see chapter 10). In *Hedley Byrne & Co* v. *Heller* the parties were not in a contractual or a pre-contractual relationship, so there could not have been an action for misrepresentation. In *Esso Petroleum* v. *Mardon* (1976), however, Mardon succeeded in an action for negligent misstatement, on the basis that he had been wrongly advised as to the amount of petrol he could expect to sell from a garage.

(b) Under the Misrepresentation Act, 1967 (MA). *Esso Petroleum* v. *Mardon* occurred before the introduction of the MA, and although it might still be necessary, or beneficial, to sue at common law, it is more likely that such actions would now be taken under the statute. The reason for this is that Section 2(1) of the MA reverses the normal burden of proof. Where a misrepresentation has been made, then under Section 2(1) it is up to the party who made the statement to show that they had reasonable grounds for believing it to be true.

3 Innocent misrepresentation

The false representation is made by a person who not only believes it to be true, but also has reasonable grounds for that belief.

7.2.2 Remedies for misrepresentation

For fraudulent misrepresentation, the remedies are rescission, and/or damages for any loss sustained. The action for damages is in the tort of deceit.

For negligent misrepresentation, the remedies are rescission, and/or damages. The action for damages is either in the tort of negligence, at common law; or under Section 2(1) of the MA 1967. Under the statute, the measure of damages will still be determined as in a tort action.

For innocent misrepresentation, the common law remedy is rescission. Under the MA, however, the Court may award damages instead of rescission, in cases where it is considered equitable to do so (Section 2(2)).

In regard to Section 2(2), it should be noted that the Court can only award damages, instead of rescission, where the remedy of rescission is still available. The importance of this lies in the fact that the right to rescind can be lost:

1 By affirmation. Where the innocent party, with full knowledge of the misrepresentation, either expressly states that he intends to go on with the agreement, or does some action from which it can be implied that he intends to go on with the agreement. Affirmation may be implied from lapse of time.

2 Where the parties cannot be restored to their original positions.

3 Where third parties have acquired rights in the subject matter of the contract.

7.2.3 Effect of the Unfair Contract Terms Act

Section 8 of the UCTA provides that any exclusion of liability for misrepresentation must comply with the requirement of reasonableness.

7.3 Duress

This concept used to be restricted to contracts entered into as a consequence of actual physical violence, or the threat of such violence to a person. Under such circumstances the contract was voidable at the instance of the innocent party.

> *Barton v. Armstrong* (1975)
>
> The defendant threatened Barton with death if he did not arrange for his company to buy Armstrong's shares in it. Barton sought to have the agreement set aside. It was found that the threats had been made, but that, in addition, Barton thought that the transaction was a favourable one.
>
> **Held:** Barton succeeded. The proper inference was that duress was present, and the burden of proof was on Armstrong to show that the threats had played no part in Barton's decision. He had failed to discharge this burden.

Originally it was held that threats to a person's goods could not amount to duress, but recently a doctrine of economic duress has been developed by the Courts. The germ of the doctrine, that an abuse of economic power can render a contract invalid, can be found in Lord Denning's decision in *D & C Builders Ltd* v. *Rees* (1966), and was developed in later cases such as *'The Siboen & The Sibotre'*; and

> *'The Atlantic Baron'* (1979)
>
> A contract had been entered into for the building of a ship. The builders then stated that they would not complete construction unless the purchasers paid an extra 10 per cent. Without the ship, the buyers would have lost a lucrative contract with a third party, to whom they had already agreed to charter the ship. The buyers paid the extra money, then, at a later date, sued to recover it, on the basis of economic duress, amongst other things.
>
> **Held:** The threat to terminate the contract did constitute economic duress, which rendered the contract voidable. In the event, the buyers' delay in bringing the action acted as an affirmation of the agreement and they lost their right to rescission.

The doctrine of economic duress finally received the approval of the House of Lords in *'The Universe Sentinel'* (1982). In order to benefit from the doctrine, the plaintiff must show the following two things:

1 that pressure, which resulted in an absence of choice on his part, was brought to bear on him; and

2 that the pressure was of a nature considered illegitimate by the Courts.

Only under such circumstances will the Court permit rescission of an agreement.

7.4 Undue influence

Transactions, either contract or gifts, may be avoided where they have been entered into as a consequence of the undue influence of the person benefiting from them. The effect of undue influence is to make a contract voidable, but delay may bar the right to avoid the agreement.

There are two possible situations relating to undue influence.

7.4.1 Special relationships

Where there is a special relationship between the parties, there is a presumption that the transaction is the consequence of undue influence. The burden of proof is on the person receiving the benefit to rebut the presumption.

> *Re Craig* (1971)
>
> After the death of his wife Mr Craig, then aged 84, employed a Mrs Middleton as his secretary-companion. In the course of the six years for which she was employed, he gave her money to the extent of some £30 000. An action was taken to have the gifts set aside.
>
> **Held:** The action succeeded. The circumstances raised the presumption of undue influence, and Mrs Middleton had failed to rebut it.

Examples of special relationships are: parent and child while still a minor; guardian and ward; religious adviser and follower; solicitor and client. The list is not a closed one, however, and other relationships may be included within the scope of the special relationship (as in *Re Craig*).

Where a special relationship exists, then an important way in which the presumption of undue influence can be rebutted is to show that independent advice was taken by the other party, although all that is necessary is to show that the other party exercised their will freely.

Even where a special relationship exists, a transaction will not be set aside unless it is shown to be manifestly disadvantageous.

> *National Westminster Bank* v. *Morgan* (1985)
>
> When a couple named Morgan fell into financial difficulties the plaintiff bank made financial arrangements which permitted them to remain in their house. The refinancing transaction secured against the house was arranged by a bank manager who called at their home; Mrs Morgan had no independant legal advice. When the husband died, the bank obtained a possession order against the house in respect of outstanding debts. Mrs Morgan sought to have the refinancing arrangement set aside, on the grounds of undue influence.
>
> **Held:** The action failed. The doctrine of undue influence had no place in agreements which did not involve any manifest disadvantage, and Mrs Morgan had actually benefited from the transaction by being able to remain in her home for a longer period.

The key element in deciding whether a relationship was a special one or not was whether one party was in a position of dominance over the other. It also decided that a normal relationship between a bank manager and his client is not a special relationship.

7.4.2 No special relationship

Where no special relationship exists between the parties, the burden of proof is on the party claiming the protection of the undue influence doctrine.

It has been suggested that undue influence and duress are simply examples of a wider principle, based on inequality of bargaining power. The existence of such a principle was suggested in a number of decisions involving Lord Denning. It was intended to provide protection for those who suffered as a consequence of being forced into particular agreements due to their lack of bargaining power. This doctrine was considered, and firmly rejected, however, by the House of Lords in *National Westminster Bank* v. *Morgan*.

7.5 Contracts and public policy

It is evident that some agreements will tend to be contrary to public policy. The fact that some are considered more serious than others is reflected in the distinction drawn between those which are said to be illegal and those which are simply void.

7.5.1 Illegal contracts

A contract which breaks the law is illegal. The general rule is that no action can be brought by a party to an illegal contract. The contract may be expressly prohibited by statute, or implicitly prohibited by the common law. The following is a list of illegal contracts:

1 contracts prohibited by statute;

2 contracts to defraud the Inland Revenue;

3 contracts involving the commission of a crime or a tort;

4 contracts with a sexually immoral element;

5 contracts against the interest of the UK or a friendly state;

6 contracts leading to corruption in public life;

7 contracts which interfere with the course of justice.

7.5.2 Void contracts

A void contract does not give rise to any rights or obligations. The contract is only void so far as it is contrary to public policy, thus not the whole agreement may be void. Severance is the procedure whereby the void part of a contract is excised, permitting the remainder to be enforced. Contracts may be void under statute, or at common law.

7.5.3 Contracts void by statute

1 Wagering contracts

A wagering contract is an agreement that, upon the happening of some uncertain event, one party shall give something of value to the other, the party who has to pay being dependent on the outcome of the event. Such contracts are governed by the Gaming Acts.

2 Restrictive trading agreements

Certain restrictive trading agreements are subject to registration and investigation under the Restrictive Trade Practices Act, 1976. If the agreements cannot be justified by the parties to them, as required under Section 10 of that Act, then they are void and unenforceable.

3 Resale price maintenance agreements

Agreements which seek to enforce minimum prices for goods through resale price maintenance agreements are void, and the enforcement of such agreements is prohibited under the Resale Prices Act, 1976. It is possible, however, for particular classes of goods to qualify for exemption from the provisions of the Act.

7.5.4 Contracts void at common law

1 Contracts to oust the jurisdiction of the Court

Any contractual agreement which seeks to deny the parties the right to submit questions of law to the Courts are void, as being contrary to public policy. Agreements which provide for compulsory arbitration are enforceable.

2 Contracts prejudicial to the status of marriage

It is considered a matter of public policy that the institution of marriage be maintained. Hence any contract which seeks to restrain a person's freedom to marry, or undermines the institution in any way, will be considered void.

3 Contracts in restraint of trade

A contract in restraint of trade is an agreement whereby one party restricts their future freedom to engage in their trade, business, or profession. The general rule is that such agreement are *prima facie* void, but they may be valid if it can be shown that they meet the following three requirements:

1 the person who imposes the restriction has a legitimate interest to protect;

2 the restriction is reasonable as between the parties;

3 the restriction is not contrary to the public interest.

The doctrine of restraint of trade is flexible in its application, and may be applied to new situations when they arise. Bearing this in mind, however, it is usual to classify the branches of the doctrine as follows:

1 Restraints on employees

An employer cannot protect himself against competition from an ex-employee, except where he has a legitimate interest to protect. The only legitimate interests recognized by the law are trade secrets and trade connection.

Even in protecting those interests, the restraint must be of a reasonable nature. What constitutes 'reasonable' in this context depends on the circumstances of the case.

> *Lamson Pneumatic Tube Co v. Phillips* (1904)
>
> The plaintiffs manufactured specialized equipment for use in shops. The defendant's contract of employment stated that, on ceasing to work for the plaintiffs, he would not engage in a similar business for a period of five years, anywhere in the Eastern hemisphere.
>
> **Held:** Such a restriction was reasonable, bearing in mind the nature of the plaintiff's business.

> *Empire Meat Co Ltd v. Patrick* (1939)
>
> Patrick had been employed as manager of the company's butcher's business in Mill Road, Cambridge. The company sought to enforce the defendant's promise that he would not establish a rival business within five miles of their shop.
>
> **Held:** The restraint was too wide and could not be enforced.

The longer the period of time covered by the restraint the more likely it is to be struck down, but in *Fitch* v. *Dewes* (1921) it was held that a life-long restriction placed on a solicitor was valid.

2 Restraints on vendors of businesses

The interest to be protected in this category is the goodwill of the business purchased, i.e. its profitability. Restrictions may legitimately be placed on previous owners to prevent them from competing, in the future, with new owners. Again, the restraint should not be greater than is necessary to protect that interest.

> *British Concrete v. Schelff* (1921)
>
> The plaintiffs sought to enforce a promise given by the defendant, on the sale of his business to them, that he would not compete with them in the manufacture of road reinforcements.
>
> **Held:** Given the small size, and restricted nature, of the business sold, the restraint was too wide to be enforceable.

In *Nordenfeld* v. *Maxim Nordenfeld Guns & Ammunition Co* (1894), however, a world-wide restraint on competition was held to be enforceable, given the nature of the business sold.

3 Restraints on distributors/solus agreements

This category of restraint of trade is usually concerned with solus agreements between petrol companies and garage proprietors, by which a petrol company seeks to prevent the retailer from selling its competitors' petrol. It is recognized that petrol companies have a legitimate interest to protect, and the outcome depends on whether the restraint obtained in protection of that interest is reasonable.

> *Esso Petroleum* v. *Harper's Garage* (1968)
>
> The parties had entered into an agreement whereby Harper undertook to buy all of the petrol to be sold from his two garages from Esso. In return Esso lent him £7000, secured by way of a mortgage over one of the garages. The monopoly right in regard to one garage was to last for 4½ years, and in regard to the other garage for 21 years. When Harper broke his undertaking, Esso sued to enforce it.
>
> **Held:** The agreements in respect of both garages were in restraint of trade. But whereas the agreement which last for 4½ years was reasonable, the one which last for 21 years was unreasonable, and void.

Until recently it was thought that *Esso* v. *Harper's* case had set down a rule that any solus agreement involving a restriction which was to last longer than five years would be void, as being in restraint of trade. In *Alec Lobb (Garages) Ltd* v. *Total Oil Ltd* (1985), however, the Court of Appeal made it clear that the outcome of each case depended on its own particular circumstances, and in that case approved a solus agreement extending over a period of 21 years.

4 Exclusive service contracts

This category relates to contracts which are specifically structured to exploit one of the parties by controlling and limiting their output, rather than assisting them. The most famous cases involve musicians.

> *Schroeder Music Publishing Co* v. *Macauley* (1974)
>
> An unknown songwriter, Macauley, entered into a five year agreement with Schroeder. Under it, he had to assign any music he wrote to them, but they were under no obligation to publish it. The agreement provided for automatic extension of the agreement if it yielded £5000 in royalties, but the publishers could terminate it at any time, with one month's notice.
>
> **Held:** The agreement was so one-sided as to amount to an unreasonable restraint of trade, and hence was void.

Sample questions

Consider the following:

1 (a) In what circumstances will a mistake avoid a contract at common law?

(b) C, who was short of money, wished to sell some jewellery. He took it to a local shop where D offered C a cheque, but C asked for cash. D then produced a card which suggested he was a wealthy businessman and C decided to take the cheque. The cheque proved worthless and D has disappeared having resold the jewellery to E for £150.

ACCA

Suggested answer

Refer to section 7.1.

(a) In answering this question the student should distinguish between what is commonly understood by mistake, and fundamental mistakes which are operative in law. The three types of mistake which have an effect on contracts should then be identified. In regard to common mistakes it should be pointed out that the only mistakes sufficiently fundamental to render a contract void involve: *res sua* and *res extincta*.

Cases: *Bell* v. *Lever Bros*, *Couturier* v. *Hastings*, and *Cooper* v. *Phipps*.

With regard to mutual mistake, it should be mentioned that the Court will apply an objective test in order to try to find the sense of the agreement, rather than simply declare the contract void.

Cases: *Smith* v. *Hughes* and *Raffles* v. *Wichelhaus*.

As for unilateral mistake, it should be stated that mistakes as to the attributes of a person do not amount to operative mistakes.

Cases: *Cundy* v. *Lindsay*, *Phillips* v. *Brooks*, and *Lewis* v. *Avery*.

It should be stated that *Ingram* v. *Little*, in which the Court reached a contrary decision, is now of doubtful authority.

(b) This question is a reversal of the fact situation in *Phillips* v. *Brooks*, but the same legal rules apply. C simply makes a mistake as to the creditworthiness of D, and as such it is not of a sufficiently fundamental nature to render the contract void. The contract is voidable for fraud, but before C has taken any steps to avoid the contract, D has already passed good title to the property. E is therefore entitled to keep the jewellery.

2 Consider this problem. Alfred is thinking of buying a microcomputer, but he knows very little about them. He visits Clive's Computer Shop and discusses a possible purchase. Clive tells him that the Sweet Special is 'the best little machine money can buy', and that 'as it is IBM compatible you can use any IBM software with it'.

Clive, however, had confused the Sweet Special with the Sweet Super. Whereas the latter is IBM compatible, the former, the Special, is not. The Super costs £1000, and the Special £500.

A week later Alfred returns and buys the Sweet Special from Clive. Only after he has spent £100 on IBM software does Alfred discover that the Special is not IBM compatible.

LLB, Staffordshire Polytechnic

Suggested answer

Refer to section 7.2.

This question is a typical misrepresentation question, and should be tackled by asking the following questions:

(a) Has there been a misrepresentation?

In this case, the statement about the machine being 'the best little machine that money can buy', is simply a sales puff; but the statement about it being IBM compatible is a misrepresentation, being a false statement of fact which induces Alfred to enter into the contract. It is clearly not a term, as it was made some time before the contract was made.

(b) What kind of misrepresentation is involved?

It is not fraudulent, as Clive did not deliberately mislead Alfred, nor was he reckless in what he said.

It is possible for Alfred to sue for negligence at common law; but it is easier to make use of Section 2(1) of the Misrepresentation Act, because it reverses the usual burden of proof. All Alfred has to show is that a false statement was made. It is then up to Clive to show that he had reasonable grounds for making the statement. If he has reasonable grounds, the misrepresentation is wholly innocent. In this case it is likely to be an example of negligent misrepresentation under Section 2(1).

(c) What remedies are available:

In this case Albert would be entitled to damages, as well as the right to rescind the contract. It should be stated that the right to rescind may be lost, and that the Court may award damages, instead of rescission, under Section 2(2) of the Misrepresentation Act.

3 Service Stations, a company whose only shareholders are Mr and Mrs Jones, carried on business as a petrol filling station. The company found itself in financial difficulty and entered into an agreement with the Black Gold Oil Company by which, for a premium of £30 000, Service Stations granted a lease of their premises to the Black Gold Oil Company for 50 years, at a nominal rent. The Black Gold Oil Company then sub-let the premises back to Service Stations for 21 years at a rent of £2000 per annum, subject to the condition that Black Gold Oil Company should supply all petrol during the currency of the sub-lease.

Advise Mr and Mrs Jones, who now wish to get out of the agreement.

LLB, Staffordshire Polytechnic

Suggested answer

This question concerns contracts in restraint of trade, and solus agreements in particular. Refer to section 7.5.4.

Contracts in restraint of trade are, *prima facie*, void as contrary to public policy; but they may be valid if the following questions are answered in the affirmative.

(a) Does the petrol company have a legitimate interest to protect? In this case the answer is yes, the interest being the protection and stability of their distribution network.

(b) Is the restriction reasonable as between the parties? It was once thought, on the basis of *Esso* v. *Harper's Garage*, that solus agreements lasting for longer than five years would be automatically void. Since *Alec Lobb* v. *Total Petroleum*, however, it is now settled that each case has to be decided on its own facts, and that solus agreements for 21 years may be valid. In this case, which is rather similar to the *Lobb* situation, it would appear that the garage company could only stay in business if it received the money from the petrol company, and as a result the restraint may be legitimate as between the parties.

(c) Is the agreement contrary to public policy? It is arguable that the loss, in terms of competition, suffered by the public is more than made up for by the benefit of the garage staying open, and that therefore the agreement is not contrary to public policy. Thus it would appear that, under the particular circumstances of the problem, the solus agreement may well be valid.

Further reading

For further reading on the topics covered in this chapter, see chapter 4.

8 Discharge of contract

Discharge of contract means the parties are freed from their obligations under the contract. A contract is discharged in one of four ways:

1 agreement;
2 performance;
3 frustration;
4 breach.

8.1 Discharge by agreement

Emphasis has been placed on the consensual nature of contract law, and it follows that what has been made by agreement can be ended by agreement. The contract itself may contain provision for its discharge, by either the passage of a fixed period of time, or the happening of a certain event. Alternatively it may provide, either expressly or by implication, that one or other of the parties can bring it to an end, as in a contract of employment.

Where there is no such provision in a contract, another contract would be required to cancel it, before all of the obligations have been met. There are two possible situations:

1 Where the contract is executory, the mutual exchange of promises to release one another from future performance will be sufficient consideration.

2 Where the contract is executed, i.e. one party has performed, or partly performed, his obligations, the other party must provide consideration in order to be released from performing his part of the contract (unless the release is made under seal). The provision of this consideration discharges the original contract, and there is said to be accord and satisfaction.

8.2 Discharge by performance

This occurs where the parties to a contract perform their obligations under it; it is the normal way in which contracts are discharged. As a general rule, discharge requires complete and exact performance of the obligations in the contract.

> *Cutter v. Powell* (1795)
> Cutter was employed as second mate on a ship sailing from Jamaica to Liverpool. The agreement was that he was to receive 30 guineas when the journey was completed. Before the ship reached Liverpool, Cutter died and his widow sued Powell, the ship's master, to recover a proportion of the wages due to her husband.
> **Held:** She was entitled to nothing as the contract required complete performance.

There are four exceptions to the general rule requiring complete performance:

1 Where the contract is divisible
In an ordinary contract of employment, where it is usual for payment to be made periodically, the harshness of the outcome of *Cutter* v. *Powell* is avoided.

2 Where the contract is capable of being fulfilled by substantial performance

This occurs where the essential element of an agreement has been performed, but some minor part remains to be done, or some minor fault remains to be remedied. The party who performed the act can claim the contract price, although they remain liable for any deduction for the work outstanding.

> *Hoenig v. Isaacs* (1952)
> Hoenig was employed by Isaacs to decorate his flat. The contract price was £750, to be paid as the work progressed. Isaacs paid a total of £400, but refused to pay the remainder as he objected to the quality of the work carried out. Hoenig sued for the outstanding £350.
>
> **Held:** Isaacs had to pay the outstanding money less the cost of putting right the defects in performance. These latter costs amounted to not quite £56.

3 Where performance has been prevented by the other party
Under such circumstances, the party prevented from performance can sue for breach of contract, or on a *quantum meruit* basis (see section 8.6).

4 Where partial performance has been accepted by the other party
This occurs in the following circumstances: A orders a case of 12 bottles of wine from B. B only has 10, and delivers those to A. A is at liberty to reject the 10 bottles if he wants to, but if he accepts them he must pay a proportionate price for them.

8.2.1 Tender of performance

This simply means an offer to perform the contractual obligations. If the buyer refuses to accept the goods offered, but later sues for breach of contract, the seller can rely on the fact that he tendered performance as discharging his liability under the contract. He is also entitled to claim for breach of contract.

> *Macdonald v. Startup* (1843)
> Macdonald promised to deliver 10 tons of oil to the defendant 'within the last 14 days of March'. He tried to deliver on Saturday March 31st at 8.30 p.m., and Startup refused to accept the oil.
>
> **Held:** The tender of performance was equivalent to actual performance, and Macdonald was entitled to claim damages for breach of contract.

Section 29(5) of the Sale of Goods Act now provides that tender is ineffectual unless made at a reasonable hour. It is unlikely that 8.30 p.m. on a Saturday evening would be considered reasonable.

8.3 Discharge by frustration

Where it is impossible to perform an obligation from the outset, no contract can come into existence. Early cases held that subsequent impossibility was no excuse for non-performance. In the 19th century, however, the doctrine of frustration was developed to permit a party to a contract, in some circumstances, to be excused performance on the grounds of impossibility arising subsequently to the formation of the contract.

A contract will be discharged by reason of frustration in the following circumstances:

1 Where destruction of the subject matter of the contract has occurred

> *Taylor v. Caldwell* (1863)
> Caldwell had agreed to let a hall to the plaintiff for a number of concerts. Before the day of the first concert the hall was destroyed by fire. Taylor sued for breach of contract.
>
> **Held:** The destruction of the hall made performance impossible, and therefore the defendant was not liable under the contract.

2 Where government interference, or supervening illegality, prevents performance
The performance of the contract may be made illegal by a change in the law. The outbreak of war, making the other party an enemy alien, will have a similar effect.

> **Re Shipton, Anderson & Co etc (1915)**
>
> A contract was made for the sale of wheat stored in a warehouse in Liverpool. Before the seller could deliver, it was requisitioned by the Government, under wartime emergency powers.
>
> **Held:** The seller was excused from performance. Due to the requisition, it was no longer possible lawfully to deliver the wheat.

3 Where a particular event, which is the sole reason for the contract, fails to take place

> **Krell v. Henry (1903)**
>
> Krell let a room to the defendant for the purpose of viewing the coronation procession of Edward VII. When the procession was cancelled due to the King's ill health, Krell sued Henry for the due rent.
>
> **Held:** The contract was discharged by frustration, as its purpose could no longer be achieved.

This only applies where the cancelled event was the sole purpose of the contract.

> **Herne Bay Steamboat Co v. Hutton (1903)**
>
> A naval review, which had been arranged as part of Edward VII's coronation celebrations, also had to be cancelled due to illness. Hutton had contracted to hire a boat from the plaintiffs for the purpose of seeing the review.
>
> **Held:** Hutton was liable for breach of contract. The sole foundation of the contract was not lost as the ship could still have been used to view the assembled fleet.

4 Where the commercial purpose of the contract is defeated

This applies where the circumstances have so changed that to hold a party to his promise would require him to do something which, although not impossible, would be radically different from the original agreement.

> **Jackson v. Union Marine Insurance Co (1874)**
>
> The plaintiff's ship was chartered to proceed to Newport to load a cargo bound for San Francisco. On the way, it ran aground. It could not be refloated for over a month, and needed repairs. The charterers hired another ship and the plaintiff claimed under an insurance policy he had taken out to cover the eventuality of his failure to carry out the contract. The insurance company denied responsibility, on the basis that the plaintiff could claim against the charterer for breach of contract.
>
> **Held:** The delay had put an end to the commercial sense of the contract. The charterers had been released from their obligations under the contract and were entitled to hire another ship.

5 Where, in the case of a contract of personal service, the party dies or becomes otherwise incapacitated

> **Condor v. Barron Knights (1966)**
>
> Condor contracted to be the drummer in a pop group. After he became ill he was medically advised that he could only play on four nights per week, not every night as required.
>
> **Held:** The contract was discharged by the failure in the plaintiff's health preventing him from performing his duties under it.

8.3.1 Situations in which the doctrine of frustration does not apply

In *Tsakiroglou & Co v. Noblee & Thorl* (1960) it was stated that frustration is a doctrine only too often invoked by a party to a contract who finds performance difficult or unprofitable, but it is very rarely relied on with success. It is, in fact, a kind of last resort, and it is a conclusion which should be reached rarely and with reluctance. A contract will not be discharged by reason of frustration in the following circumstances:

1 Where the parties have made express provision in the contract for the event which has occurred. In this case, the provision in the contract will be applied.

2 Where the frustrating event is self-induced.

> *Maritime National Fish Ltd* v. *Ocean Trawlers Ltd* (1935)
>
> Maritime were charterers of a ship, equipped for otter trawling, owned by Ocean Trawlers. Permits were required for otter trawling, and Maritime, who owned four ships of their own, applied for five permits. They were only granted three permits, however, and they assigned those permits to their own ships. They claimed that their contract with Ocean Trawlers was frustrated, on the basis that they could not lawfully use the ship.
>
> **Held:** The frustrating event was a result of their action in assigning the permits to their own ships, and therefore they could not rely on it as discharging their contractual obligations.

3 Where an alternative mode of performance is still possible.

> *Tsakiroglou & Co.* v. *Noblee & Thorl* (1962)
>
> A contract was entered into to supply 300 tons of Sudanese groundnuts c.i.f. Hamburg. It had been intended that the cargo should go via the Suez canal, and the appellants refused to deliver the nuts when the canal was closed. It was argued that the contract was frustrated, as to use the Cape of Good Hope route would make the contract commercially and fundamentally different from that which was agreed.
>
> **Held:** The contract was not fundamentally altered by the closure of the canal, and, therefore was not discharged by frustration.

4 Where the contract simply becomes more expensive to perform.

> *Davis Contractors* v. *Fareham U.D.C.* (1956)
>
> The plaintiffs contracted to build 78 houses in 8 months, at a total cost of £94 000. Due to shortage of labour it actually took 22 months to build the houses, at a cost of £115 000. They sought to have the contract set aside as frustrated, and to claim on a *quantum meruit* basis.
>
> **Held:** The contract had not been frustrated by the shortage of labour, and the plaintiffs were thus bound by their contractual undertaking as regards the price.

5 It used to be the case that frustration did not apply in regard of leases to land, but the House of Lords in *National Carriers Ltd* v. *Panalpina Ltd* (1981) decided that the doctrine could be applied in cases involving leases.

8.3.2 The effect of frustration

At common law, the effect of frustration was to make the contract void as from the time of the frustrating event. It did not make the contract void *ab initio*, i.e. from the beginning. The effect of this was that each party had to perform any obligation which had become due before the frustrating event, and was only excused from obligations which would arise after that event. This could lead to injustice. In *Krell* v. *Henry* the plaintiff could not claim the rent, as it was not due to be paid until after the coronation event had been cancelled. The outcome was different in a similar case, however, where the rent had to be paid immediately on the making of the contract.

> *Chandler* v. *Webster* (1904)
>
> The plaintiff had already paid £100 of the total rent of £141 15s for a room from which to watch the coronation procession, before it was cancelled. He sued to recover his money.
>
> **Held:** Not only could he not recover the £100, but he also had to pay the outstanding £41 15s as the rent had fallen due before the frustrating event had taken place.

8.3.3 Law Reform (Frustrated Contracts) Act, 1943

The statute intervened in 1943, and the position is now as follows:

1 Any money paid is recoverable.

2 Any money due to be paid ceases to be payable.

3 The parties may be permitted, at the discretion of the Court, to retain expenses incurred from any money received; or recover those expenses from money due to be paid before the frustrating event. If no money was paid, or was due to be paid, before the event, then nothing can be retained or recovered.

4 Where a party has gained a valuable benefit under the contract he may, at the discretion of the Court, be required to pay a reasonable sum in respect of it.

The Act does not apply to the following types of contract:

(a) contracts for the carriage of goods by sea;

(b) contracts of insurance;

(c) contracts for perishable goods.

8.4 Discharge by breach

A breach of contract may occur in three ways:

1 where a party, prior to the time of performance, states that he will not fulfil his contractual obligation;

2 where a party fails to perform his contractual obligation;

3 where a party performs his obligation in a defective manner.

8.4.1 Effect of breach

Any breach will result in the innocent party being able to sue for damages. In addition, however, some breaches will permit the innocent party to treat the contract as discharged. In this situation they can refuse either to perform their part of the contract, or to accept further performance from the party in breach. The right to treat a contract as discharged arises in the following instances:

1 Where the other party has repudiated the contract before performance is due, or before he has completed performance.

2 Where the other party has committed a fundamental breach of contract. As has already been pointed out in section 6.2, there are two methods of determining whether a breach is fundamental or not; one relying on the distinction between conditions and warranties, the other relying on the seriousness of the consequences that flow from the breach.

8.4.2 Anticipatory breach

This arises where one party, prior to the actual due date of performance, demonstrates an intention not to perform his contractual obligations. The intention not to fulfil the contract can be either express or implied.

1 Express

This occurs where a party actually states that he will not perform his contractual obligations:

> *Hochster v. De La Tour* (1853)
>
> In April De La Tour engaged Hochster to act as his courier on his European tour, starting on 1st June. On 11th May De La Tour wrote to Hochster stating that he would no longer be needing his services. The plaintiff started proceedings for breach of contract on 22nd May, and the defendant claimed that there could be no cause of action until 1st June.
>
> **Held:** The plaintiff was entitled to start his action as soon as the anticipatory breach occurred (when De La Tour stated he would not need Hochster's services).

2 Implied

This occurs where a party carries out some act which makes performance impossible.

> *Omnium D'Enterprises* v. *Sutherland* (1919)
>
> The defendant had agreed to let a ship to the plaintiff. Prior to the actual time for performance, he sold the ship to another party.
>
> **Held:** The sale of the ship amounted to repudiation of the contract and the plaintiff could sue from that date.

With regard to anticipatory breach, the innocent party can sue for damages immediately, as in *Hochster* v. *De La Tour*.

Alternatively they can wait until it is actually the time for performance before taking action. In the latter instance, they are entitled to make preparations for performance, and claim the agreed contract price, even though this apparently conflicts with the duty to mitigate losses (see section 8.5.5).

> *White & Carter (Councils)* v. *McGregor* (1961)
>
> McGregor contracted with the plaintiffs to have advertisements placed on litter bins which were supplied to local authorities. The defendant wrote to the plaintiffs asking them to cancel the contract. The plaintiffs refused to cancel, and produced, and displayed, the adverts as required under the contract. They then claimed payment.
>
> **Held:** The plaintiffs were not obliged to accept the defendant's repudiation. They were entitled to perform the contract and claim the agreed price.

Where the innocent party elects to wait for the time of performance, he takes the risk of the contract being discharged for some other reason, such as frustration, and thus of losing his right to sue.

> *Avery* v. *Bowden* (1855)
>
> Bowden chartered the plaintiff's ship in order to load grain at Odessa within a period of 45 days. Although Bowden later told the ship's captain that he no longer intended to load the grain, the ship stayed in Odessa in the hope that he would change his mind. Before the end of the 45 days, the Crimean war started and thus the contract was discharged by frustration. Avery then sued for breach of contract.
>
> **Held:** The action failed. Bowden had committed anticipatory breach, but the captain had waived the right to discharge the contract on that basis. The contract continued and was brought to an end by frustration, not by breach.

8.5 Remedies for breach of contract

The principle remedies for breach of contract are damages, *quantum meruit*, and specific performance and injunction.

8.5.1 Damages

The estimation of what damages are to be paid by a party in breach of contract can be divided into two parts: remoteness and measure.

8.5.2 The remoteness of damages

What kind of damage can the innocent party claim? This involves a consideration of causation, and the remoteness of cause from effect, in order to determine how far down a chain of events a defendant is liable. The rule in *Hadley* v. *Baxendale* states that damages will only be awarded in respect of losses which:

1 arise naturally, i.e. in the natural course of things; or which

2 both parties may reasonably be supposed to have contemplated, when the contract was made, as a probable result of its breach.

> *Hadley* v. *Baxendale* (1854)
>
> Hadley, a miller at Gloucester, had engaged the defendant to take a broken mill-shaft to Greenwich so that it could be used as a pattern for a new one. The

defendant delayed in delivering the shaft, thus causing the mill to be out of action for longer than it would otherwise have been. Hadley sued for loss of profit during that period of additional delay.

Held: It was not a natural consequence of the delay in delivering the shaft that the mill should be out of action. The mill might, for example, have had a spare shaft. So part 1 of the rule stated above did not apply.

In addition Baxendale was unaware that the mill would be out of action during the period of delay, so part 2 of the rule did not apply, either.

The effect of the first part of the rule in *Hadley* v. *Baxendale* is that the party in breach is deemed to expect the normal consequences of the breach, whether they actually expected them or not.

Under the second part of the rule, however, the party in breach can only be held liable for abnormal consequences where he has actual knowledge that the abnormal consequences might follow.

Victoria Laundry Ltd v. *Newman Industries Ltd* (1949)

The defendants contracted to deliver a new boiler to the plaintiffs, but delayed in delivery. The plaintiffs claimed for normal loss of profit during the period of delay, and also for the loss of abnormal profits from a highly lucrative contract which they could have undertaken, had the boiler been delivered on time.

Held: Damages could be recovered in regard to the normal profits, as that loss was a natural consequence of the delay. The second claim failed, however, on the grounds that the loss was not a normal one, but was a consequence of an especially lucrative contract, about which the defendant knew nothing.

The decision in the *Victoria Laundry* case was confirmed by the House of Lords in *The Heron II*, although the actual test for remoteness was reformulated in terms of whether the consequence should have been 'within the reasonable contemplation of the parties' at the time of the contract.

The Heron II (*Czarnikow* v. *Koufos*) (1967)

The defendants contracted to carry sugar from Constanza to Basra. They knew that the plaintiffs were sugar merchants, but did not know that they intended to sell the sugar as soon as it reached Basra. During a period when the ship was delayed, the market price of sugar fell. The plaintiffs claimed damages for the loss from the defendants.

Held: The plaintiffs could recover. It was common knowledge that the market value of such commodities could fluctuate, therefore the loss was within the reasonable contemplation of the parties.

As a consequence of the test for remoteness, a party may be liable for consequences which, although within the reasonable contemplation of the parties, are much more serious in effect than would be expected by them.

H. Parsons (Livestock) Ltd v. *Uttley Ingham & Co* (1978)

The plaintiffs, who were pig farmers, bought a large food hopper from the defendants. While erecting it, the plaintiffs failed to unseal a ventilator on the top of the hopper. Because of lack of ventilation, the pig food stored in the hopper became mouldy. The pigs which ate the mouldy food contracted a rare intestinal disease and died.

Held: The defendants were liable. The food affected by bad storage caused the illness as a natural consequence of the breach, and the death from such illness was not too remote.

8.5.3   The measure of damages

Damages in contract are intended to compensate an injured party for any financial loss sustained as a consequence of another party's breach. The object is not to punish the party in breach, so the amount of damages awarded can never be greater than the actual loss suffered. The aim is to put the injured party in the same position he would have been in had the contract been properly performed.

8.5.4   The market rule

Where the breach relates to a contract for the sale of goods, damages are usually assessed in line with the market rule. This means that if goods are not delivered under a contract, the buyer is entitled to go into the market and buy similar goods, and pay the market price prevailing at that time. He can then claim the difference in price between what he paid and the original contract price as damages. Conversely, if a buyer refuses to accept goods under a contract, the seller can sell the goods in the market, and accept the prevailing market price. Any difference between the price he receives and the contract price can be claimed in damages.

8.5.5   The duty to mitigate losses

The injured party is under a duty to take all reasonable steps to minimize his loss. So in the above examples, the buyer of goods which are not delivered has to buy the replacements as cheaply as possible; and the seller of goods which are not accepted has to try to get as good a price as he can when he sells them.

> *Payzu v. Saunders* (1919)
>
> The parties entered into a contract for the sale of fabric, which was to be delivered and paid for in instalments. When the purchaser, Payzu, failed to pay for the first instalment on time, Saunders refused to make any further deliveries unless Payzu agreed to pay cash on delivery. The plaintiff refused to accept this and sued for breach of contract.
>
> **Held:** The delay in payment had not given the defendant the right to repudiate the contract. As a consequence, he had breached the contract by refusing further delivery. The buyer, however, should have mitigated his loss by accepting the offer of cash on delivery terms. His damages were restricted, therefore, to what he would have lost under those terms, namely, interest over the repayment period.

8.5.6   Non-pecuniary loss

At one time, damages could not be recovered where the loss sustained through breach of contract was of a non-financial nature. The modern position is that such non-pecuniary damages can be recovered.

> *Jarvis v. Swan Tours Ltd* (1973)
>
> The defendant's brochure stated that various facilities were available at a particular ski resort. The facilities available were in fact much inferior to those advertised. The plaintiff sued for breach of contract.
>
> **Held:** Jarvis was entitled to recover, not just the financial loss he suffered, which was not substantial, but also for loss of entertainment and enjoyment. The Court of Appeal stated that damages could be recovered for mental distress in appropriate cases, and this was one of them.

8.5.7   Liquidated damages and penalties

It is possible for the parties to a contract to make provisions for possible breach by stating in advance the amount of damages that will have to be paid in the event of any breach occurring. Damages under such a provision are known as liquidated damages. They will only be recognized by the Court if they represent a genuine pre-estimate of loss, and are not intended to operate as a penalty against the party in breach. If the Court considers the provision to be a penalty, it will not give it effect, but will award damages in the normal way.

> *Dunlop v. New Garage & Motor Co* (1915)
>
> The plaintiffs supplied the defendants with tyres, under a contract designed to achieve resale price maintenance. The contract provided that the defendants had to pay Dunlop £5 for every tyre they sold in breach of the resale price agreement. When the garage sold tyres at less than the agreed minimum price, they resisted Dunlop's claim for £5 per tyre, on the grounds that it represented a penalty clause.
>
> **Held:** In this situation the provision was a genuine attempt to fix damages, and was not a penalty.

8.6 *Quantum meruit*

This means that a party should be awarded 'as much as he had earned', and such an award can be either contractual or quasi-contractual (see section 8.9) in nature. If the parties enter into a contractual agreement without determining the reward that is to be provided for performance, then in the event of any dispute, the Court will award a reasonable sum. Payment may also be claimed on the basis of *quantum meruit*, where a party has carried out work in respect of a void contract.

> *Craven-Ellis* v. *Canons Ltd* (1936)
>
> The plaintiff had acted as the managing director of a company under a deed of contract. As, however, he had not acquired any shares in the company, as required by its articles, his appointment was void. He sued to recover remuneration for the service he had provided prior to his removal.
>
> **Held:** Although he could not claim under contract, he was entitled to recover a reasonable sum on the basis of *quantum meruit*.

8.7 Specific performance

It will sometimes suit a party to break his contractual obligations, and pay damages, but through an order for specific performance the party in breach may be instructed to complete his part of the contract. The following rules govern the award of such a remedy.

1 An order of specific performance will only be granted in cases where the common law remedy of damages is inadequate. It is not usually applied to contracts concerning the sale of goods where replacements are readily available. It is most commonly granted in cases involving the sale of land, where the subject matter of the contract is unique.

2 Specific performance will not be granted where the Court cannot supervise its enforcement. For this reason it will not be available in respect of contracts of employment or personal service.

> *Ryan* v. *Mutual Tontine Westminster Chambers Association* (1893)
>
> The landlords of a flat undertook to provide a porter, who was to be constantly in attendance to provide services such as cleaning the common passages and stairs, and delivering letters. The person appointed spent much of his time working as a chef at a nearby club. During his absence his duties were performed by a charwoman or by various boys. The plaintiff sought to enforce the contractual undertaking.
>
> **Held:** Although the landlords were in breach of their contract, the Court would not award an order of specific performance. The only remedy available was an action for damages.

3 Specific performance is an equitable remedy which the Court grants at its discretion. It will not be granted where the plaintiff has not acted properly on his part. Nor will it be granted where mutuality is lacking; thus a minor will not be granted specific performance, because no such order would be awarded against him.

8.8 Injunction

This is also an equitable order of the Court, which directs a person not to break their contract. It can have the effect of indirectly enforcing contracts for personal service.

> *Warner Bros* v. *Nelson* (1937)
>
> The defendant, the actress Bette Davis, had entered a contract which stipulated that she was to work exclusively for the plaintiffs for a period of one year. When she came to England the plaintiffs applied for an injunction to prevent her from working for someone else.
>
> **Held:** They were entitled to the order. The Court rejected her argument that granting it would force her either to work for the defendants, or not to work at all.

An injunction will only be granted to enforce negative covenants within the agreement, and cannot be used to enforce positive obligations.

> *Whitwood Chemical Co* v. *Hardman* (1891)
>
> The defendant had contracted to give the whole of his time to the plaintiffs, who were his employers, but he occasionally worked for others. The plaintiffs applied for an injunction to prevent him working for anyone else.
>
> **Held:** No injunction was granted; Hardman had said what he would do, not what he would not do; and, therefore, there was no negative promise to enforce.

8.9 Quasi-contractual remedies

This is based on the assumption that a person should not receive any undue advantage from the fact that there is no contractual remedy to force him to account for it. An important quasi-contractual remedy is an action for money paid and received.

If no contract comes into existence for reason of a total failure of consideration, then under this action, any goods or money received will have to be returned to the party who supplied them.

Sample questions

1 (a) Simon leases a flat on the top floor of a large block of flats for a period of 99 years. After he has been in possession for five years, a fire breaks out (cause unknown) which completely destroys the whole block. It is estimated that rebuilding will take three years. Advise Simon.

(b) Tom agrees to hire a room to celebrate his engagement to Ursula. He agrees to pay Viceroy Hotels Ltd £200, of which £50 is to be paid in advance and the remainder at the end of the party. Viceroy Hotels spend £150 on food for the party. On the night before the party is due to take place, Tom goes drinking with his friends. The car which he is driving is involved in an accident. Tom is injured and telephones the hotel from his hospital bed, cancelling the arrangement. Advise Tom.

ILE

Suggested answer

This problem relates to discharge of a contract by frustration (see section 8.3).

Part (a) deals with whether the doctrine applies to leases, and if so, under what circumstances, and with what effect. In *National Carriers Ltd* v. *Panalpina Ltd* the House of Lords decided that frustration was applicable to leases, but it also stated that it would hardly ever be applied in practice. In the *National Carriers* case, the lessee, who had a lease for 10 years, after 5 years of occupation, lost the use of the premises for 20 months. The Court decided that, given the length of the continuance of the lease, the interruption did not amount to frustration. As Simon is only losing 3 years out of a 99-year lease, it is very unlikely that he will be successful in an attempt to have the contract discharged for frustration. As a result he will be bound by its terms.

The outcome of part (b) depends on whether or not the frustrating event is self induced. It is not clear whether Tom was drunk, or even that he was drinking alcohol, when he was driving the car. If he were drunk then he would not be in a position to claim frustration, as his own actions brought about the frustrating event (*Maritime National Fish Ltd* v. *Ocean Trawlers Ltd*).

If Tom was not to blame, then he may be able to claim frustration. It is then a matter of determining how the various financial matters are to be dealt with.

Under the Law Reform (Frustrated Contracts) Act, 1943, Tom would be released from paying the outstanding £150. The hotel would be entitled to retain the £50 already paid, but cannot recover the other £100 that they have spent in preparation, as further payment by Tom was not due before the frustrating event occurred.

2 What remedies are available to an innocent party for a breach of contract?

ACCA

Suggested answer

This question is very straightforward and simply requires consideration of the various remedies discussed in section 8.5: what the remedies are, when they will be granted, and what their effects are.

3 (a) Describe the rules governing remoteness of damage and the measure of damages in the law of contract.

(b) H promised to deliver goods to G on a specified date. There was a term in the contract which provided for the payment of liquidated damages of £500 in the event of a breach of contract. He delivered goods of the right quality and quantity but two weeks late. G accepted the goods, but later G decided to sue H for breach of contract and to claim £500 damages. Comment on the situation.

ACCA

Suggested answer

(Refer to section 8.5.)

(a) With regard to remoteness, reference should be made to the rules stated in *Hadley* v. *Baxendale* and the subsequent reformulation of the rule in terms of whether the consequence was within the reasonable contemplation of the parties at the time they made the contract, stated in the *Heron II*. It should be stated that the party in breach will be liable for other losses where he was aware of any special circumstances which gave rise to them, as in *Victoria Laundry* v. *Newman Industries*.

With regard to the measure of damages, reference should be made to the fact that the award should accurately reflect the plaintiff's loss. Mention should be made of the market rule, and the duty to mitigate losses, citing *Payzu* v. *Saunders*. The possibility of liquidated damages as a pre-estimate of loss should be mentioned. Finally it might be mentioned that damages can now be recovered for non-economic losses, citing *Jarvis* v. *Swan Tours*.

(b) H's delay in delivering the goods amounts to a breach of contract. It is likely that the question of time of delivery would be seen as a condition of the contract, thus giving G the right to treat the contract as repudiated. G would have lost the right to treat the contract as being repudiated by his acceptance of the goods. He would, however, still be entitled to damages for the breach. The question is then whether the £500 is to be regarded as liquidated damages or a penalty clause. The outcome depends on whether or not it is a genuine pre-estimate of loss (*Dunlop* v. *New Garage Co*).

In this case the £500 has to be paid no matter how serious, or trivial, the breach. It is likely, therefore, to be interpreted as a penalty clause.

4 (a) What matters will a Court take into account in deciding whether or not to grant an injunction?

(b) Mark takes the lease of a 'service' flat. Under the terms of the lease the landlords, Noble Properties plc, agree *inter alia* to provide cleaning services for all stairways and corridors. The company also agrees that their house manager, Owen, will deliver milk, newspapers, mail etc. to Mark's flat. Owen, however, takes a part-time job as a chef at Ryan's cafe and consequently the corridors are dirty and no mail, milk or newspapers are delivered.

Advise Mark who now seeks a decree of specific performance.

ILE

Suggested answer

(a) This question relates to the equitable remedies of injunction, and specific performance. Refer to section 8.8.

The Court will only grant an injunction to enforce negative covenants in agreements, and will not be granted to enforce positive promises: *Whitwood Chemical Co* v. *Hardman*. It can, however, be used as an indirect way of enforcing contracts for personal service (*Warner Bros* v. *Nelson*).

(b) This question invites the student to consider the remedy of specific performance. Such a remedy will not be granted to enforce contracts of personal service, so Owen cannot be ordered to carry out his contractual duty. Nor will specific performance be granted in circumstances which would require continuous supervision by the Court.

As a result Mark will not be able to get an order of specific performance against Noble Properties.

This problem is closely based on the circumstances in *Ryan* v. *Mutual Tontine Westminster Chambers Association* (1893) in which the plaintiff had to settle for damages when his claim for specific performance was rejected for the foregoing reasons.

Further reading

For further reading on the topics covered in this chapter, see chapter 4.

9 Agency

9.1 Definition of agency

An agent, in legal terms, is a person who is a representative of another legal party, called a principal. The agent has powers to make contracts between his principal and one or more third parties. It is an unusual relationship in contract law, because parties normally act for themselves.

The law must protect:

1 the interests of the principal, who is represented;

2 the interests of the third party, who is not negotiating directly with the 'other side';

3 the interests of the agent, who is acting on someone else's behalf.

An agent may be an employee of the principal, or an independent contractor. The general rule governing agency is that once the contract has been formed between the principal and a third party, the agent has no further obligations under that contract, but there are exceptions to this rule. Typical questions on agency revolve around three areas: the rights and duties of the agent, the authority of the agent and the relationship between the principal, agent and third party. There may also be questions which include points about the formation or ratification of an agency agreement.

9.2 Creation of agency

No one can claim to be the agent of a principal unless the principal consents to that agency.

> *White* v. *Lucas* (1887)
>
> A firm of estate agents tried to act on behalf of the owner of a property. The owner denied the firm permission to act for him, but sold the property to someone introduced by the estate agents.
>
> **Held:** The estate agents had no right to remuneration since the property owner had not agreed that they should act for him.

If the agency is created by deed, it is called 'power of attorney'. An agency contract may be created in a variety of ways:

1 by express contract (oral or written);

2 by estoppel;

3 by implication;

4 by ratification;

5 by necessity.

It is wise to analyse a situation given in a problem, to check that the agency relationship exists.

9.2.1 Agency created by express contract

This describes the situation where the terms of the agency contract were agreed between the parties in writing or by word of mouth.

9.2.2 Agency created by estoppel

If a person acts in such a way that he is precluded from denying that he has given authority to another to act on his behalf, a contract of agency will arise from the doctrine of estoppel. For example, an agent may have ceased to work for his principal, but the principal does not inform his clients; or the principal may be aware of the agent's negotiations, and yet has not tried to deny that the agent represents him.

The fact that the principal is 'estopped' from denying the agency contract is very similar to the principal being 'stopped' from denying the agency contract, but with the added weight of legal implications, i.e. he or she cannot deny it in court.

> *Freeman & Lockyer* v. *Buckhurst Park Properties Ltd* (1964)
>
> A property company had four directors. One director effectively controlled the company, and made contracts as if he were managing director, although he had no authority to do so. The other directors were aware of these activities but took no action. The company was sued on the basis of one of the contracts so formed.
>
> **Held:** The company was estopped from denying that the active director was its agent. This effectively created agency by estoppel. Thus the contract formed by the active director as agent was held to be valid.

9.2.3 Agency created by implication

Agency created by implication normally means that positive action has been taken on behalf of the principal, who intends that the agency contract should be formed. It is best used in contrast to express agency to highlight the lack of direct written or verbal agreement. The agreement is implied, e.g. through actions, or by law. Some textbooks use the expression 'implied agency' rather loosely.

9.2.4 Agency created by ratification

An agency can be created by ratification when a person has no authority, but purports to contract with a third party on behalf of a principal. Ratification is the express acceptance by the principal of that contract with the third party, and such ratification relates back to the making of the contract by the agent.

9.2.5 Agency created by necessity

An agency contract may be created by necessity in some limited circumstances. A person may be bound by such a contract, even if he declines to ratify it.

There are several important conditions which must apply in the formation of such an agency relationship:

1 there must be 'necessity', in the sense of some form of emergency.

2 the agent must find it impossible to obtain instructions from the principal.

> *Springer* v. *Great Western Railway Company* (1921)
>
> A consignment of tomatoes arrived at Weymouth after a delayed and stormy journey at sea. There was a railway strike which would have caused further delay. The railway company therefore decided to sell the tomatoes locally. They were sued for damages by the consignee.
>
> **Held:** The railway company could not claim to be agents of necessity, because they could have communicated with the consignee and obtained instructions.

3 The agent must act in good faith, in the interests of the principal.

Recent affirmation of the agency of necessity has taken place in the House of Lords in the case of *China Pacific SA* v. *Food Corporation of India, The Winson* (1981). In this case Lord Simon of Glaisdale implied that an agency of necessity may still arise whenever the limitations (1 and 2 above) are satisfied, provided that some sort of contract already exists.

9.3 Rights and duties of an agent

The common law has imposed a number of duties on the agent. It has also established various rights which enable the agent to make claims. These rights and duties may give rise to legal claims for damages by the principal against his agent, and vice versa.

9.3.1 Rights of an agent

An agent has rights to:

1 Claim indemnity, i.e. expenses justifiably incurred, for work done.

2 Claim remuneration, i.e. payment, where this is expressly or impliedly agreed in the contract.

Problem cases arise when the remuneration has not been agreed in advance. In such cases, the courts will stick as closely as possible to the words of the contract. They will not seek to override the original agreement, even if the conclusions to be drawn seem to be unjust or unfair.

There can be a claim in *quantum meruit* in the appropriate circumstances, but this is not always the case.

> *Re Richmond Gate Property Co Ltd* (1965)
>
> The express contract stated that the remuneration payable would be such a sum as the directors should determine, for the managing director. No such sum had been determined.
>
> **Held:** No remuneration could be claimed.

3 Exercise a lien, i.e. a right to retain the principal's goods, where they have lawfully come into his possession as agent, and hold them against any debts outstanding to him in consequence of that particular agency. The lien is normally a particular lien, relating to particular goods, and not a general lien relating to any monies owed.

General liens do apply in some instances, as a result of well-established practice, e.g. with solicitors, bankers, stockbrokers.

9.3.2 Duties of an agent

An agent is obliged to perform certain duties, which are listed below (1-5).

1 To perform tasks according to the instructions of the principal

These instructions may be specified in the contract, or given to the agent according to the terms of the contract.

> *Turpin* v. *Bilton* (1843)
>
> An insurance broker agreed, for a consideration, to insure the plaintiff's ship. He failed to do so. The ship was lost.
>
> **Held:** The broker was liable to make good the losses incurred.

2 To exercise due care and skill

The level of skill to be exercised would be that appropriate to the agent's professional capacity, e.g. a solicitor should show appropriate knowledge of legal implications, whereas another type of agent might not, in those circumstances, be expected to demonstrate equivalent knowledge of law.

An unpaid (gratuitous) agent would also be liable for damages, if he failed to fulfil this duty, but his duty may not be regarded as so onerous when the damages are assessed as if he was paid.

It is possible to sue the agent in contract, or for the tort of negligence, but the damages are assessed using roughly the same principles, so that the outcome would be the same.

> *Keppel* v. *Wheeler* (1927)
>
> Agents were employed to sell a block of flats. They received an offer from X, which the owners accepted 'subject to contract'. The agents subsequently received a higher offer from Y. The agents did not pass this latter offer on to the owners. Later, after the sale of the property to X, the agents arranged a resale beween X and Y.
>
> **Held:** The agents had to pay damages to the principal equal to the differences between X's offer and Y's offer. They were successful, however, in a counterclaim for remuneration from the principal, because they had honestly believed that their duties to the principal had ceased when the owners accepted the first offer 'subject to contract'.

> *Baxter* v. *Gapp & Co Ltd* (1939)
>
> Some estate agents made an excessive valuation of freehold land, which was relied on by the plaintiff when advancing money for a mortgage.

> **Held:** The agents had not fulfilled their duty of care and skill. They were liable for the loss suffered as a result of lending the excess money.

It is possible that this duty of care and skill could conflict with a duty to obey the instructions of the principal. It is best, in these circumstances, for the agent to warn the principal that his instructions are not adequate, which would show the agent exercising proper skill. It is unlikely, however, that the agent will be liable to pay damages if he has obeyed the instructions of his principal.

3 To keep accounts

There is an implied duty to keep proper accounts of all transactions entered into on behalf of the principal. The agent must ensure that he keeps his own property separate from that of his principal.

4 To act personally

An agent owes a duty to his principal to act personally, unless he has expressly or impliedly been authorized to delegate work to another person. The legal maxim *delegatus non potest delegare* (a delegate cannot himself delegate) is normally applied. However, there are several exceptions to this general rule about delegation, e.g. a solicitor acting for his client might instruct a stockbroker. Alternatively, the principal may agree to delegation. In these exceptional circumstances, the question arises, 'what is the relationship between the sub-agent and the principal?'. If the delegation to the sub-agent is unauthorized, there will be no contractual relationship between the sub-agent and the principal. Where the delegation to the sub-agent is authorized, the position in tort is still unclear. Recent trends may indicate that the sub-agent may be liable to damages.

5 To accept fiduciary duties

The word 'fiduciary' comes from the same Latin base as *fido*. *Fido* (a traditional name for a trustworthy dog) means 'I trust'. Thus fiduciary duties are duties of trust and good faith. They include such matters as:

(a) Not to permit a conflict of interest

An agent should not allow his personal interests to conflict with the interests of his principal. If there is a breach of this duty, the principal can set aside the contract so affected, and claim any profit which has been made by the agent.

> *McPherson* v. *Watt* (1877)
>
> A solicitor acted for two ladies in the sale of some houses. He purchased the property himself, using his brother as a nominee.
>
> **Held:** The House of Lords refused to grant an order for specific performance of the contract of sale. The solicitor was in breach of his duty as an agent, by allowing a conflict of interests to arise.

A similar consideration means that an agent must not sell his own property to his principal, without the principal's knowledge. Such transactions are permissible if the principal is fully informed.

> *Harrods Ltd* v. *Lemon* (1931)
>
> The plaintiffs were acting as estate agents for the vendor of some property, and as surveyors for the prospective purchaser. When they realized their position they informed the vendor, and she allowed them to continue acting for her.
>
> **Held:** The vendor could not refuse payment on the grounds that the agents may have had a conflict of interests, as she had been fully informed of the situation.

(b) Not to make a secret profit, or misuse confidential information

An agent who uses his position as an agent to secure financial advantage for himself is in breach of good faith.

> *Boardman* v. *Phipps* (1967)
>
> The agents were acting for the trustees, and attended the annual general meeting of a company in which the trust had a major shareholding. It was part of their job to negotiate with the directors of the company about matters which related to the

> trust. Whilst doing this, they obtained certain information which prompted them to personally acquire shares in the company. They made a substantial profit.
>
> **Held:** The agents were in a fiduciary position. They had made a profit using this position, and therefore they should account for it to the trust.

Any financial gain made by an agent in the course of carrying out his principal's work, which is kept secret from the principal, is a secret profit, and therefore recoverable by the principal.

> *Hippisley v. Knee Bros* (1905)
>
> The plaintiffs employed the defendants, who were auctioneers, to sell some pictures for them for a lump sum payment. In the expense account, the defendants debited the gross amount of the printer's bill, and the full cost of newspaper advertising. In fact the defendants had received discounts on these two items.
>
> **Held:** The amounts of the discount were a secret profit, and, as such, they were recoverable by the principal, even though the defendants had acted without fraudulent intent.

A typical example of misuse of confidential information is where an employee is about to leave his employment, and set up his own business, and he solicits his employer's clients for the new business, e.g. as a hairdresser.

9.4 The authority of an agent

The very fact that the agent is capable of binding the principal in contractual situations means that the agent possesses certain authority. The contract made by the agent must be within the limits of his authority if it is to be binding on the principal. The authority of the agent can be actual or apparent.

9.4.1 Actual authority

Actual authority can arise in either of two ways. These are:

1 express authority, which is explicitly or expressly granted;

2 implied authority, which arises from the conduct of the parties, or from the usual assumptions in those circumstances. For example, the agent is given a particular capacity which allows him to make contracts, such as seem necessary and normal to that particular job. If such implied authority is limited, this fact must be communicated to third parties who might make contracts through the agent.

> *Watteau v. Fenwick* (1893)
>
> The owner of a beerhouse employed the previous owner as manager, and forbade him to purchase certain articles, including cigars. The manager purchased cigars from a third party, who sued the principal for payment.
>
> **Held:** The principal had to pay. It was within the usual authority of a manager of such an establishment to purchase cigars, and any restrictions on such usual authority must be communicated to third parties.

Implied authority can arise from trade or custom.

9.4.2 Apparent authority

Apparent authority is the authority the principal represents to third parties as having been given to the agent. It is a form of agency by estoppel. The expression 'ostensible authority' is also used sometimes to describe this situation.

A standard example of circumstances in which such authority may arise is in a partnership, where one partner is allowed to negotiate with greater authority than would normally be allowed, and partners are subsequently bound by contracts made within the limit of his apparent authority.

A common problem which arises in the agency situation, is to determine whether the principal is bound if the agent sells goods below a minimum fixed price. The principal will obviously be bound if the agent makes a sale within his actual authority, but if the agent sells at a price outside his authority, the sale is void unless the principal has conferred apparent authority on the agent, covering that situation. The principal may be estopped from denying the agent's authority. This often occurs in actual cases.

There are certain exceptions to this general statement, such as where the agent is a mercantile agent or factor, who can pass on a good title to a third party provided that:

1 he is in possession of the goods for sale or pledge; *or*
2 the third party acts in good faith, without notice of the agent's lack of authority.

> *Oppenheim* v. *Attenborough & Son* (1908)
>
> Diamonds were given to a diamond broker, who pledged them to X.
>
> **Held:** X received a good title, as he had received the goods in good faith, even though it was not within the normal authority of a diamond broker to pledge diamonds.

If an agent exceeds his authority, he may be liable to pay damages to the third party for breach of warranty of authority.

9.4.3 Breach of warranty of authority

If an agent contracts with a third party on behalf of a principal, he impliedly warrants that the principal exists, and that he has contractual capacity. The agent also implies that he, as agent, has authority to make contracts on behalf of the principal. If any of these facts prove to be untrue, then the third party can sue the agent for breach of warranty of authority.

Such a breach may be possible even though the agent was unaware, at the time of negotiation, that he lacked authority.

> *Yonge* v. *Toynbee* (1910)
>
> A solicitor was conducting legal proceedings on behalf of a client, who was later certified to be insane. The solicitor continued to act for the client, without any knowledge of the disability.
>
> **Held:** The solicitor was liable to pay damages for the third party, for breach of warranty of authority.

9.5 Who can sue and be sued?

9.5.1 Principal's existence disclosed

Where the agent has authority, and the principal's existence (not necessarily his name) is disclosed to the third party, the general rule is that only the principal and third party have rights and obligations under the contract. Exceptionally, the agent may be made a party to the contract, expressly or by implication.

Foreign principal: there used to be a strong presumption that when an agent acted for a foreign principal, the agent incurred personal liability. This was only a presumption, and could be rebutted.

> *The Santa Carina* (1977)
>
> The agent had a foreign principal, and the third party wished to sue the agent.
>
> **Held:** The agent was not liable, since the third party believed he had contracted with the principal.

9.5.2 Principal's existence not disclosed

Where the agent has authority, but the principal's existence is not disclosed to the third party (i.e. there is an undisclosed principal, rather than a principal who is simply unnamed as in the last example), and if the agent purports to act on his own behalf, then:

1 the agent can enforce the contract against the third party;

2 the principal can enforce the contract against the third party;

3 the third party can choose to enforce the contract against the agent or the principal.

The principal may not sue the third party if the contract is inconsistent with the existence of an agency, e.g. a contract of personal service.

Similarly, the third party cannot sue the principal if the terms of the contract are inconsistent with those of an agency contract. If the third party shows, unequivocally, that he has chosen to sue one party (either the principal or the agent), he is then barred from suing the other one.

> *Clarkson, Booker Ltd* v. *Andjel* (1964)
>
> An agent had not disclosed that he was purchasing goods on behalf of a principal. The third party sent letters to both agent and principal, demanding payment, and then issued a writ against the principal. The principal went into liquidation. A second writ was issued against the agent.
>
> **Held:** The third party had not withdrawn his demands addressed to the agent, and he had not, by issuing a writ against the principal, unequivocally elected to hold only the principal liable.

9.5.3 Agent has no authority

Where the agent has no authority, but purports to act for a principal, the third party is allowed to sue the agent on the contract.

9.5.4 Payment by means of the agent

The general rule is that, if the principal pays the agent, who does not pay the third party, the principal is still liable to the third party.

> *Irvine & Co* v. *Watson & Sons* (1880)
>
> A principal engaged an agent to buy oil. The agent made a contract with a third party. The name of the principal was not disclosed to the agent. The terms of the contract stated 'cash on delivery', but the third party did not insist on payment at the time. The principal paid the agent, believing that he had paid for the oil. The agent defaulted, and the third party sued the principal for payment.
>
> **Held:** The principal was liable to the third party. A condition of pre-payment was not sufficient to lead the principal to assume that payment had been made, in the absence of trade custom.

Consider the situation in which the third party pays the agent. The question arises 'Would the third party have to pay twice if the agent defaulted?'.

In order to pay the agent, the third party must have notice that the agent is authorized to receive payment. Clearly this cannot be the case if the third party is not aware of the agency. In these circumstances, he would not be liable again to the principal.

9.6 Termination of agency

An agency can be terminated by act of the parties, or by operation of law.

9.6.1 By act of the parties

The parties may agree mutually to terminate the agency contract. In normal circumstances, either side may give notice of termination. If such notice, on behalf of the principal, is a breach of the agency contract, the principal may be liable to pay damages to the agent.

> *Turner* v. *Goldsmith* (1891)
>
> A shirt manufacturer had agreed to use an agent for five years, as a traveller, on commission. After two years the factory burnt down, and the manufacturer did not resume business. The agent sued for breach of contract.
>
> **Held:** The agent was entitled to damages, based on the amount of commission he might have earned in that time. The agent had, however, a duty to mitigate damages.

If the principal is declared bankrupt, the agent is not liable for contracts negotiated before the date of the receiving order.

In some circumstances, the law holds that the agency agreement is irrevocable. This is normally where the agent has 'authority coupled with an interest', e.g. an agent is owed money by the principal, and that was a reason for the formation of the agency.

9.6.2 By operation of law

Certain special types of agency may be expected from the general rules, but, normally, an agency will cease when:

1 the contract is executed, or a fixed period specified if the contract has elapsed;

2 there is death, insanity or bankruptcy of either party (see *Yonge* v. *Toynbee* (1910));

3 there is frustration of contract. This terminates the agency contract, according to the usual laws of contract.

Sample questions

1 What is the difference between actual and apparent authority of an agent?

Suggested answer

The following points should be considered:

The actual authority of an agent is express, or implied, i.e. it is created by the agency contract or it is implied into the contract by law. The case of *Watteau* v. *Fenwick* can be used here.

Apparent authority, on the other hand, is ostensible authority. It occurs when the principal represents to a third party that such authority has been given. This can happen by the process of estoppel. It has happened, for instance, when partners have allowed one particular partner to take a leading role in their negotiations.

Apparent authority can also exist when an agent goes beyond his actual authority, but acts within the usual authority given to that type of agent. If the third party wishes to enforce the contract made with the principal, he will claim that the agent had apparent authority to act as he did.

2 P delivers goods to agent A and instructs A that they are not to be sold for less than £1000. Describe the legal position of the parties in the following cases:

(a) A sells the goods to T (third party) for £700.

(b) A buys the goods himself, using a nominee, for £1000, and gives P the money. Soon after, A sells the goods to S for £1200.

(c) A sells the goods to T for £1100. T feels he has a bargain, and gives A a present of £50.

Suggested answer

The following points should be considered:

(a) The sale is void, unless the agent had apparent authority or the principle of estoppel applies. The agent has acted outside his authority.

(b) A made a secret profit, and could be criticised for permitting a conflict of interest between himself and his principal. He must return the secret profit of £200 to P.

(c) A has not acted in the best interests of his principal, and can be sued for breach of fiduciary duty. He has let his personal interests conflict with those of his principal, and he has made a secret profit (see *Boardman* v. *Phipps* (1967)).

3 (a) When, if ever, is an agent personally liable upon contracts made by him on behalf of his principal?

(b) P appointed A to sell radios on his behalf. A sold radios to X without disclosing that he was negotiating the contract as an agent. X paid the agreed price, but the radios were not delivered to him, so he wishes to sue for the recovery of the purchase price. In the meantime, A has sold the radios to Y, who offered him the gift of a car in return for arranging the deal.

What are the respective rights of X and P in these circumstances?

ACCA

Suggested answer

The following points should be considered:

(a) The agent is liable if the principal is undisclosed, because the third party has no means of identifying the principal, or indeed knowing that there was a principal. The agent is possibly liable if the principal is a foreign principal as in *Teheran (Europe) Ltd v. S.T. Belton Ltd* (1968).

The agent is also liable if he has not actual authority, but just purports to be acting for a principal.

Clearly the agent is also liable if the contract provides for that.

(b) X can sue A or P. P can sue A for breach of duty to exercise due care and skill, and breach of fiduciary duty, becaue A should not have made a secret profit i.e. the car. The case of *Keppel* v. *Wheeler* would be appropriate, and for fiduciary duty *Boardman* v. *Phipps*. X may lose the goods if Y has a claim to them under the Sale of Goods Act.

4 In relation to the law of agency, discuss:

(a) the nature of the duties owed by the agent to the principal;

(b) the legal affect of ratification.

CIS

Suggested answer

The following points should be considered:

(a) Duties of the agent to the principal

  (i) to obey instructions;

  (ii) to exercise due care and skill;

  (iii) to act personally;

  (iv) a fiduciary duty:

     −not to make a secret profit;

     −not to permit a conflict of interests;

     −not to misuse confidential information;

  (v) to account.

(b) This relates back to the making of the contract.

If the principal expressly accepts the contract and all its terms, and if it is possible for the terms to be carried out given that the starting date of the contract is the date the contract was originally made, then ratification is possible.

Further reading

Fridman *Law of Agency* (Butterworths)

Marsh and Soulsby *Business Law* (McGraw-Hill)

10 Negligence I

In the following four chapters we shall consider selected aspects of the law of tort, in particular negligence, employer's liability, and vicarious liability. A typical examination problem in any of these areas is likely to involve the application of each element of the tort and therefore you will need to revise the whole topic for your examination. A typical essay question, however, may be more selective in the area which it covers, e.g. an essay in negligence may require a discussion of breach of duty and not require reference to duty of care and resultant damage.

10.1 Definition of tort

A tort is a wrongful act against an individual (or body corporate) and/or his property, which gives rise to a civil action (usually for damages, although other remedies are available). Principally, liability is based on fault, with the exception of the tort of *Rylands* v. *Fletcher*, and to some extent, vicarious liability, breach of statutory duty and trespass. The motive of the defendant in committing the tort is generally irrelevant.

There is a wide variety of torts, e.g. trespass to the person, goods and land, nuisance, defamation, etc. However, in a course on business law, negligence is the one tort which is likely to be dealt with in detail.

In this and the following chapters, negligence will be considered in some detail, and reference will also be made to economic torts.

10.2 Negligence as a tort

Negligence is the most important of all the torts, not only because an understanding of it is vital to the comprehension of other torts, such as employer's liability or occupier's liability, but also because it is constantly developing and keeping up with social and economic changes. Negligence as a tort has extended, for example, into the fields of product liability, professional negligence and economic loss, all of which were originally only compensated for if there was in existence a valid contract – in other words, no contract, no claim.

After a period of continual development in the scope and application of this tort, the signs are that the Courts are beginning to be more cautious. They are aware of the economic implications on the public and private sector if they continue to extend the net of this tort. Whether this should be an issue for the Courts is always open to debate, but if the Courts are to be pragmatic, then they may have no choice but to be cautious in the current economic climate.

There are specific elements of the tort which have to be established, in the correct order, if a claim by an injured party is to succeed.

The burden of proof is on the plaintiff, to show on a balance of probabilities, that the following exists:

1 a duty of care;

2 a breach of duty;

3 resultant damage.

Each of these will be covered in detail, as well as the limits of compensation in negligence.

10.2.1 Duty of care

The onus is on the plaintiff to establish that the defendant owes him a duty of care. The test for establishing whether a duty of care exists arises out of the case of *Donoghue* v. *Stevenson* (1932).

Prior to this case, the duty of care was owed only in limited circumstances, e.g. railway accidents. Now it is said that categories of negligence are never closed. Therefore where there is unintentional damage, there is potentially an action in negligence.

Donoghue v. Stevenson (1932)

A lady went into a café with her friend, who bought her a bottle of ginger beer. After she had drunk half of the ginger beer from the bottle, she poured the remainder into a glass. She then saw the remains of a decomposed snail in the bottom. She suffered nervous shock as well as physical after-effects. She sued the manufacturer on the basis that the snail must have got into the bottle at the manufacturer's premises, as the bottle top was securely sealed when her friend bought it.

Held: A manufacturer owes a duty of care to the ultimate consumer of his goods. He must therefore exercise reasonable care to prevent injury to the consumer. The fact that there is no contractual relationship between the manufacturer and the consumer is irrelevant to this action.

The most important aspect of this case is the test laid down by Lord Atkin. He decided that reasonable care must be taken to avoid acts and omissions, which could reasonably be foreseen to be likely to injure a neighbour.

He then decided that a 'neighbour' in law could be defined as:

> any person so closely and directly affected by my act that I ought reasonably to have them in contemplation as being so affected when I am directing my mind to the acts and omissions which are called in question.

It follows that if a duty of care is to exist, the question for the Court is somewhat hypothetical, in that the Court does not look at the reality – not **did** you contemplate the affect on the injured party of your actions, but **should** you have done so? This does not require reference to specific identity of the injured person, merely to the class of person, e.g. pedestrians, children etc. Unless it is established that the injured person is one's neighbour, there can be no duty of care.

The following case reaffirms the approach in *Donoghue* v. *Stevenson*, even though the test is expressed as a 'two-stage test'.

Anns v. Merton London Borough Council (1978)

Merton Borough Council had issued bye-laws relating to the depth of foundations for buildings being erected within their authority. All builders had to notify the Council before foundations were covered, and then the Council could exercise their power to inspect them. In 1970, a block of maisonettes built eight years previously showed signs of structural damage, due to inadequate foundations. The foundations had never been inspected by the Council. Two of the plaintiffs were not the original lessees, i.e. they had no contract with the builder, so they brought an action in negligence against the Borough Council for failing to inspect the foundations.

Held: The Borough Council were liable, because they had failed to give proper consideration to the exercise of a power bestowed on them by statute. A duty of care was owed to owners and occupiers. This duty had been breached, if, in failing to carry out an inspection, the Council had not properly exercised a discretion and taken reasonable care to ensure that the foundations complied with the bye-laws. The duty would also have been breached if the foundations had been inspected, but the inspector had failed to exercise reasonable care in doing his job.

Lord Wilberforce's decision regarding the introduction of the 'two-stage test' is important. He says the question of establishing duty of care had to be approached in two stages:

1 Is there between the alleged wrongdoer and the person who has suffered damage a sufficient relationship of proximity or neighbourhood such that, in the reasonable contemplation of the former, carelessness on his part may be likely to cause damage to the latter?

2 If the first question is answered in the affirmative, are there then any considerations which ought to negate, reduce or limit the scope of the duty or the class of persons to whom it is owed, or the damages to which a breach of duty may give rise?

The first question clearly corresponds with the neighbour test in *Donoghue* v. *Stevenson*, although it is referred to as the proximity test. The second question introduces the consideration of public policy issues, which may be grounds for limiting the situations where a duty of care is found to exist. Where new situations are concerned, the following are some of the policy arguments which, if justified, may prevent a duty of care from being actionable:

1 The 'floodgates' argument, i.e. will an extension of duty to cover this situation lead to a flood of litigation?

2 Will it lead to an increase in the number of fraudulent claims, either against insurance companies or in the Courts?

3 What are the financial or commercial consequences of extending the duty?

The test in *Anns* v. *Merton London Borough Council* has been criticized in *Peabody Donation Fund* v. *Sir Lindsay Parkinson & Co Ltd* (1985). However, it could be argued that it came to the same conclusion, but expressed in a different way!

In the *Peabody* case the Court stressed that the proximity test has to be satisfied before a duty of care could be found to exist. Furthermore, the scope of the duty depended upon all of the circumstances of the case, and whether a particular scope of duty ensnares the wrongdoer depends on whether it is 'just and reasonable' for it to do so. Of course, the range of meanings which can be given to these words are infinite. In real terms, a consideration of public policy grounds for limiting the scope is the likely outcome.

There have been recent attempts to limit the scope of the test for establishing duty of care, as laid down by *Anns* v. *Merton L.B.C.* In *Leigh & Sillivan Ltd* v. *Aliakmon Shipping Co Ltd* (1986) (known as *The Aliakmon*), the facts of which are not particularly relevant here, Lord Brandon stated that, when Lord Wilberforce laid down the two-stage test in *Anns*, he was:

> dealing with the approach to the questions of existence and scope of duty of care in a novel type of factual situation which was not analogous to any factual situation in which the existence of such a duty had already been held to exist. He was not suggesting that the same approach should be adopted to the existence of a duty of care in a factual situation in which the existence of such a duty had repeatedly been held not to exist.

By limiting the application of the test in *Anns* to new situations, it would seem that after *The Aliakmon*, as far as existing situations are concerned, if a duty of care has been found to exist (or vice versa) in a given situation, there is no scope to change the law. Obviously this test case can be distinguished in future cases, and the House of Lords is not bound by its own decisions.

However, a further criticism was made of the decision in the *Anns* case in *Yuen Kun-yeu* v. *Attorney-General of Hong Kong* (1987), where Lord Keith stated:

> Their Lordships venture to think that the two-stage test formulated by Lord Wilberforce for determining the existence of a duty of care in negligence has been elevated to a degree of importance greater than its merits, and greater perhaps than its author intended.... It is clear that foreseeability does not of itself and automatically lead to a duty of care.... Foreseeability of harm is a necessary ingredient but it is not the only one. Otherwise there would be liability in negligence on the part of one who sees another about to walk over a cliff with head in the air, and forebears to shout a warning.... The speech of Lord Atkin [in *Donoghue* v. *Stevenson*] stressed not only the requirement of foreseeability of harm but also that of a close and direct relationship of proximity.... The second stage of Lord Wilberforce's test is one which will rarely have to be applied. It can only arise in a limited category of cases where, notwithstanding that a case of negligence is made out on the proximity basis, public policy requires that there should be no liability....

Following the decisions considered above, there must now be considerable doubt on the use of the test in *Anns* as a general test for establishing duty of care. It seems that it is once more safe to rely on *Donoghue* v. *Stevenson*, although the issue of public policy was relevant to the decision in *Hill* v. *Chief Constable of West Yorkshire Police* (1988), where it was held that as a matter of law and for public policy reasons there was insufficient proximity between the police and a murder victim to establish a duty of care in negligence. An action against the police for failing to identify and apprehend the 'Yorkshire Ripper', where that failure resulted in further murders, would therefore fail.

10.3 Duty of care for negligent misstatements

The importance of the neighbour or proximity test can be seen in the extension of the duty of care to cover negligent misstatements which result in economic loss. This arose out of the case of *Hedley Byrne & Co Ltd* v. *Heller & Partners Ltd* (1964). Prior to this case there was only liability for negligent misstatements causing physical damage, intentionally dishonest or fraudulent statements, or where there was a fiduciary or contractual relationship between the parties.

> *Hedley Byrne & Co Ltd* v. *Heller & Partners Ltd* (1964)
>
> Hedley Byrne asked their bank to make enquiries into the financial position of one of their clients. The bank made enquiries of Heller's bank, who gave a favourable reply about the client's financial position, adding the words 'without responsibility'. Hedley Byrne relied on this advice and lost a lot of money when their clients went into liquidation. However, they lost their action against the bank, because of the exclusion clause, which was held to be valid. The importance of the case lies in the dictum on negligent misstatements.
>
> **Held:** A duty of care exists where 'one party seeking information and advice was trusting the other to exercise such a degree of care as the circumstances required, where it was reasonable for him to do that, and where the other party gave the information or advice when he knew, or ought to have known, the enquirer was relying on him'.

Liability for negligent misstatements is based on the existence of a special relationship, i.e. the defendant must hold himself out in some way as having specialized knowledge, knowing that any information he gives will be relied upon by the plaintiff. Obviously lawyers, accountants, bankers, surveyors etc. come within this 'special relationship'. However, there is no liability for information given on a purely social occasion. The principle laid down in the *Hedley Byrne* case has been applied on numerous occasions, not always successfully:

See *Esso Petroleum Co Ltd* v. *Mardon* (1975), *Mutual Life Ltd* v. *Evatt* (1971), *Dutton* v. *Bognor Regis UDC* (1972), and *Ministry of Housing & Local Government* v. *Sharp* (1970).

10.4 Breach of duty

Once the plaintiff has established that the defendant owes him a duty of care, he must establish that the defendant is in breach of this duty. Once more, there is a test for establishing breach of duty. It was laid down in *Blyth* v. *Birmingham Waterworks Co* (1856).

A breach of duty occurs if the defendant:

> ... fails to do something which a reasonable man guided upon those considerations which ordinarily regulate the conduct of human affairs would do,
> or does something which a prudent and reasonable man would not do.

The test is an objective test, judged through the eyes of the reasonable man. However, the degree or standard of care to be exercised by such a person will vary, as there are factors, such as the age of the plaintiff, which can increase the standard of care to be exercised by the defendant. The test therefore is flexible. The factors outlined below are relevant.

10.4.1 The likelihood of injury

In deciding whether the defendant has failed to act as the reasonable man would act, the degree of care must be balanced against the degree of risk involved if the defendant fails in his duty. It follows, therefore, that the greater the risk of injury, or the more likely it is to occur, the more carefully the defendant will have to act to fulfil his duty.

> *Bolton* v. *Stone* (1951)
>
> A cricket ground was surrounded by a 17-foot wall, and the pitch situated some way from the road. A batsman hit the ball exceptionally hard, driving it over the wall, where it struck the plaintiff who was standing on the highway.
>
> **Held:** The plaintiff could not succeed in his action, as the likelihood of such injury occurring was very small, as was the risk. The slight risk was outweighed by the height of the wall and the fact that a ball had only been hit out of the ground 6 times in 30 years.

10.4.2 'Egg shell skull' rule

The degree of care to be exercised by the defendant may be increased if the plaintiff is very young, old or less able-bodied in some way. The rule is that 'you must take your victim as you find him'.

> *Haley* v. *London Electricity Board* (1965)
>
> The defendants, in order to carry out repairs, had made a hole in the pavement. Haley, who was blind, often walked along this stretch of pavement. He was normally able to avoid obstacles by using his white stick. The precautions taken by the Electricity Board would have prevented a sighted person from injuring himself, but not a blind person. As a result Haley fell, striking his head on the pavement, and consequently he became deaf.
>
> **Held:** The Electricity Board were in breach of their duty of care to pedestrians. They had failed to ensure that the excavation was safe for all pedestrians, not just sighted persons. It was clearly not reasonably safe for blind persons, yet it was foreseeable that they could use this pavement.

There are other cases which you might wish to refer to in this field: *Gough* v. *Thorne* (1966) (young children), *Daly* v. *Liverpool Corporation* (1939) (old people), and *Paris* v. *Stepney BC* (1951) (disability).

10.4.3 Cost and practicability

Another factor in deciding whether the defendant is in breach of his duty to the plaintiff is the cost and practicability of overcoming the risk. The foreseeable risk has to be balanced against the measures necessary to eliminate it. If the cost of these measures far outweighs the risk, the defendant will probably not be in breach of duty for failing to carry out these measures.

> *Latimer* v. *AEC Ltd* (1953)
>
> A factory belonging to AEC became flooded after an abnormally heavy rainstorm. The rain mixed with oily deposits on the floor making the floor very slippery. Sawdust was spread on the floor but there was insufficient to cover the whole area, although most of the floor was covered. Latimer, an employee, slipped on a part of the floor to which sawdust had not been applied.
>
> **Held:** AEC Ltd was not in breach of their duty to the plaintiff. It had taken all reasonable precautions and had eliminated the risk as far as it practicably could without going so far as to close the factory. There was no evidence to suggest that any reasonably prudent employer would have closed down the factory and as far as the Court was concerned the cost of doing that far outweighed the risk to the employees.

However in *Haley* v. *London Electricity Board* (1965) the provision of two foot high barriers around excavations in the pavement was practicable and would have eliminated the risk to blind people.

10.4.4 Social utility

The degree of risk has to be balanced against the social utility and importance of the defendant's activity. If the activity is of particular importance to the community, then in the circumstances, the taking of greater risks may be justified.

> *Watt v. Hertfordshire CC* (1954)
>
> The plaintiff, a fireman, was called out to rescue a woman trapped beneath a lorry. The lifting jack had to be carried on an ordinary lorry, as a suitable vehicle was unavailable. The jack slipped, injuring the plaintiff.
>
> **Held:** The employer was not in breach of duty. The importance of the activity and the fact that it was an emergency was found to justify the risk involved.

10.4.5 Common practice

If the defendant can show that what he has done is common practice, then this is evidence that a proper standard of care has been exercised. However if the common practice is in itself negligent, then his actions in conforming to such a practice will be actionable. See *Paris* v. *Stepney BC* (1951).

10.4.6 Skilled persons

The standard of care to be exercised by people professing to have a particular skill is not to be judged on the basis of the reasonable man. The actions of a skilled person must be judged by what the ordinary skilled man in that job or profession would have done, e.g. the reasonable doctor, plumber or engineer. Such a person is judged on the standard of knowledge possessed by the profession at the time the accident occurred. Obviously there is an onus on the skilled person to keep himself abreast of changes and improvements in technology.

> *Roe v. Ministry of Health* (1954)
>
> A patient was paralysed after being given a spinal injection. This occurred because the fluid being injected had become contaminated with the storage liquid, which had seeped through minute cracks in the phials.
>
> **Held:** There was no breach of duty as the doctor who administered the injection had no way of detecting the contamination at that time.

Furthermore the common practice of the profession may, if followed, prevent liability.

> *Bolam v. Friern Hospital Management Committee* (1957)
>
> Bolam broke his pelvis whilst undergoing electro-convulsive therapy treatment at the defendant's hospital. He alleged that the doctor had not warned him of the risks, nor had he been given relaxant drugs prior to treatment, and no one had held him down during treatment.
>
> **Held:** The doctor was not in breach of duty (and there was therefore no vicarious liability), because this form of treatment was accepted at that time by a certain body of the medical profession.

10.4.7 *Res ipsa loquitur*

The burden of proof in establishing breach of duty normally rests on the plaintiff. In certain circumstances, the inference of negligence may be drawn from the facts. If this can be done, the plaintiff is relieved of the burden, which moves to the defendant, to rebut the presumption of negligence. This is known as *res ipsa loquitur*, i.e. the thing speaks for itself. It can only be used where the only explanation for what happened is the negligence of the defendant, yet the plaintiff has insufficient evidence to prove his negligence. There are three criteria for the maxim to apply:

1 Sole management or control

It must be shown that the damage was caused by something under the sole management or control of the defendant, or by someone for whom he is responsible or whom he has a right to control.

2 The occurrence cannot have happened without negligence

This depends on the facts of each case. If there are other possible explanations as to how the incident occurred, *res ipsa loquitur* will fail.

> *Mahon* v. *Osborne* (1939)
>
> A patient died after a swab was left in her body after an operation. No one could explain how this had happened.
>
> **Held** *Res ipsa loquitur* applied.

3 Cause of the occurrence is unknown

If the defendant can put forward a satisfactory explanation of how the accident occurred which shows no negligence on his part, then the maxim is inapplicable.

> *Pearson* v. *NW Gas Board* (1968)
>
> The plaintiff's husband was killed, and her house destroyed, when a gas main fractured. She pleaded *res ipsa loquitur*. However the Gas Board put forward the explanation that the gas main could have fractured due to earth movement after a heavy frost.
>
> **Held:** This explanation was plausible and as it showed no negligence on their part, they were not liable.

If the defendant can rebut the presumption of negligence by giving a satisfactory explanation, it is open to the plaintiff to establish negligence in the normal way. In practice, he is unlikely to succeed as if he had sufficient evidence in the first place he would not have pleaded *res ipsa loquitur*!

Sample questions

| Sample questions on the topic of negligence can be found at the end of Chapter 11.

Further reading

| For further reading on the topics covered in this chapter, see chapter 13.

11 Negligence II

In this chapter on negligence we shall be considering the third element which has to be established before liability in negligence can exist, that of resultant damage. We shall also be looking briefly, in the final part of the chapter, at the economic torts.

Firstly, let us remind ourselves of the elements of negligence, as outlined in the flow chart below.

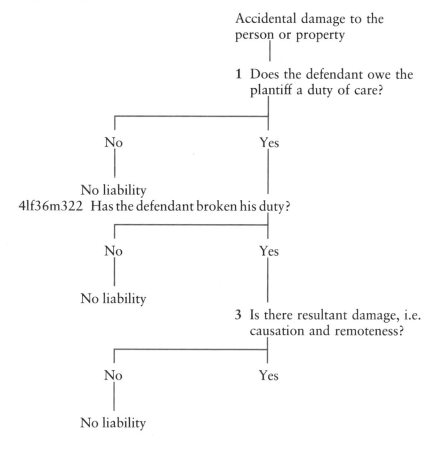

Accidental damage to the person or property

1 Does the defendant owe the plantiff a duty of care?

No   Yes

No liability

4lf36m322 Has the defendant broken his duty?

No   Yes

No liability

3 Is there resultant damage, i.e. causation and remoteness?

No   Yes

No liability

11.1 Resultant damage

The plaintiff must show that he has suffered some 'injury', though not necessarily physical. Furthermore he must show that this injury was caused by the defendant's negligence. This is known as 'causation'. There is a test which can be used to establish whether the defendant's negligence was the cause of the injury to the plaintiff.

11.1.1 The 'but for' test

In order to satisfy this test, the plaintiff must show that 'but for the defendant's actions the damage would not have occurred'. If the damage would have occurred irrespective of a breach of duty on the part of the defendant, then the breach is not the cause.

> *Cutler* v. *Vauxhall Motors Ltd* (1971)
> The plaintiff suffered a grazed ankle while at work, due to the defendant's negligence. The graze became ulcerated because of existing varicose veins, and the plaintiff had to undergo an immediate operation for the removal of the veins.

> **Held:** The plaintiff could not recover damages for the operation, because the evidence was that he would have to undergo the operation within five years, irrespective of the accident at work.

There can be problems, where there are two or more independent tortfeasors, in establishing how far each one is responsible for the damage caused.

> *Baker v. Willoughby* (1970)
>
> The plaintiff injured his leg through the defendant's negligence, leaving him partially disabled. Subsequently the plaintiff was shot in the same leg by another person, and as a result the leg had to be amputated. It was likely that the leg would in any case have had to be amputated as a result of the shooting.
>
> **Held:** The first defendant was liable for the plaintiff's disability (not the amputation) for the rest of his life. Irrespective of the amputation, it would have been a continuing disability, and this was reflected in the responsibility imposed on the defendant. The liability for the existing disability did not cease when the second incident took place.

The importance of establishing causation in an action for negligence was confirmed by the House of Lords in *Wilsher* v. *Essex Area Health Authority* (1988); the onus to do so clearly being on the plaintiff.

The 'but for' test can be used to establish causation on the facts. However, once this has been established it does not mean that the defendant will be liable for all of the damage to the plaintiff. There must be causation in law. This can be seen through the maxim *novus actus interveniens*: a new intervening act.

11.1.2 *Novus actus interveniens*

Where there is a break in the chain of causation, the defendant will not be liable for damage caused after the break. The issue is whether the whole sequence of events is the probable consequence of the defendant's actions, and whether it is reasonably foreseeable that these events may happen. This break in the chain is caused by an intervening act, and the law recognizes that such acts fall into three categories.

1 A natural event

> *Carslogie Steamship Co Ltd* v. *Royal Norwegian Government* (1952)
>
> A ship owned by Carslogie had been damaged in a collision caused by the defendant's negligence. The ship was sent for repair, and on this voyage suffered extra damage, caused by the severe weather conditions. This resulted in the repairs taking 40 days longer than anticipated.
>
> **Held:** The bad weather acted as a new intervening act, for which the defendant was not liable. The effect of the new act in this case prevented the plaintiff from recovering compensation for the time it would have taken to repair the vessel in respect of the collision damage, as the ship would have been out of use due to the damage caused by the weather.

2 Act of a third party

> *Lamb* v. *Camden London BC* (1981)
>
> Due to the defendant's negligence, a water main was damaged, causing the plaintiff's house to be damaged. The house was then vacated until it had been repaired, but while the house was empty, squatters moved in and caused further damage to the property.
>
> **Held:** The defendants were not liable for the squatters' damage. Although it was a reasonably foreseeable risk, it was not a likely event. Furthermore, it was not the duty of the Council to keep the squatters out.

3 Act of the plaintiff himself

> *McKew* v. *Holland, Hannen and Cubbitts (Scotland) Ltd* (1969)
>
> The plaintiff was injured while at work. As a result, on occasions his leg gave way without warning. While coming downstairs on one occasion his leg gave way, so he

jumped, rather than fall head first. This resulted in a badly injured ankle.

Held: The defendants were not liable for this additional injury. The plaintiff had not acted reasonably in attempting to negotiate the stairs without assistance, and his actions amounted to a *novus actus interveniens.*

Where it is the act of the plaintiff which breaks the chain, it is not a question of foresight but of unreasonable conduct.

11.1.3   Remoteness of damage

It must be understood that, even where causation is established, the defendant will not necessarily be liable for all of the damage resulting from the breach. This was not always the case, and the way in which the law has developed must be considered.

Re Polemis (1921)

The plaintiff's ship was destroyed by fire when one of the employees of the company to whom the ship had been chartered negligently knocked a plank into the hold. The hold was full of petrol vapour. The fall of the plank caused a spark as it struck the side and this ignited the vapour.

Held: The defendants were liable for the loss of the ship, even though the presence of petrol vapour and the causing of the spark were unforeseen. The fire was the direct result of the breach of duty and the defendant was liable for the full extent of the damage even where the manner in which it took place was unforeseen.

The case of *Re Polemis* is no longer regarded as the current test for remoteness of damage, even though it has not been distinguished or overruled. The accepted test at present arose out of:

The Wagon Mound (No 1) (1961)

The defendants negligently allowed furnace oil to spill from a ship into Sidney harbour. The oil spread, and came to lie beneath a wharf owned by the plaintiffs. The plaintiffs had been carrying out welding operations and, on seeing the oil, they stopped welding in order to ascertain whether it was safe to continue to weld. They were assured that the oil would not catch fire and so resumed welding. Molten metal fell onto cotton waste floating in the water, causing it to catch fire. This in turn ignited the oil and this fire spread to the plaintiff's wharf.

Held: The defendants were in breach of duty. However, they were only liable for the damage caused to the wharf and slipways through the fouling by the oil. They were not liable for the damage caused by fire because damage by fire was at that time unforeseeable. This particular oil had a high ignition point, and it could not have been foreseen that it would ignite on water. The Court refused to apply the rule in *Re Polemis.*

The test of reasonable foresight arising out of the *Wagon Mound* clearly takes into account such things as scientific knowledge at the time of the negligent act. The question to be asked in determining the extent of liability is 'is the damage of such a kind as the reasonable man could have foreseen?' This does not mean that the defendant should have foreseen precisely the sequence or nature of the events. Lord Denning in *Stewart* v. *West African Air Terminals* (1964) said:

It is not necessary that the precise concatenation of circumstances should be envisaged. If the consequence was one which was within the general range which any reasonable person might foresee (and was not of an entirely different kind which no one would anticipate), then it is within the rule that a person who has been guilty of negligence is liable for the consequences.

This is illustrated in the case of:

Hughes v. *Lord Advocate* (1963)

Employees of the Post Office, who were working down a manhole, left it without a cover, but with a tent over it and lamps around it. A child picked up a lamp and went into the tent. He tripped over the lamp, knocking it into the hole. An explosion occurred, in which the child was burned. The risk of the child being

> burned by the lamp was foreseeable, but the vapourization of the paraffin in the lamp, and its ignition, were not foreseeable.
>
> **Held:** The defendants were liable for the injury to the plaintiff. It was foreseeable that the child might be burned, and it was immaterial that neither the extent of his injury nor the precise chain of events leading to it were foreseeable.

The test of remoteness is not easy to apply. The cases themselves highlight the uncertainty of the Courts. It is a flexible test and is certainly subject to public policy issues as introduced by the Courts. See *Doughty* v. *Turner Manufacturing Co Ltd* (1964) and *Tremain* v. *Pike* (1969).

11.1.4 Nervous shock

Nervous shock is a form of personal injury which may give rise to an action for damages. If damages are to be recoverable, nervous shock must take the form of a recognized mental illness; mental suffering, such as grief, is not recoverable. No physical injury need be suffered. The basis of liability for nervous shock depends on whether this type of injury was reasonably foreseeable – see *Bourhill* v. *Young* (1943).

As far as the Courts are concerned, persons claiming for nervous shock fall into one of several distinct categories.

1 The claimant experiences shock and illness after fearing for their own safety

> *Dulieu* v. *White* (1901)
>
> A pregnant woman was serving in a public house when the defendant's employee negligently drove a carriage into the front of the building. The plaintiff was not physically injured, but suffered severe shock, leading to illness.
>
> **Held:** She was allowed to recover damages as the shock and illness arose out of fear of immediate personal injury to herself.

2 Where the claimant fears for the personal injury of a close relative

> *Hambrook* v. *Stokes Bros* (1925)
>
> A lorry began to roll down a hill, out of control. A mother had just left her children when she saw the lorry go out of control, but she could not see her children; she merely heard the crash. She was told that a child with glasses had been hurt, and one of her children wore glasses. She suffered shock which was so severe it eventually led to her death.
>
> **Held:** Her estate could recover damages, even though her illness was caused by fear for her children, not for herself. The defendant should have foreseen that his negligence might put someone in such fear of bodily injury that they would suffer nervous shock; and that this could be extended to cover fear for one's children.

> *McLoughlin* v. *O'Brian* (1983)
>
> A mother was told in her home that her family had been injured in a road accident two miles away. She suffered illness caused by the shock of hearing this news, and later by seeing her family in hospital before they had received any treatment, i.e. while still covered in blood.
>
> **Held:** She could recover damages, as the shock was a foreseeable consequence of the defendant's negligence. The Courts felt that the proximity of the claimant to the accident was relevant. However, 'proximity' here meant closeness in time and space. Furthermore, the shock must be caused by the sight or hearing of the event, or its immediate aftermath.

3 Where the claimant suffers nervous shock through seeing injury to others, even though he is in no danger himself

> *Dooley* v. *Cammel Laird & Co* (1951)
>
> A faulty rope was being used on a crane to secure a load which was being loaded into the hold of a ship. The rope broke, causing the load to fall into the hold where

people were working. The crane driver suffered shock arising out of a fear for the safety of his fellow employees.

Held: The crane driver could recover damages, as it was foreseeable that he was likely to be affected if the rope broke.

Chadwick v. British Transport Commission (1967)

Chadwick took part in the rescue operations after a train crash. He suffered a severe mental condition as a result of the horrific scenes there. He had a previous history of mental illness.

Held: BTC were liable. It was reasonably foreseeable that in the event of an accident someone other than the defendant's employees (servants) would intervene and suffer injury. Injury by shock to a rescuer was reasonably foreseeable, even if he suffered no physical injury.

See *Bourhill* v. *Young* (1943) for a consideration of the position of the innocent passer-by, who merely witnesses the aftermath of an accident.

It is certainly possible to extend the claims for nervous shock to liability for negligent misstatement. For example, if a bank gives negligent advice about an investment, and the person acting on this advice loses his life savings and suffers a nervous breakdown, then damage for this is likely to be recoverable. The Financial Services Act, 1986, however, considerably restricts the circumstances in which banks and other institutions are able to give financial advice.

11.1.5 Economic loss

Liability in negligence for economic loss is a comparatively recent development.

Spartan Steel & Alloys Ltd v. *Martin & Co* (1973)

The plaintiffs manufactured steel alloys, 24 hours a day. This required continuous power. The defendants' employees damaged a power cable, which resulted in a lack of power for 14 hours. There was a danger of damage to the furnace, so this had to be shut down and the products in the process of manufacture removed, thereby reducing their value. The plaintiffs also suffered loss of profits.

Held: The defendants were liable for physical damage to the products and the loss of profit arising out of this. There was, however, no liability for economic loss unconnected with the physical damage, i.e. the extra melts which could have passed through the furnace.

The rule that economic loss is only recoverable where it is directly the consequence of physical damage has been challenged in:

Junior Books Co Ltd v. *Veitchi Ltd* (1983)

Veitchi, the defendants, were specialist flooring contractors and were engaged as sub-contractors to lay a factory floor which was part of a building being erected for Junior Books. There was no contractual relationship between the parties. It was alleged that the floor was defective, in that it was of the wrong composition and construction. It cracked badly, and as a result the plaintiff suffered loss and damage. The plaintiff claimed for the relaying of the floor, the storage of books during the relaying, removal of machinery, loss of profits through closure, wages of employees who could not work because of the closure, overheads and investigations into the treatment of the floor.

Held: Veitchi owed Junior Books a duty of care, because of the proximity test. There was no reason why the duty of care should be restricted in any way. The defendants were clearly in breach of duty and the economic loss as well as the physical damage was reasonably foreseeable. The plaintiff therefore succeeded in obtaining damages for the full extent of his claim.

The importance of proximity was highlighted in the following case:

Muirhead v. *Industrial Tank Specialities Ltd* (1986)

The plaintiff bought a large tank in which to keep lobsters as part of his business.

Water had to be constantly pumped round the tank. The pump supplied with the tank broke down and the entire stock of lobsters died. The plaintiff had relied on the advice of the supplier of the tank and pump, and had had no contact with the manufacturer. The reason the pump failed was due to its unsuitability for UK voltage. However, he brought an action against the manufacturer claiming the loss of the lobsters and economic loss including loss of profits.

Held: If proximity could be established between the manufacturer and the plaintiff, and the latter could show reliance on the manufacturer rather than the supplier, then the duty of care would be established in respect of pure economic loss. However, on the facts there was no proximity or reliance and therefore the claim for economic loss would fail.

Nevertheless, the plaintiff would succeed in his claim for the loss of the lobsters, which was physical damage, and any consequent financial loss, as this was reasonably foreseeable.

There have been two significant attempts to limit claims for economic loss arising out of an action in tort and, more specifically, negligence.

Simaan General Contracting Co v. *Pilkington Glass Ltd* (1988)

Pilkington supplied glass units to a sub-contractor for installation in a building. The units did not comply with the specifications agreed between the building owner and the main contractors.

Held: Pilkington were not liable to the main contractor for the economic loss suffered by them as a result of the rejection of the units. There was no physical damage; the defects in the units merely related to the colour as specified in the contract between the building owner and the main contractor and therefore this case could be distinguished from *Junior Books*.

Greater Nottingham Co-operative Society Ltd v. *Cementation Piling & Foundations Ltd* (1988)

Cementation were sub-contractors to the main contractor in a contract to extend the Society's premises at Skegness. Cementation agreed to undertake the pile driving and due to their negligence, adjoining premises were damaged. The Society paid for remedial work, for which Cementation agreed liability. The Society however claimed additional damages for economic loss arising out of the negligence of the sub-contractors.

Held: Whilst the proximity of the relationship between the Society and the sub-contractor was of significance, it did not permit the society to recover damages for economic loss which was not referable to physical injury. As a result, the claim for expenses incurred due to delayed completion were not recoverable.

11.2 Defences

11.2.1 Contributory negligence

Where the plaintiff is found in some way to have contributed through his own fault to his injury, the amount awarded as damages will be reduced accordingly – Law Reform (Contributory Negligence) Act, 1945. The onus is on the defendant to show that the plaintiff was at fault and that this contributed to his injury.

If the Court is satisfied that the plaintiff is at fault, it will reduce the amount of damages by an amount which is just and reasonable, depending on the plaintiff's share of the blame. For example, damages are often reduced by anything from 10 per cent to 75 per cent. However a 100 per cent reduction has been made – see *Jayes* v. *IMI (Kynoch) Ltd* (1985).

11.2.2 *Volenti non fit injuria*

Volenti, or consent, may be a defence to an action arising out of injury caused by the future conduct of the defendant, which involves the risk of a tort being committed. *Volenti* may arise from the express agreement of the plaintiff and defendant, or it may be implied from the plaintiff's conduct.

> *ICI* v. *Shatwell* (1965)
>
> The plaintiff and his brother ignored the safety precautions issued by their employer, and breached regulations in testing detonators. As a result, the plaintiff was injured in an explosion. The action against the employer was based on vicarious liability and breach of statutory duty on the part of the plaintiff's brother.
>
> **Held:** The defence of *volenti* would succeed. The plaintiff not only consented to each act of negligence and breach of statute on the part of his brother, but also participated in it quite willingly.

It must be stressed that this particular case highlights the extreme circumstances where *volenti* is likely to succeed.

However, if the defence is to succeed it must be shown that the plaintiff was fully informed of the risks when he gave his consent.

> *Dann* v. *Hamilton* (1939)
>
> A girl accepted a lift in the car of a driver whom she knew to be drunk. She could have used alternative transport. She was injured as a result of his negligent driving.
>
> **Held:** Although she knew of the risk, this was insufficient to support the defence of *volenti*. It was necessary to show that she had consented to the risk, which could not be established. She therefore succeeded in her action against the driver.

Following this case, it is doubtful whether this defence will succeed where the implied consent is given before the negligent act occurs.

In practice the Courts do not look favourably on this defence in respect of negligent actions and therefore it is not usually pleaded. However, the defence of contributory negligence may succeed on the same facts – see *Dann* v. *Hamilton*.

11.3   Economic torts

The following is a brief outline of the economic torts. As they are complex in nature, it is unlikely that they will be dealt with in great detail in a business law course designed for non-lawyers. These torts give a right of action to persons whose contract or business suffers at the hands of a third party.

11.3.1   Interfering with a contract or inducing a breach of contract

The essentials are:

1 There must be in existence a valid contract between the plaintiff and another person.

2 The defendant must know of the existence of the contract.

> *Emerald Construction Co* v. *Lowthian* (1966)
>
> Officials of a bricklayers' trade union put pressure on building contractors to end their system of 'labour only' sub-contracts, whereby the plaintiff supplied the workers to them. The officials knew of the existence of the contracts, but not the precise nature of the terms.
>
> **Held:** It was sufficient that the union officials knew of the existence of the contract. There was no need to know the actual terms, as for the most part a total disregard for terms was shown by the defendants' actions in attempting to bring about the termination of the contract.

3 The defendant must intend to interfere with the contractual relationship, or induce a breach of contract.

4 The plaintiff must suffer damage.

At one time it was thought that an action would only lie if there had been an actual breach of contract as a result of the defendant's actions. However, as a result of the decision in *Merkur Island Shipping Co* v. *Laughton* (1983), the plaintiff will have an action in respect of the interference with the contract, even though a breach of contract does not take place. In this particular case, an act of interference prevented the plaintiff from performing his part of the contract but, because of the wording of the charterparty, this did not actually amount to a breach of contract.

Interference or inducement can take place by:

1 Persuasion, i.e. the link must be made between the defendant's actions and the breach or non-performance in the form of causation.

2 Prevention of the performance of the contract. It is open to question whether the 'prevention' has to take the form of 'unlawful means', i.e. should it amount to a crime or tort?

> *GWK Ltd v. Dunlop Rubber Co Ltd* (1926)
>
> The plaintiff contracted with a car manufacturer that the plaintiff's tyres would be displayed on the manufacturer's cars at an exhibition. The defendant removed the plaintiff's tyres from the cars at the exhibition and replaced them with tyres which they had manufactured.
>
> **Held:** This amounted to the physical prevention of the performance of the contract between the plaintiff and the car manufacturer and was therefore actionable. The unlawful means was the trespass by the defendant on the goods of the plaintiff.

11.3.2   Intimidation

The essentials of this economic tort are laid down in *Morgan v. Fry* (1968):

1 There must be a threat by one person to use unlawful means to compel another to obey his wishes, i.e. there must be a coercive element; *and*

2 the person so threatened must comply with the demand, rather than risk the threat being carried out.

> *Rookes v. Barnard* (1964)
>
> The plaintiff was employed by BOAC. There was an agreement between BOAC and the trade union that all employees would be members of the union. The plaintiff resigned from the union. The three defendants were union officials who threatened BOAC with a strike if the plaintiff was not 'removed'. BOAC dismissed the plaintiff. Any strike would have amounted to 'unlawful means', as there was a 'no strike' agreement between BOAC and its employees.
>
> **Held:** The individual actions of the defendants amounted to intimidation, and their combined action amounted to a conspiracy to commit the tort of intimidation.

11.3.3   Conspiracy

Conspiracy is an agreement of two or more persons to do an unlawful act, or lawful act by unlawful means, resulting in damage to the plaintiff.

This tort has the following requirements:

1 An agreement, undertaking or concerted action to cause injury to the plaintiff;

2 There must be at least two parties to the agreement.

> *Lonrho v. Shell Petroleum* (1981)
>
> The plaintiff alleged that it had suffered damage as a result of a conspiracy between the defendants, Shell Petroleum and other bodies to break the sanctions imposed by an Order in Council in Southern Rhodesia by continuing to deliver oil to that country. This effectively prolonged the use of sanctions and prevented the plaintiff from using their pipeline to Southern Rhodesia.
>
> **Held:** There was no actionable conspiracy. There was no evidence of an intention to cause any loss or damage to the plaintiff. The predominant purpose of a conspiracy must be to harm the plaintiff in his trade or business and the onus is on the plaintiff to show this.

> *Metall und Rohstoff AG v. Donaldson Lufkin & Jenrette Inc* (1988)
>
> In this case it was decided that the decision in *Lonrho* was confined to conspiracy to injure a man in his trade or business. However, the tort of conspiracy was not limited to such cases.

11.3.4 Passing off

This tort provides protection for a person whose competitors attempt to pass off their goods or services as his. The law recognizes that a person's trade name and reputation are capable of protection. The requirements of the tort are as follows:

1 There must be economic competition between the defendant and the plaintiff, i.e. they must be trade rivals in some way.

2 There must be an intention or calculated act to deceive.

3 The plaintiff need not prove damage.

The tort can occur in a number of ways:

1 Use of trade marks
Where the defendant makes use of the plaintiff's trade marks on his goods, the plaintiff may bring an action in tort for passing off. Protection is also afforded under the Trade Marks Act, 1938, if the trade mark is registered.

2 Use of trade names
The plaintiff may be able to prevent – usually by injunction – the defendant from using the same name or a similar trade name to himself. This also covers descriptions applied to goods.

> *Warnink v. Townend* (1979)
>
> The plaintiffs manufactured advocaat from eggs and spirits. The defendants manufactured a drink which they called 'Old English Advocaat', made from dried eggs and sherry. This product was cheaper than Warninks product because of the cheaper ingredients used.
>
> **Held:** Warninks were entitled to an injunction to prevent the defendants using the word 'advocaat' for their product. The word 'advocaat' had an exclusive meaning, indicating that spirits were used in its manufacture.

Also, if the defendant's own trade name is similar to that of the plaintiff, an injunction may be awarded if there is unavoidable confusion in the eyes of the public. This is only likely to occur where the plaintiff and defendant are in the same competitive markets.

Finally, the appearance, or get-up, of a product may be protected by an action for passing off.

> *Reckitt & Coleman Products Ltd v. Borden Inc* (1988)
>
> Since 1956, the plaintiffs had sold lemon juice in a particular type of plastic container which resembled a real lemon, and which was known as 'Jif' lemon. The defendants attempted to market and sell a similar item. The particular get-up of the Jif product had become identified in the eyes of the public with the product of the plaintiff.
>
> **Held:** The manufacturers of Jif lemon juice had established a proprietary right in the particular get-up of their product. Any trader therefore was under a duty to ensure that there were sufficient distinguishing features between the get-up of their products and that of the plaintiffs.

Sample questions

1 What factors are taken into account in considering whether the defendant is in breach of his duty owed to the plaintiff?

Suggested answer

You should refer to the test expounded in *Blythe v. Birmingham Waterworks Co* – the defendant should act as the reasonable man would act. The test is objective and consideration should be made of the other factors which are relevant; foresight and the likelihood of injury (*Bolton* v. *Stone*); the egg-shell skull rule (*Haley* v. *London Electricity Board*); cost and practicability (*Latimer* v. *AEC*); and social utility (*Watt* v. *Hertfordshire CC*).

The standard of care may be increased where the defendant has particular skills, e.g. as a doctor, and such people are judged on the basis of whether they have acted as the reasonably skilled member of their profession (*Roe* v. *Minister of Health*). The standard of care may also have to be considered in the light of common practice at the time of the accident (*Bolam* v. *Friern Hospital Management Committee*).

2 Widsworth District Council is in the process of carrying out road repairs. Their employees damage a water main, which results in the loss of water supply to the local steam laundry. The laundry is forced to send work to its nearest rival and send many of its employees home. Advise Widsworth District Council.

Suggested answer

In answering this problem you need to establish the three elements of liability in negligence, i.e. duty of care, breach of duty and resultant damage. In considering duty, you will need to establish that a duty of care was owed to the plaintiff using the neighbour test in *Donoghue* v. *Stevenson*. Having established duty you would need to show that the local authority had failed to act reasonably and were therefore in breach of duty – consideration of the factors affecting breach should be considered here i.e. foresight, cost and practicability etc. Finally, you need to establish resultant damage, i.e. causation in fact and law – the 'but for' test and the issue of remoteness of damage as in the *Wagon Mound (No 1)*. In considering the extent of the liability of the local authority the question of liability for economic loss is important and the following cases should be referred to – *Spartan Steel & Alloys Ltd* v. *Martin & Co*, *Junior Books* v. *Veitchi*, *Muirhead* v. *Industrial Tank Specialities*, *Simaan General Contracting Co* v. *Pilkington Glass Ltd*.

3 What are the essential elements which have to be established on the part of the plaintiff for there to be liability in negligence?

Suggested answer

You must establish, in turn, the following for there to be liability in negligence:

Duty of care – reference should be made to the test for establishing duty i.e. the neighbour test in *Donoghue* v. *Stevenson* as well as *Anns* v. *Merton London BC*, although the limitation on the use of *Anns* in the light of recent cases must be mentioned – *The Aliakmon*.

Once the plaintiff has established duty of care he must show that the defendant is in breach of duty, i.e. the reasonable man test in *Blythe* v. *Birmingham Waterworks*; there should also be reference to the other factors – foresight, cost and practicability, the egg-shell skull rule. Although the onus is usually on the plaintiff, mention should be made of *res ipsa loquitur*.

The plaintiff must finally show resultant damage in the form of causation i.e. the 'but for' test and the test for remoteness of damage in the *Wagon Mound*.

4 Frank is considering buying a hotel. His friend James, an architect, surveys the property and informs him it is in good order. His bank manager, Mr Bloggs, looks at the last financial statement of the hotel and advises him that the hotel seems to be a very lucrative proposition. After Frank has purchased the hotel he discovers it needs £3000 worth of repairs and the opening of it has to be delayed for six months. He also discovers that the bank manager has mis-interpreted the financial statement and the hotel has never made adequate profits. Advise Frank.

LLB, Staffordshire Polytechnic

Suggested answer

This problem involves liability for negligent mis-statement. In establishing duty of care it is necessary to show that there is a special relationship between the parties as in *Hedley Byrne* v. *Heller & Partners*. In this particular case, even though James is a friend, he may still have held himself out as being a competent surveyor; Frank will have to show that James knew that Frank would rely on his skill and judgment, which should not prove to be too difficult.

A special relationship will also have to be established between Mr Bloggs and Frank, which again should not pose a problem. The issue of breach of duty then needs to be considered. The issue being: have James and Mr Bloggs respectively acted as a reasonable surveyor and bank manager. If the repairs could have been detected by the reasonable surveyor and the reasonable bank manager would not have made the mistake made by Mr Bloggs, breach can be shown.

The issue of resultant damage in the form of causation must be considered as well as the extent of liability for such things as economic loss.

5 (a) What is meant by duty of care in negligence?

(b) Explain the rule that 'you must take your victim as you find him'.

Suggested answer

(a) In this part of the question you need to be prepared to discuss not only the basic test as laid down in *Donoghue* v. *Stevenson*, i.e. that a duty of care is owned to one's neighbour but also the development of the test in *Anns* v. *Merton London BC* and the suggested limitation on the use of the test in *Anns* as expounded in *Peabody Donation Fund* v. *Sir Lindsay Parkinson & Co Ltd*, *The Aliakmon* and *Yuen Kun-yue* v. *Attorney-General of Hong Kong*.

(b) This rule, often called the 'egg-shell skull' rule, is important in establishing breach of duty and whether the defendant has acted reasonably. It is clear from the rule that the defendant must be prepared for certain categories of plaintiff to be less careful and he must therefore increase his standard of care, e.g. to the blind person as in *Haley* v. *London Electricity Board*; to young children – *Gough* v. *Thorne*; to workmen with a disability – *Paris* v. *Stepney BC*.

6 A heavy rainfall has flooded Blooming Bakers shop leaving the floor slippery. One of the employees is given some sawdust to put on the floor but there is insufficient to cover all of the slippery area. Maisey, a customer, who has a defective hip joint and is therefore unsteady on her feet, enters the shop and slips on the floor. She is taken to hospital, where an operation is carried out on her damaged leg. However due to the mis-reading of the x-rays she is left with a worse limp than before. Advise Blooming Bakers.

Suggested answer

In deciding whether there is liability in negligence, you must establish that the shop owed their customer a duty of care, that they were in breach of duty and that there was resultant damage. In establishing duty of care, you should refer to the neighbour test in *Donoghue* v. *Stevenson* and in this particular instance applying that test it should be easy to establish that a duty of care was owed to Maisey.

Breach of duty is decided on the basis of whether BB have acted reasonably, considering the risk and the cost and practicability of remedying the situation. You should consider whether they could have been expected to do more in the circumstances – *Latimer* v. *AEC*. There is also the point that they must take their victim as they find her, as she has a defective hip joint – *Haley* v. *London Electricity Board*.

Finally, in considering resultant damage and the extent of BB's liability, although BB caused the initial injury it must be decided whether there has been a *novus actus interveniens* which would make the hospital liable for some of the damage.

7 (a) What must be established for an action to lie for inducing or interfering with a contract?

(b) What amounts to the tort of intimidation?

Suggested answer

(a) The tort of interfering or inducing a breach of contract may take place in a number of ways, e.g. persuasion or coercion. You will need to refer to the following points in order to establish liability:

The existence of a valid contract between the plaintiff and a third party.

The defendant must know of the existence of the contract.

The defendant must intend to interfere or induce a breach of contract.

The plaintiff must show that he has suffered some damage.

(b) Intimidation can be the act of an individual or the combined actions of several, which can amount to conspiracy to commit the tort of intimidation. Intimidation exists where one person is forced to act in a certain way because of threats made by another. The coercive action must amount to unlawful means, e.g. the threat of assault. The tort will only arise where the person who has been intimidated gives into the intimidation and as a result another person suffers.

Further reading

For further reading on the topics covered in this chapter, see chapter 13.

12 Employers' liability

Under the heading of employers' liability we shall only be considering the liability of the employer for accidents to his employees, which arise out of the employer's breach of his personal duties owed to his employees. The liability of the employer for injuries to victims of his employee's torts is considered under vicarious liability, which is dealt with in the next chapter.

Employers' liability arises out of the law of negligence, and if it is studied after the tort of negligence, it poses fewer problems for the student. Employers' liability is merely a specialized aspect of negligence, tied in with the employer/employee relationship.

It gives the employee the right to sue the employer when he is injured at work for negligent acts arising in the course of his employment. In order to ensure that the employer can pay any award of damages, the Employers' Liability (Compulsory Insurance) Act, 1969 imposes a duty on employers to take out the necessary insurance cover.

12.1 Duty of care

The employer's duty of care is owed to each individual employee, and cannot be delegated by the employer to anyone else. However, the duty is only owed whilst the employee is acting within the course of his employment, i.e. if he is doing something reasonably incidental to his main job.

> *Davidson v. Handley-Page Ltd* (1945)
>
> The plaintiff slipped and hurt his leg whilst standing on a duck-board at the sink. He was washing his tea-cup after his tea break. The duck-board had become slippery because water was constantly splashed upon it.
>
> **Held:** The employer was in breach of his duty because the employee was carrying out a task which was reasonably incidental to his job—tea breaks being an accepted part of working life!

As the duty is of a personal nature, the standard of care will vary with the individual needs of each employee. It follows, therefore, that special regard must be made for the old, young, inexperienced and less able-bodied. The general nature of the duty can be expressed as follows:

> The employer must take reasonable care in the way he conducts his operations, so as not to subject his employees to unnecessary risks. See *Smith* v. *Baker & Sons* (1891).

12.2 Scope of the employer's duty

This was defined in *Wilsons & Clyde Coal Co* v. *English* (1938). Following this case the employer's duty extends to the provision of:

1 competent fellow employees;

2 safe plant and appliances;

3 a safe place of work;

4 safe systems of work.

12.2.1 Competent fellow employees

The employer must ensure that all his staff are competent to do the job for which they have been employed. He must therefore make sure that they have the necessary experience, or be prepared to train them accordingly. If one of his employees is injured as a result of the incompetence of a fellow employee, then the employer will be liable. The word 'incompetence' covers a multitude of sins. Much of the case law arises out of practical jokes at work. In this situation, whether the employer is liable will depend on the depth of his knowledge about the incompetent employee.

O'Reilley v. *National Rail & Tramway Appliances Ltd* (1966)

O'Reilley was employed with three others to break up scrap from railways. His colleagues persuaded him to hit with his sledge-hammer a shell case embedded between the railway sleepers. When he did this the shell exploded.

Held: The employer was not in breach of his duty because he had no previous knowledge that these workers played practical jokes. He therefore had not failed to employ competent fellow employees.

The previous conduct of the 'incompetent employee' is relevant. If there have been any occurrences which should act as a warning to the employer, yet he does nothing about his employee, then the employer will be liable for any injury or damage arising out of his employee's incompetence.

Hudson v. *Ridge Manufacturing Co Ltd* (1957)

Hudson was on his way to the sick room when a fellow employee tripped him up and broke his wrist. This employee was known as a practical joker and had been warned by his employer to stop fooling about.

Held: The employer was in breach of his duty because he was aware of his employee's tendency to fool about. He should have done more to curb his employee even if this meant dismissal.

12.2.2 Safe plant and appliances

The employer must not only provide his employees with the necessary plant and equipment to do the job safely, but must also ensure that such plant and equipment is safe, i.e. properly maintained. For example, guards must be provided on dangerous machinery to protect the employee from injury, and these guards must be inspected regularly to ensure that they are securely in position and are not damaged in any way.

Bradford v. *Robinson Rentals Ltd* (1967)

Bradford was employed as a driver. He was required to drive over 400 miles in extremely cold weather in a van with a broken window and a heater which did not work. He suffered severe frostbite.

Held: The van was not safe, and therefore the employer had failed in his duty to provide safe plant and equipment. Although the conditions were extreme, it was foreseeable that the employee would suffer some 'injury' if sent out on a long journey in a van in that condition.

Taylor v. *Rover Car Co Ltd* (1966)

Taylor was using a hammer and chisel when a piece of metal flew off the chisel and blinded him in one eye. This batch of chisels was in a defective state when supplied by the manufacturers.

Held: Taylor's employer was liable, because four weeks previously a similar incident had occurred, albeit without anyone being injured. This meant that the employer should have known of the likelihood of such an accident occurring. To avoid this, the chisels should have been taken out of use and returned to the manufacturer.

If the previous incident in Taylor's case had not occurred, Taylor's only remedy at that time would have been against the manufacturer.

However, the Employers' Liability (Defective Equipment) Act, 1969 provides that where an employee is injured at work as a consequence of defective equipment supplied by his employer, and the defect is the fault of a third party, e.g. the manfacturer, the employer will be deemed to be negligent and therefore responsible for the injury. This statute removes the need to establish foresight on the part of the employer in cases like Taylor's.

12.2.3 A safe place of work

The employer must ensure that his employees are not exposed to any dangers arising out of the place where the employee is expected to work. This covers any place under the control of the employer, including access and egress.

> *Smith* v. *Vange Scaffolding & Engineering Co Ltd* (1970)
>
> Smith was employed by Vange on a building site. There were other contractors on site. As Smith returned to the changing hut at the end of the working day, he tripped over the cable of a welding machine, which had been left there by a contractor. Vange was aware of the obstructions on site, which made access to and from the place of work difficult and dangerous, but he had not complained to the other contractors.
>
> **Held:** The employer had failed in his duty to his employee, because he was aware of the situation and should have made the necessary complaints to the main contractor. It was foreseeable that such an accident might occur and reasonable precautions should have been taken.

12.2.4 Safe system of work

The duty of the employer to provide a safe system of work extends to a consideration of the following by the employer: the physical layout of the job; safety notices; special procedures; protective clothing; training and supervision.

In order to fulfil this duty, the employer must take into account all **foreseeable** eventualities, including the actions of his employees. Any system, to be safe, must reduce the risks to the employee to a minimum. It is accepted that not all risks can be eliminated. Furthermore, the employer must do more than introduce a safe system of work, he must ensure that it is observed by his employees. The case law highlights the breadth of this duty.

> *Charlton* v. *Forrest Printing Ink Co Ltd* (1980)
>
> One of Charlton's duties was to collect the firms' wages every Friday from the bank. He was issued with instructions to vary the time and route, because of a previous robbery. He ignored this and kept to a regular collection pattern. One day he suffered severe injuries when he was attacked and robbed.
>
> **Held:** There was a foreseeable risk to the employee, but his employer had done what was necessary to minimize the risk and therefore there was no breach of duty. The Court felt that it was in order for a small firm to collect its own payroll.

Decisions like the above may well be different if made today, as the social, economic and political situation changes. For example, even small firms may be expected to use a security firm nowadays to collect wages from the bank, in the light of the increase in the number of violent robberies.

> *Woods* v. *Durable Suites Ltd* (1953)
>
> Woods worked in the veneer department at Durable Suites. He was an extremely experienced employee. As there was a risk of dermatitis from the synthetic glues, his employer posted up a notice specifying the precautions to be taken. Woods had also been instructed personally by the manager in the protective measures, but had not observed them fully. As a result, he contracted dermatitis.
>
> **Held:** The employer was not liable for failing to provide a safe system of work, because the company had taken all reasonable care in posting up notices and providing barrier cream etc. They were under no obligation, given the age and experience of Woods, to provide someone to watch over him to make sure he followed the precautions.

Constant supervision, on the whole, is not necessary where the employees have the necessary experience and have been trained or instructed accordingly.

> *Bux* v. *Slough Metals Ltd* (1974)
>
> Bux's job involved the removal of molten metal from a furnace, and the pouring of this metal into a die-casting machine. Goggles were supplied and Bux was made aware of the risks. He refused to wear the safety goggles because they misted up

and he complained to the supervisor, who informed him that no other goggles were available. He was injured when molten metal splashed into his eye.

Held: The employer was liable. Where work is of a particularly hazardous nature, the employer must do more than merely provide safety equipment—he should constantly urge his employees to use or wear such safety equipment, as is deemed necessary.

See *McDermid* v. *Nash Dredging & Reclamation Co Ltd* (1987).

12.3 Breach of duty

The burden is on the employee to show that the employer is in breach of his duty. As the duty does not impose strict liability, the employee must prove that his employer has been negligent, or he can plead *res ipsa loquitur*. The most important question to ask in establishing breach of duty is: Has the employer failed to act like any reasonable employer?

If the employer has taken all reasonable precautions, considering all of the circumstances of the case, then he will not be liable (see *Latimer* v. *AEC Ltd* (1953)).

The standard of care will vary in respect of the individual needs of each employee. The employer must have special regard for the old, young, inexperienced and employees with special disabilities, i.e. the standard of care will be increased.

Paris v. *Stepney District Council* (1951)

Paris worked for the Council in one of their garages. One of his frequent jobs was to chip out rust from under buses and other vehicles owned by the Council. At that time it was not customary to provide safety goggles for such work. Paris was already blind in one eye. One day as he was chipping out rust a fragment of rust entered his good eye and he was made totally blind.

Held: The employer had failed to exercise the necessary standard of care. It was foreseeable that there was an increased risk of greater injury to this particular employee because of the nature of his existing disability. He should therefore have been provided with safety goggles, which at the very least would have reduced the risk.

This case illustrates the basic rule that 'You must take your victim as you find him', otherwise known as the 'egg-shell skull rule'. The application of this rule can be seen in the following case.

James v. *Hepworth & Grandage Ltd* (1968)

The employers erected large notices in their foundry, instructing their employees to wear spats to protect themselves from burns to the legs caused by molten metal. James could not read and no one had explained the notice to him. He did not wear the spats and as a result he suffered severe burns to his legs and feet.

Held: The employer was not in breach of duty in this particular case, even though they had not specifically instructed James in the wearing of spats. As all the other employees were wearing spats, James had ample opportunity to observe them and ask for a pair for himself. The Court presumed (not necessarily correctly) that as James had failed to make enquiries, he would not have worn the spats even if he had understood the notices.

As employment of Indian, Caribbean and other immigrants has increased, the Courts have recognized that it is foreseeable that some of these employees may have a poor understanding of the English language, and as a result the standard of care is increased.

Hawkins v. *Ian Ross (Castings) Ltd* (1970)

The employer employed a large number of Asians as labourers. Hawkins was carrying a ladle of molten metal with the assistance of one such labourer. When he shouted to him to stop, the labourer did not understand and carried on walking. Hawkins overbalanced and was injured by the molten metal.

> **Held:** The employer had failed in his duty, because where he chooses to employ labourers or indeed any staff who may not have a good understanding of the English language, the standard of care is increased. Furthermore, this increase is not confined to the particular employee, but is extended to their workmates, as there is a foreseeable increase in the risks to them of having to work with people who do not understand instructions.

12.4 Causation and resultant damage

The employee must show that he has suffered injury as a result to the employer's breach of duty. 'Injury' is not confined to physical injury, but includes damage to personal property, loss of earnings etc. The test for establishing liability is the one used in negligence, i.e. the 'but for' test. The question which has to be answered by the Court therefore is: but for the employer's breach of duty, would the employee have been injured? If the answer is no, causation is established.

> *McWilliam v. Arrol & Co Ltd* (1962)
> McWilliam, a steel erector employed by Arrol, fell from scaffolding and was killed. The employer had provided safety harnesses in the past, but as they had not been worn, they had been removed to another site.
> **Held:** Although the employer was in breach of his duty, he was not liable, because it could not be proved that McWilliam would have worn the harness even if it had been available. The 'but for' test was not satisfied.

Even after causation has been established, the employer is not necessarily liable for all the damage to his employee. He will only be liable for foreseeable damage. This does not mean that the precise nature or extent of the injury has to be foreseen, only that some harm will result from the breach of duty. However, there is a legal limit to the extent of liability as expounded in *the Wagon Mound (No 1)* (1961). Applying this rule, the employer will only be liable for the foreseeable consequences of his breach. This does not mean that he has to foresee the exact consequences of his actions, but he will not be liable for the completely unexpected.

> *Doughty v. Turner Manufacturing Co Ltd* (1964)
> A lid made of asbestos and cement covering a bath of sulphuric acid was knocked accidentally into the acid. A chemical reaction took place between the cover and the acid. In the eruption which followed, Doughty was severely burned.
> **Held:** The employer was not liable, because the only harm which could be foreseen from the incident was splashing. A chemical reaction of this type was at the time unknown and therefore unforeseeable.

> *Smith v. Leech, Brian and Co Ltd* (1962)
> Smith's lip was splashed with molten metal. At the time his lip contained cancerous tissue which became malignant as a result of the burn. He subsequently died.
> **Held:** The employer was liable for his death from cancer, because the risk of being splashed with molten metal was foreseeable. Smith's death therefore was merely an extension of the foreseeable injury, which was a burn. The 'egg-shell rule' is also applicable.

12.5 Remedies and defences

The same remedies which are available for actions in negligence are also available for employers' liability, and will not be dealt with separately, the principal one being damages.

There are no defences which are unique to this particular tort.

However, the main ones pleaded are contributory negligence, which obviously can have a significant effect on the amount of damages awarded; and *volenti*, which has not proved popular with the Courts, especially in the field of negligence.

Sample questions

1 In reality, employer's liability is no more or no less than a study to take reasonable care for the safety of his employees. Discuss.

LLB, Staffordshire Polytechnic

Suggested answer

This question requires the consideration of employer's liability as a negligence-based tort. The duty is a personal one owed to each individual employee. Each duty should be referred to with reference to the case law:

1 Duty to provide competent fellow employees: *O'Reilley* v. *National Rail & Tramway Appliances Ltd* (1966).

2 Duty to provide a safe place of work: *Smith* v. *Vange Scaffolding Co Ltd* (1970).

3 Duty to provide safe plant and appliances: *Taylor* v. *Rover Car Co Ltd* (1966).

4 Duty to provide safe system of work: *Woods* v. *Durable Suites* (1953). The point should be made that even where an injured employee is shown to be owed a duty of care, the employer will not be liable unless he can be shown to be in breach of his duty. The risk of injury must be foreseeable and the employer must have failed to exercise the standard of care of the reasonable man: *Latimer* v. *AEC*. The standard of care varies depending on the risk and the employee: *Paris* v. *Stepney DC*. It must then be shown that the failure to exercise reasonable care resulted in the injury to the employee. This requires application of the 'but for' test and if necessary the rules relating to the remoteness of damage will apply: *Doughty* v. *Turner Manufacturing*.

2 (a) What is the extent of the 'egg-shell skull' rule as it applies to employees?

(b) Melt-It Ltd have recently erected warning notices instructing employees to wear safety boots and glasses in the metal cutting area. Mr Patel has been employed in this area for six months as a labourer. He cannot read English and does not receive any verbal instructions regarding the notices. He is injured when a sheet of metal is dropped on his foot. He already has a badly bruised toe and as a result of the accident gangrene sets in and the toe has to be amputated. Advise Mr Patel.

LLB, Staffordshire Polytechnic

Suggested answer

(a) The 'egg-shell skull' rule affects the standard of care owed by the employer to his employee. As a general rule, the old, young, inexperienced and disabled are owed a greater duty of care because the risk of injury to these categories of people is usually increased. This can be seen in *Paris* v. *Stepney DC*. In the relationship between the employer and employee, the Courts are prepared to extend the special categories of people to include those who do not understand English, either because they are illiterate, or because they are from another country and have not yet had a chance to master the language. It is obvious that if such people are employed in potentially hazardous occupations without being informed of the risks or the safety procedures, other than by written notices, then there will be an increased risk of injury to themselves, and also to the people who have to work with them (*James* v. *Hepworth & Grandage Ltd* (1968), and *Hawkins* v. *Ian Ross* (*Castings*) *Ltd* (1970)).

(b) In this problem, each element of the tort of employers' liability must be considered. It must be established that Melt-It owe Mr Patel a duty of care and what that particular duty is. Clearly, there is an employer/employee relationship. The duty is concerned with safe system of work – provision of safety footwear and safe working procedures. Then breach of duty must be established. This requires consideration of the risks and the 'egg-shell skull' rule. Apply *James* v. *Hepworth* and *Hawkins* v. *Ian Ross* (*Castings*). There is a foreseeable risk of injury. Once breach is established, has the breach caused the injury? Certainly the 'but for' test is satisfied, but what is the extent of the employer's liability in this case? The rule regarding remoteness must be considered – *Doughty* v. *Turner Manufacturing* and *Smith* v. *Leech, Brain*.

3 Consider the employer's position in the following situations:

(a) Mike is burned by a welding torch when Bob starts to fool around and pretend the torch is a flame thrower.

(b) Graham loses a finger in an unguarded drilling machine. The guard has been removed because it was broken. Graham had been heard to remark that he would rather work the machine without a guard.

(c) Gavin was on the way to the washroom when he slipped in a pool of water from a leaking pipe. His employer had put down sawdust but there was not enough to cover the whole floor.

Suggested answer

(a) This requires consideration of the duty to provide competent employees. The knowledge of the employer is relevant if there have been previous incidents involving Bob. (*Hudson* v. *Ridge Manufacturing.*)

(b) Duty to provide safe plant and appliances. The employer may escape liability if it can be shown that the employee would not have used the guard even if it had been available. (*McWilliam* v. *Arrol Ltd.*)

(c) Gavin was within the course of his employment in going to the washroom (*Davidson* v. *Handley-Page*) he is therefore owed a duty of care. The employer is under a duty to provide a safe place of work, but is he in breach of this duty? He need only take reasonable care which depends on the risk (*Latimer* v. *AEC*). The issue is whether the employer should have obtained more sawdust if he had done nothing to have the pipe repaired.

4 Mark, a labourer, was asked to operate an overhead crane which was used to carry metal tubes the length of the factory. This job was usually done by an experienced man and supervised by the foreman. On the day in question it was supervised by the managing director's son, Peter, who was working in the factory during his vacation from college. The tubes were normally attached to the crane by a metal chain; Mark used a fibre rope which was badly worn. Peter walked in front of the load to warn people to get out of the way. He stopped to chat to a female employee; Mark did not know how to stop the crane. The rope holding the tubes gave way and the tubes fell on Peter. Advise Peter.

Suggested answer

In this problem, all elements of this tort must be considered. Firstly, is Peter owed a duty of care? Even though he is only working at the factory temporarily, he is probably to be regarded as an employee. There are no other factors which state anything to the contrary. Which of the duties are applicable here? The duty to provide competent fellow employees – an inexperienced man, Mark, has been chosen to do the work of an experienced man; safe system of work – the procedure for moving the tubes is not safe; and safe plant – the badly worn fibre rope should have been taken out of use. The employer, given the risks involved and the likelihood of injury in using inexperienced people to do this job, has failed to act like any reasonable employer. The employer's breach has caused the injury to Peter, but has Peter contributed to his injury in any way? At the very least he should not have stopped to chat to the female employee and it could be argued that if he had noticed how worn the rope was, he should not have used it. Although the onus was on the employer to take the rope out of use, it is likely that any award of damages will be reduced. Also the issue of *volenti* as a possible defence should be raised although this defence is unlikely to succeed as there was clearly a failure on the part of the employer and therefore this problem can be distinguished from the facts in *ICI Ltd* v. *Shatwell*.

Further reading

For further reading on the topics covered in this chapter, see chapter 13.

13 Vicarious liability

As a general rule, vicarious liability only arises out of the employer/employee relationship, although it can be found in the principal/agent relationship and, as an exceptional case, in the employer/independent contractor relationship. It is always dependent upon a special relationship. This chapter concentrates on the employer/employee relationship, in order to show how this particular liability arises.

13.1 Meaning of vicarious liability

Literally, this means that one person is liable for the torts of another, even though the former does not have primary liability, i.e. is not at fault. The employer is therefore liable for the torts of his employee. This liability only arises while the employee is acting within the course of his employment, which is considered later. The concept has found favour with the Courts and the plaintiffs because, realistically, the employer is likely to have the money to pay for any claim for damages. This does not mean that the employee will escape liability. The employer can insist that he is joined in any action and if the employer is found to be liable, he may insist on an indemnity from his employee. The effect of this is that the employee will have to pay towards the damages imposed on the employer – see the Civil Liability (Contribution) Act, 1978, which provides for this.

It must not be forgotten that this tort depends on the primary liability of the employee being established. Once this is done, the plaintiff has the option to sue the employer, the employee or both.

13.2 Employer/employee relationship

It may be necessary, at the outset, for the plaintiff to establish that there is in existence an employer/employee relationship, i.e. a contract of service as opposed to a contract for services. In the majority of cases this may not be an issue, but just because the word 'employee' is used in an agreement, does not automatically mean that it is a contract of service. There are defined tests for establishing this relationship. These are considered in detail in chapter 14. The tests are outlined below:

1 Control test
This requires consideration of who has the ultimate right to control the person concerned – *Mersey Docks and Harbour Board* v. *Coggins & Griffiths (Liverpool) Ltd* (1947).

2 Integration test
The issue here is how far the person is integrated into the business – *Whittaker* v. *Minister of Pensions & National Insurance* (1967).

3 Multiple test
This is the most important test, as it incorporates both tests referred to above. Control, integration and all relevant terms of the contract – tax, national insurance, etc., must be considered – *Ready Mixed Concrete (SE) Ltd* v. *Minister of Pensions & National Insurance* (1968).

13.3 Scope of vicarious liability

Once it is established that there is in existence a contract of service, and that the employee has committed a tort, i.e. has primary liability, the vicarious liability of the employer can be considered. This stage is important, because the employer will only be liable if the employee is 'acting within the course of his employment'. It is therefore essential to consider what is meant by this in law. If the employee is outside the scope of his employment, the injured person has no choice but to sue the employee, who may not be in a financial position to compensate him.

13.3.1 Course of employment

The interpretation given by the Courts is wide, as in the past they have favoured making the employer liable, if it is possible to do so. The onus is on the employee to show that he is a servant, and that his tortious act was committed whilst he was going about his employer's business. Once this is established, the onus moves to the employer, who must show that the tortious act was one for which he was not responsible. As a general rule, to be within the course of employment, one of the following must be established:

1 The act must be incidental to the job the employee was employed to do.

2 The act was authorized by the employer, either expressly or impliedly.

3 The authorized act was carried out in a wrongful, negligent or unauthorized manner.

The best way to consider the scope of these points is through the case law. This clearly illustrates how far the Courts are prepared to go. The following cases relate to situations where the employee was found to be 'within the course of his employment'.

> *Century Insurance Co Ltd* v. *Northern Ireland Road Transport Board* (1942)
>
> Davison was employed as a tanker driver for the NIRTB. He was delivering petrol at a garage. Whilst the underground storage tank was being filled with petrol, Davison lit a cigarette and threw away the lighted match. The petrol vapour ignited, resulting in an explosion. The employer's insurance company claimed that the driver's actions regarding the cigarette were outside the course of his employment, and therefore the employer was not liable and the insurance company would not have to pay any compensation.
>
> **Held:** The employer was vicariously liable for the negligent act of his employee. The lighting of the cigarette was an act of convenience on the part of the employee, and although it was not necessarily for the employer's benefit, it did not prevent him from being held liable. It was the time and place at which the employee struck the match which was negligent. The employee was seen to be carrying out the job he was employed to do in a negligent manner.

From this case it can be seen that such acts as taking a tea-break, having a cigarette, going to the washroom, etc. are all acts which are incidental to the main job, although it is still necessary to consider all the facts of the case at the time of the tortious act. The next case is regarded as the leading authority in respect of actions which are specifically prohibited by the employer.

> *Rose* v. *Plenty* (1976)
>
> Plenty was employed as a milkman by the Co-operative Dairy. A notice had been posted up in the depot which prohibited all milkmen from using young children in delivering milk, or giving lifts to them on the milk float. Plenty ignored this notice and engaged the assistance of Rose, a boy aged 13 years. Rose was injured whilst riding on the milk float, through the negligent driving of Plenty.
>
> **Held:** Applying the decision in *Limpus* v. *London General Omnibus Co* (1862), as the prohibited act was being done for the employer's purpose i.e. the delivery of milk, and not for the employee's own benefit or purpose, Plenty was within the course of his employment and therefore the employer was vicariously liable.

Obviously, where the employee carries out a prohibited act, all the circumstances will have to be considered to see if he remains within the course of his employment. However, the key to establishing vicarious liability in such cases is to ask the question: 'Who is the intended beneficiary of the prohibited action?' Furthermore, the attitude of the Courts can be clearly seen in *Rose* v. *Plenty*. Indeed, in that case, Lord Denning applied his own earlier judgment from *Young* v. *Edward Box & Co Ltd* (1951), where he said:

> In every case where it is sought to make the master liable for the conduct of his

servant the first question is to see whether the servant was liable. If the answer is yes, the second question is to see whether the employer must shoulder the servant's liability.

Generally, it is the employer who will have the money to pay the compensation, because of his insurance cover, and therefore if it is at all possible to do so, he will be made responsible for his employee's tortious acts. Vicarious liability extends to acts which may be crimes as well as torts, e.g. assault, fraud.

> *Poland* v. *Parr & Sons* (1927)
>
> Hall was employed as a carter by Parr. He honestly believed that Poland, aged 12 years, had stolen or was about to steal some sugar from his wagon. Hall hit the boy so hard on the back of the head that he stumbled under the wheels of the wagon and injured his leg.
>
> **Held:** The employer was vicariously liable for Hall's actions. An employee is impliedly authorized, as a general rule, to carry out acts for the protection of his employer's property; and unless he does more than is required of him in the circumstances, he will remain within the course of his employment. It was felt in this case that Hall had not used excessive force, which might have taken him outside the course of his employment.

This raises the issue of implied authority on the part of the employee. The exercise of this authority is to some extent at the discretion of the employee. The Courts will consider whether an employee has gone too far in exercising his discretion, and in the current climate may feel that the use of any force will take an employee outside the course of his employment.

The following cases consider the situation where the employee is put in a position of trust and he uses that position in order to commit a crime or tort.

> *Morris* v. *Martin & Sons Ltd* (1966)
>
> Morris's mink wrap was sent by her furrier to Martins to be cleaned. Whilst there, an employee of Martins, who had been entrusted with the cleaning of the fur, stole it – the tort of conversion.
>
> **Held:** The employers were liable for the act of conversion of their employee. Martins Ltd were bailees for reward of the fur and were therefore under a duty to take reasonable care of it. It was then entrusted to an employee so that he could carry out an act which was within the course of his employment, i.e. clean it. What the employee did in stealing the fur was merely an abuse of his job.

There is a limit on the application of the rule *Morris* v. *Martin & Sons*. It can make the employer vicariously liable where the goods come into the employee's possession as part of his job. If, for example, an employee not involved in the cleaning of the fur, had stolen it, the employer would not have been vicariously liable.

> *Heasmans* v. *Clarity Cleaning Co Ltd* (1988)
>
> An employee of a firm contracted to clean offices, whose job involved the cleaning of telephones, dishonestly made use of the telephones to make private calls.
>
> **Held:** The telephone calls were outside the purpose for which this man was employed. For an employer to be liable for the criminal acts of his employees, there must be some nexus between the criminal act of the employee and the circumstances of his employment. In this case, the requirement to dust the telephones merely provided the employee with an opportunity to commit the crime. Access to the premises was insufficient to establish a nexus.

The lengths to which the Courts may be prepared to go can be seen in the following:

> *Lloyd* v. *Grace, Smith & Co* (1912)
>
> Lloyd went to the defendant solicitors to discuss some properties she had for investment purposes. She saw their managing clerk, who persuaded her to sell the properties and to sign some documents which, unknown to her, transferred the properties to him. He then disposed of them for his own benefit.

> **Held:** The solicitors were liable for the fraudulent act of their employee, even though they did not benefit from the fraud. They had placed him in a position of responsibility which enabled him to carry out the fraud. Also, as far as the general public was concerned, he was in a position of trust and appeared to have the authority for his actions.

The facts of the *Lloyd* case are rather special, and the decision is based on the specific relationship between solicitor and client, which is one of trust. The Court did not regard 'benefit to the employer' as an issue. This does not mean, however, that it should not be a matter for consideration in other cases.

13.3.2 Outside the course of employment

Cases where the Courts have found the employee to be outside the course of his employment can now be considered. A significant aspect of these decisions is deviation by the employee from the job he is employed to do.

> *Hilton v. Thomas Burton (Rhodes) Ltd* (1961)
>
> Four workmen were allowed to use their employer's van, as they were working on a demolition site in the country. At lunchtime they decided to go to a café some seven miles away. Before reaching the café, they changed their minds and set off to return to the site. On the return journey one of them was killed through the negligent driving of the van driver.
>
> **Held:** The employer was not vicariously liable. By travelling such a distance to take a break, they were no longer doing something incidental to their main employment; nor were they doing anything for the purpose of their employment; nor were they doing anything for the purpose of their employer's business. As far as the Court was concerned, they were 'on a frolic of their own'.

Following this case it is pertinent to ask: How far has the employee deviated from his course of employment? This is a question of degree, dependent on the facts of the case. There are cases dealing with prohibited acts which have reached the decision that the employee was outside the course of his employment. However, these decisions were before *Rose* v. *Plenty* (1965), generally seen as the watermark case for such decisions. The following cases illustrate the developments in the law.

> *Twine v. Bean's Express Ltd* (1946)
>
> Drivers employed by Bean's were specifically prohibited from giving lifts. One driver gave a lift to Twine, who was injured as a result of his negligent driving. The driver was on a specific delivery route, and did not deviate from this route in giving Twine a lift.
>
> **Held:** The employer was not liable for the injury to Twine. The act of giving a lift was not done for the purpose of the employer, but for the benefit of Twine. Twine was therefore a trespasser on the vehicle, and the employer owed no duty to trespassers.

It should be noted that even trespassers may now be owed a duty of care, especially children. See *Herrington* v. *British Railways Board* (1971), and the Occupiers' Liability Act, 1984.

> *Warren v. Henleys Ltd* (1948)
>
> A petrol pump attendant employed by Henleys used verbal abuse, wrongly accusing Warren of trying to drive away without paying for the petrol he had put in the tank of his car. Warren called the police and told the attendant that he would be reported to his employer. The attendant then physically assaulted Warren.
>
> **Held:** The employer was not liable. The act of violence was not connected in any way to the discharge of the pump attendant's duties. When he assaulted Warren he was not doing what he was employed to do, but was acting in an unauthorized manner. The act was carried out in relation to a personal matter affecting his personal interests.

13.4 Principal and agent

The rules relating to the vicarious liability of a principal for the tortious acts of his agent operate in the same way as those for the employer/employee. However, the key to the principal's liability will be based on whether the agent has exceeded his authority. As can be seen in chapter 9 on agency, an agent's authority can be extremely wide, in that it can be express, implied, ostensible or usual. There is therefore more scope for making the principal vicariously liable – see *Lloyd* v. *Grace, Smith & Co* (1912).

13.5 Employer and independent contractor

As a general rule, the employer is not liable for the torts of any independent contractor he chooses to employ. However, he may be made a joint tortfeasor with the independent contractor in the following situations where he has:

1 Ratified or authorized the tortious act.

2 Contributed to the commission of the tort by the independent contractor, either by the way in which he directed the work or by interfering with the work.

3 Been negligent in the selection of his independent contractor:

> *Balfour* v. *Barty-King* (1957)
> Barty-King's water-pipes were frozen. She asked two men at a nearby building site to help unfreeze them. They did this by using a blow-lamp, rather than a heated brick, on the lagged pipes in her loft. The lagging caught fire and the fire spread to the adjoining premises.
> **Held:** Barty-King was jointly liable for the negligence of the contractor. She had chosen them, invited them into her premises and then left them to do the job. She should have exercised more care, not only in her selection, but also in overseeing their work.

4 A non-delegable duty, e.g. under the Factory Act, 1961 and related statutes. See *Wilsons & Clyde Coal* v. *English* (1938).

5 Asked the independent contractor to carry out work which is particularly hazardous, or is situated on the highway:

> *Salisbury* v. *Woodland* (1970)
> The independent contractor was contracted to fell a tree in his client's garden close to the highway. He was an experienced tree-feller but was negligent in felling the tree. Telephone lines were brought down and the plaintiff, whilst attempting to move the wires from the highway, was struck by a car.
> **Held:** The person employing the independent contractor was not liable. The work was not being carried out on the highway – near to the highway is not the same thing. Furthermore this work would only be regarded as extra-hazardous if it had been carried out on the highway. The independent contractor must bear sole responsibility.

The criteria for judging whether work is particularly hazardous involves looking at where the work is to be carried out; whether members of the public are at risk and what the dangers are.

> *Honeywell & Stein Ltd* v. *Larkin Bros Ltd* (1934)
> A contractor was employed to take flash-light photographs in a cinema. At that time, flash-light photographs involved the ignition of magnesium powder. Through the negligence of the photographer in igniting the magnesium close to some curtains, a fire broke out.
> **Held:** The 'employer' of the contractor was liable, because this was to be regarded as an extra-hazardous activity because of the risks involved and the special dangers to others.

Sample questions

1 What is the significance of the tests for establishing the existence of a contract of service as opposed to a contract for services to vicarious liability?

BTEC HND, Staffordshire Polytechnic

Suggested answer

This question requires consideration of the tests for establishing whether someone is employed under a contract of service as opposed to a contract for services. The tests should be considered in chronological order and reference should be made to the relevant case law as follows:

1 The control test: who had ultimate control of the employee (*Mersey Docks & Harbour Board* v. *Coggins & Griffiths* (1947)).

2 The integration test: is the employee part of the organization (*Whittaker* v. *Minister of Pensions & National Insurance* (1967)).

3 The multiple test: incorporates the other tests and considers the other terms of the contract (*Ready-Mixed Concrete Ltd* v. *Minister of Pensions and National Insurance* (1968)).

In many cases, it is clear that the person who has committed the tort is an employee – however, where there is a doubt, the tests will have to be applied. If it is concluded that there is in existence a contract of service, as long as the employee is found to be acting within the course of his employment the employer will be vicariously liable for this tort. If the person in question is found to be employed under a contract for services or is acting outside the course of his employment he will be personally liable and there will be no vicarious liability. The finding may be crucial to the person injured because it will probably make a difference as to whether he receives any award of damages in a lump sum, i.e. through the employer's insurance company, or in small instalments over a long period of time, i.e. if the employee is personally liable.

A person who is firmly established as an independent contractor is likely to have insurance protection.

2 Advise the employer in the following situations:

(a) Mark gives a lift in his employer's van to a hitch-hiker even though he has been told by his employer that this is prohibited. The hitch-hiker is injured when the van is involved in an accident caused by Mark's negligent driving.

(b) Elsie decides to leave the factory for five minutes in her tea-break in order to buy a packet of cigarettes. She rushes across the road without looking and causes a car to swerve into a bus shelter.

(c) Clara, a cashier and a black-belt karate expert, grabs hold of a man at the supermarket where she works, and uses so much force she breaks his arm. She suspects him of shop-lifting.

Suggested answer

(a) The issue here is whether the prohibited act takes Mark outside the course of his employment. Following *Rose* v. *Plenty*, if the prohibited act is done for the benefit or purpose of the employer's business, the employee will still be within the course of his employment. It is extremely unlikely that giving a lift to a hitch-hiker will in any way benefit the employer, and following *Twine* v. *Bean's Express* the Court would probably conclude that Mark was outside the course of his employment and his employer would not be vicariously liable. He would therefore be personally liable.

(b) The issue here is whether Elsie, by leaving the factory in her tea-break, has taken herself outside the course of her employment. It is established that having a tea-break is reasonably incidental to one's main employment – *Davidson* v. *Handley-Page*. Therefore going to the canteen or smoking a cigarette in break time are actions which are within the course of employment. However, leaving the premises in a tea-break may not be reasonably incidental – it will depend on the nature of the job and any rules laid down by the employer. Even if she is found to be doing something reasonably incidental to her main job, she may still be outside the course of her employment, because the actual task she was undertaking in no way benefited or was for the purpose of the employer.

(c) The issue here is whether Clara, as a cashier, was acting within the course of her employment in apprehending the man. Following *Poland* v. *Parr* it is likely to be part of her job to protect her employer's property. Therefore she is probably within the course of her employment when she grabs him. However, she may have taken herself outside the course of her employment if she is found to have used excessive force – *Warren* v. *Henleys Ltd*. If this is the case she will be personally liable and her employer will be vicariously liable.

3 Explain the circumstances when an employer can be said to be vicariously liable for the torts of his employee. Illustrate your answer with cases.

LLB degree, Staffordshire Polytechnic

Suggested answer

This question requires consideration of the basic rules relating to vicarious liability. Firstly it must be stressed that the employer can only be considered liable where the employee is found to have primary liability for a tort. Once primary liability of the employee is established, the employer will only be liable where the employee is found to be acting within the course of his employment. As this is the essence of vicarious liability, the legal interpretation of this phrase must be considered.

The employee is said to be acting within the course of his employment where he is doing something incidental to his main job, as in *Davidson* v. *Handley-Page*; and where he is doing what he is supposed to do, but in a wrongful or negligent manner – *Century Insurance* v. *NIRTB*. Furthermore, even where the employee carries out a prohibited act, he may still be within the course of his employment as long as this act was done for the benefit or purpose of the employer's business – *Rose* v. *Plenty*.

In many cases it is a question of deviation from the main purpose of the employment which is at issue. Deviation can only be assessed as a matter of degree, depending on the facts of the particular case – *Hilton* v. *Thomas Burton Ltd*. It may well be that Lord Denning's approach in *Young* v. *Edward Box* is the correct one, i.e. should the employer shoulder the servant's liability?

4 Nigel took his Ferrari sports car to be serviced at Fellini's, his local car dealer. Bent, a new mechanic, was given the keys to the car and told to drive it round to the service bay. Bent decided to take it for a joy-ride instead. Whilst driving it he lost control and hit a lamp-post and a pedestrian. Dave, another mechanic, took a Porsche for a test drive after a service. He took his son Roy as a passenger even though this was prohibited by his employer. Through Dave's negligence the car was involved in an accident and Roy was hurt. Advise Fellini.

Suggested answer

In advising Fellini, the first issue must be whether there was primary tortious liability on the part of the mechanics, Bent and Dave.

By stealing the car, Bent committed the tort of conversion and trespass to goods, and also a crime – theft. The employer can be liable where the employee has committed both – *Morris* v. *Martin*. Dave, by his careless driving, has committed the tort of negligence. There is therefore primary liability.

The next issue is: are the two mechanics acting within the course of their employment? Bent is entrusted with the car to take it round to the service bay. In taking the car on a joy-ride he is abusing his position, but following *Morris* v. *Martin*, he is probably within the course of his employment. Fellini is the bailee for reward and is responsible for taking reasonable care of the car, so Fellini will be vicariously liable for Bent's actions.

As far as Dave is concerned, he is within the course of his employment when he takes the car for a test drive. He commits a prohibited act by taking his son Roy with him. Does this prohibited act take him outside the course of his employment? Applying *Rose* v. *Plenty*, Roy would not be regarded as a trespasser, but it is still difficult to see why Dave's actions could be for the benefit of his employer – *Twine* v.

Bean's Express Ltd. This situation is clearly different from *Rose* v. *Plenty*, where the boy was actually helping with the milkround. It seems likely that if Fellini's insurance covers this accident, then the Court may make Fellini shoulder any claim. If the difference between this case and *Rose* v. *Plenty* is accepted, Roy will only have a claim against his father, Dave.

Further reading

Baker, C. D. *Tort* (Sweet & Maxwell)
Street, H. *Street on Torts* (Butterworths)
Jones, M. *Tort* (Financial Training Publications)

14 The contract of employment

In the following four chapters we shall be considering various aspects of employment law, in particular the contract of employment, unfair dismissal, redundancy, and health and safety at work. A typical examination question in any of these areas may either be problem or essay-based, or even both, i.e. part (a) a short essay and part (b) a problem, usually on a different aspect from part (a). It is therefore advisable to look at past examination papers in order to obtain some guidance on the types of examination questions in the employment law field.

In this chapter, we shall be considering the formation of the contract of employment, the relationship of the employer and employee, and the terms incorporated into the contract.

14.1 What is meant by the term 'contract of employment'?

It is important to understand what is meant by this term. Employees are employed under a contract of employment or contract **of** service, whereas self-employed persons, i.e. independent contractors, are employed under a contract **for** services. As we shall see, there are tests which enable the Courts to distinguish between the two types of contract where there are disputes. The following example should help you to distinguish between employees and independent contractors. If you employ a plumber to install your washing machine, you do not become an employer, as he is an independent contractor, although he may be employed by a firm of plumbers. If you employ a gardener, as a general rule he will become your employee and you will therefore be responsible for deductions from his salary, e.g. tax, national insurance etc.

It is important for you to understand why there is a need to distinguish between contract of service, or employment, and contract for services. If a person is employed under a contract of service he is afforded a certain amount of statutory and common law protection, whereas a person employed under a contract for services is not, although exceptions can be found in the Equal Pay Act, 1970, the Sex Discrimination Act, 1965 and the Race Relations Act, 1976 and the tort of negligence.

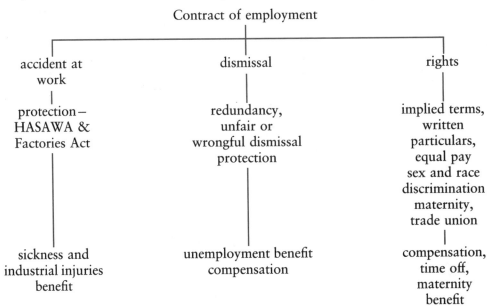

Contract of employment

accident at work	dismissal	rights
protection— HASAWA & Factories Act	redundancy, unfair or wrongful dismissal protection	implied terms, written particulars, equal pay sex and race discrimination maternity, trade union
sickness and industrial injuries benefit	unemployment benefit compensation	compensation, time off, maternity benefit

14.2   Employee or independent contractor?

Although for the majority of people at work there is no problem in deciding whether they are employees or independent contractors, there may be occasions where the distinction is not clear. Over the years the Courts have devised tests for establishing employee status. These tests will be considered in chronological order, as the last test to be developed is in current vogue with the Courts. (You should therefore ensure that you stress this in any examination answer.)

1 Control test

In applying this test the question to be asked is does the person who is to be regarded as the employer control the employee or servant. That is, does he have the right and ability to control? Control extends not only to what the employee does, but how he does it.

If the answer is in the affirmative, there is an employer-employee relationship, and the existence of a contract of employment. The reasoning behind this question is that an independent contractor may be told what to do, but probably has discretion about how to do it. However, in the modern workplace this question has become rather irrelevant and therefore use of this test has declined.

> *Walker v. Crystal Palace Football Club* (1910)
>
> Walker was employed as a professional footballer with the defendant club. It became necessary to decide whether he was employed under a contract of service or a contract for services.
>
> **Held:** He was employed under a contract of service/employment, because he was subject to the control of his master in the form of training, discipline and method of play.

Although the control test is no longer the sole test for establishing the existence of a contract of employment, you should appreciate that it still has an important role to play in subsequent tests.

2 Integration test

This was the next test to be developed as the deficiences of the control test had been highlighted. In applying this test, the question to be asked is how far is the servant/ employee integrated into the employer's business.

If it can be shown that the employee is fully integrated into the employer's business, then a contract of employment is in existence. It is clear that an independent contractor does not become part of the employer's business. This test arose out of the case of:

> *Stevenson, Jordan and Harrison Ltd v. MacDonald and Evans* (1952)
>
> Here Lord Denning expressed the following view:
> 'One feature which seems to run through the instances is that, under a contract of service, a man is employed as part of the business and his work is done as an integral part of the business; whereas, under a contract for services, his work, although done for the business, is not integrated into it but is only accessory to it.'

The integration test is illustrated by the case of:

> *Whittaker v. Minister of Pensions & National Insurance* (1967)
>
> Whittaker was employed as a trapeze artiste in a circus. She claimed industrial injuries benefit as a result of an accident sustained at work. Initially this was refused, on the basis that she was not an employee of the circus. She was, however, able to show that for at least half of her working day she was expected to undertake general duties other than trapeze work, such as acting as usherette and working in the ticket office.
>
> **Held:** Her general duties showed that she was an integral part of the business of running a circus and was therefore employed under a contract of employment.

Although this test developed due to the impracticalities of the control test, it never gained popularity with the Courts; however, it was successfully used in cases such as *Cassidy v. Ministry of Health* (1951) to establish that highly-skilled workers such as doctors and engineers can be employed under a contract of employment. The control test was clearly inapplicable in these situations.

3 Multiple test

This test is by definition much wider than both the control test and the integration test. It requires numerous factors to be taken into account in deciding whether a person is employed under a contract of service or a contract for services. It arose out of the case of:

> *Ready Mixed Concrete (South East) Ltd v. Minister of Pensions & National Insurance* (1968)
>
> RMC previously employed a number of lorry drivers under a contract of employment. The company then decided to dismiss the drivers as employees. However, it allowed them to purchase their vehicles, which had to be painted in RMC colours. The contract between the drivers and the company stated that the drivers were independent contractors. This was disputed by the Minister, who believed the drivers were employees, and therefore RMC were liable for national insurance contributions.
>
> There were a number of stipulations under the contract. The drivers had to wear the company's uniform; the company could require repairs to be carried out to the vehicles at the driver's expense. The vehicles could only be used for carrying RMC's products for a fixed period, and the drivers were told where and when to deliver their loads. However, if a driver was ill he could use a substitute driver to do the deliveries for him.
>
> **Held:** McKenna J. stated that a contract of service exists if three conditions are fulfilled:
>
> 1 The servant agrees that, in consideration of a wage or other remuneration, he will provide his own work and skill in the performance of some service for his master.
>
> 2 He agrees, expressly or impliedly, that in the performance of that service he will be subject to the other's control in a sufficient degree to make that other master.
>
> 3 The other provisions of the contract are consistent with its being a contract of service.
>
> In this case it was decided that the drivers were independent contractors, as there were factors which were inconsistent with the existence of a contract of employment, e.g. the ability to provide a replacement driver if the need arose.

Although the decision in *Ready Mixed Concrete* has been criticized, the test has been approved and applied in subsequent cases.

The multiple test has proved to be most adaptable, as it merely involves looking for factors which are not inconsistent with the existence of a contract of employment. However, you should note that an element of control is also relevant, and it is important to appreciate that there is no exhaustive list. The Courts will ask questions such as: Who pays the wages? Who pays income tax and national insurance? Is the person employed entitled to holiday pay etc? It will treat as irrelevant the fact that there is a contract in which someone is termed 'independent contractor' when the other factors point to him being an employee.

> *Market Investigations Ltd v. Minister of Social Security* (1969)
>
> Market Investigations employed Mrs Irving as an interviewer on an occasional basis. If she was selected from the pool of interviewers maintained by the firm, she was not obliged to accept the work. However, if she accepted she was given precise instructions concerning the methods to be used in carrying out the market research, and the time in which the work had to be completed. She could, however, choose the hours she wanted to work and do other work at the same time, as long as she met Market Investigations' deadlines.
>
> **Held:** She was an employee of the company every time she decided to undertake work for them. It was felt that the question to be asked was 'is the person who has engaged himself to perform these services performing them as a person in business on his own account?' If the answer is yes, then there is a contract for services; if the answer is no, there is a contract of service.

Obviously, as in the *RMC* case, there are other factors which may have to be taken into account, although the Courts are reluctant to state what other factors should be considered other than control. It is important that the multiple test is flexible, so that it can adapt with changes in the labour environment.

14.2.1 Effect

As we saw earlier, it is important to establish whether a person is an employee primarily because of the protection afforded to him by statute and under the common law, although you should appreciate that for financial reasons, e.g. tax, 'employer' and 'employees' may prefer to have the contract classified as one for services. The tests have also been used to clarify the position of employees who are lent out as part of their job, to other employers. This is particularly important in respect of who should be vicariously liable for the employee's torts.

> *Mersey Docks & Harbour Board* v. *Coggins & Griffiths (Liverpool) Ltd* (1947)
>
> Mersey Docks hired out a crane and driver to C & G to assist in the loading of a ship. C & G paid his wages. Whilst the crane driver was doing his work, he negligently injured an employee of the stevedores, C & G. The issue to be decided by the Courts was whether the Board or the stevedores were vicariously liable for the crane driver's negligence.
>
> **Held:** The Harbour Board remained the employer of the crane driver. He was under their ultimate control as to the work he was doing, even though he was under the temporary direction of the stevedores.

The Courts are reluctant to find that there has been a transfer of employment where employees are loaned out unless there is consent on the part of the employee, or there is an agreement stating the position regarding possible liability.

14.3 Formation of the contract of employment

14.3.1 Formalities

In general terms there are no formalities involved in the formation of a contract of employment. The contract itself may be oral or in writing, with the exception of apprenticeship deeds and articles for merchant seamen, which have to be in writing. It follows, therefore, that within reason the parties (i.e. the employer and employee) to the contract can decide on whatever terms they choose. The problem with this, as will be appreciated, is that one of the parties has the stronger bargaining position! However, the contract is subject to the implied terms at common law which will be considered subsequently and may be subject to express terms incorporated through collective agreements negotiated by trade unions.

14.3.2 Written particulars

Although the contract of employment itself need not be in writing, the employee must be given written particulars of the main terms. This is required by the Employment Protection (Consolidation) Act, 1978 (EPCA), Section 1. These written particulars must be supplied not later than the end of the thirteenth week after the commencement of the employment. The particulars must contain the following information:

1 The names of the parties and the date on which the employment commenced; and, if there is a change of employer resulting in continuity of employment, the date on which continuity commences must be specified.

2 The rate of pay, or the method of calculating it.

3 The intervals at which wages or salary are to be paid, e.g. weekly or monthly.

4 The terms and conditions relating to hours of work.

5 The terms and conditions relating to holidays and holiday pay.

6 The terms relating to sickness or injury and sick pay.

7 Details of pension rights.

8 The length of notice which the employee must give, and is entitled to receive, on termination of his employment.

9 A job title and description.

These form the basis of the written particulars. In addition the employer must specify the following:

1 Any disciplinary rules which apply to the employee or reference to the document containing them.

2 The person to whom the employee can apply if he is dissatisfied with any disciplinary decision relating to him.

3 The company's grievance procedure, including the person to whom the employee can apply if he has a grievance relating to his employment.

Any agreed changes must be communicated to the employee in writing within one month. Instead of supplying the written particulars, it is permissible for the employer to refer the employee to a document which contains all these particulars, such as a collective agreement, as long as it is reasonably accessible. If the employer fails to provide a statement, within Section 1 the employee may apply to an industrial tribunal in order for it to determine which particulars ought to be included in the statement.

The following employees do not qualify for written particulars under Section 1, but may be given written contracts or similar particulars:

1 employees who work less than 16 hours per week;

2 registered dock workers;

3 merchant seamen; and

4 crown employees.

14.4 Express terms

The express terms are those agreed upon by the employer and employee on entering into the contract of employment. They may be oral or in writing, and will cover such matters as the point on the salary scale at which the employee will commence employment. A breach of an express term of the contract may result in the dismissal of the employee, and if it is a breach by the employer, may enable the employee to resign and bring an action for constructive dismissal. A collective agreement made between the employer, or his association, and a trade union may be expressly incorporated into the contract of employment. Such agreements usually provide a comprehensive set of terms and conditions for particular types of employees. The trade union is more likely to have equal bargaining power with the employer. Where collective agreements are expressly incorporated under Section 1 of the EPCA, 1978, they will bind the employer and the employee.

14.5 Implied terms

Implied terms may arise out of the custom and practice of a particular industry, e.g. deductions from wages for bad workmanship were accepted as a term of contract in the cotton industry. The Courts may be the final arbiter as to whether an implied term is incorporated into a contract. Collective agreements may become implied terms of a contract, even if there is no reference to the agreement in the written particulars. However, such incorporation will depend on knowledge by the employee and acceptance by his local union representative.

14.6 Implied duties

A number of duties are implied into the contract of employment. These duties have arisen out of the common law, and can be overridden by express terms. A breach by the employee may result in disciplinary action, or even dismissal; a breach by the employer may result in legal proceedings before a tribunal.

14.6.1 Duties imposed by the employer

1 To provide work

As a general rule, an employer will not be in breach of the implied duty to provide work, as long as he continues to pay his employees, even though there may be no work available. However, in certain situations the employer may be liable for failing to provide work; for example, if a reduction in the employee's earnings occurs. This is most likely to affect those employees on piece-work or commission, although this will usually be covered by the express terms – see *Devonald & Co v. Rosser & Son* (1906). Furthermore, if the employee needs to work in order to maintain particular skills, then to deny him this right may also be a breach of this duty. Such cases are rare.

Collier v. *Sunday Referee Publishing Co Ltd* (1940)

Collier was employed as a sub-editor with the defendant's newspaper. The defendant sold the newspaper and continued to pay the plaintiff, although he was not provided with any work. Collier claimed the company was under a duty to supply work.

Held: There was a breach of the duty to provide work in this case, as the plaintiff had been appointed to a particular job which had been destroyed on the sale of the newspaper. However, Asquith J. stated the following principle: 'It is true that a contract of employment does not necessarily, or perhaps normally, oblige the master to provide the servant with work. Provided I pay my cook her wages regularly she cannot complain if I choose to eat all my meals out.'

Langston v. *Amalgamated Union of Engineering Workers* (1974)

Langston refused to join the trade union. He was suspended from work on full pay after the union put pressure on his employer.

Held: Where a person employs a skilled employee who needs practice to maintain or develop those skills, there may be an obligation to provide a reasonable amount of work.

2 To pay wages

As a general rule, the employer must pay his employees their wages, even if there is no work available. As we have seen in relation to piece-workers, this means that they should be given the opportunity to earn their pay. However, it is possible for the employer to exclude or vary this implied term by stipulating that there will be no pay where there is no work available.

3 To indemnify the employee

Where the employee, in the course of his employment, necessarily incurs expenses on behalf of his employer, he is entitled to be reimbursed by the employer. This extends to such items as postage, parking fees, damage to property etc.

4 Mutual respect

The employer is under a duty to treat his employees with respect. In deciding whether there has been a breach of this term, the actions of the employer are of great importance.

Donovan v. *Invicta Airways Ltd* (1970)

Donovan, an airline pilot, was subjected to abusive conduct by his employer on a number of occasions. As a result, Donovan resigned.

Held: In this particular case the incidents were not substantial enough to treat the contract as broken. However, it is clear that there is now a duty under which all of the parties to the contract of employment must treat each other with due consideration and courtesy.

5 To provide a reference

There is no duty on the employer to provide a reference. However, should he do so, he must ensure that it is not defamatory of the employee, nor must it be misleading to the prospective employer, as this could result in an action for negligent misstatement. The former employee may also have an action in negligence against his ex-employer.

> *Lawton* v. *BOC Transhield Ltd* (1987)
>
> Lawton, a former employee of BOC, requested BOC to provide his new employers with a reference. The reference provided was unfavourable, and as a result Lawton was dismissed. Lawton alleged that BOC were negligent in providing an inaccurate or unfair reference.
>
> **Held:** BOC owed Lawton a duty of care. However, there was no breach, as the opinions expressed were those of a reasonably prudent employer, in that they were honest and accurate.

6 To provide for the safety of the employee

This duty is based on the law of negligence. You should refer to chapter 12 on employers' liability for a detailed exposition of this area.

14.6.2 Duties imposed on the employee

1 To obey lawful and reasonable orders

If an order given by the employer is reasonable and lawful, it must be obeyed. Indeed, failure to obey may give the employer the right to dismiss the employee. Whether an order is lawful and reasonable is a question of fact in each case, depending upon the nature of the job.

> *Pepper* v. *Webb* (1969)
>
> An employer instructed his gardener to carry out certain planting work in the garden. The gardener swore at his employer and indicated that he was not prepared to obey the instructions.
>
> **Held:** The employee was in breach of his implied duty, as the orders were not only lawful but reasonable in the circumstances.

2 To act faithfully

This duty is fundamental to the relationship of the employer and employee. The employee's first loyalty must be to his employer. The duty encompasses such matters as confidentiality, not working in competition with the employer, etc.

> *Faccenda Chicken Ltd* v. *Fowler & Others* (1985)
>
> In this case it was decided that the scope of the duty to act faithfully varied according to the nature of the contract of employment. An employee who therefore makes or copies a list of his employer's customers for use after his employment ends will have broken this duty.

> *Hivac Ltd* v. *Park Royal Scientific Instruments Ltd* (1949)
>
> Employees of the plaintiff company were found to be working in their spare time for a company which was in direct competition with their employer. The employees concerned were doing the same job at both establishments.
>
> **Held:** The employees were under a duty not to work for a competitor of their employer where this work would conflict with their duty of fidelity, and may inflict harm on their employer's business.

This aspect of the duty will only apply where there is a conflict of interest – for example, where the employee chooses to work for a competitor in his spare time and where there is a risk that confidential information may be disclosed. If, for example, the employee was a car mechanic by day and worked in a public house at night, there would be no breach of duty.

The employer may prevent his employees from either working for rival firms, or setting up a business in competition with him after they have left their employment, by including in the contract of employment an express term which restricts the employees' future employment in some way. Such clauses are known as covenants in restraint of trade. Many professional people such as solicitors, accountants, etc. will have this type of clause in their contracts. Such clauses are only valid if they are reasonable in all the circumstances of the case.

> ### *Home Countries Dairies Ltd* v. *Skilton* (1970)
>
> Skilton was a milkman. His contract of employment contained a clause which provided that, for a period of one year after the termination of his contract with Home Counties Dairies, he would not sell milk or dairy produce to any person who had been a customer of the dairy for the last six months of his contract and whom he had served then. Soon after leaving his employment he set up his own milk round in the same area as he had worked for the dairy company.
>
> **Held:** The former employer was awarded an injunction to prevent Skilton from working this area. The clause in his contract was valid as the time limit was reasonable, in order to protect the interests of the dairy.

Under the heading of fidelity, the employee must not disclose confidential information which he has acquired in the course of his employment. The duty extends to trade secrets, the financial state of the company, new designs etc.

> ### *Cranleigh Precision Engineering Co Ltd* v. *Bryant* (1965)
>
> Bryant was the managing director of a firm which designed swimming pools. He left the company and started his own business, using information which he had gained from his previous employment.
>
> **Held:** Bryant was in breach of the implied term in his contract of employment, as he could only have gained the information from his previous employment. He had made improper use of information gained in confidence, to the detriment of his former employer.

3 To use skill and care

The employee is under a duty to use reasonable skill and care in the performance of his job. If he does so and incurs loss or damage, the employer will indemnify him. However, should the employee be grossly incompetent, the employer may have grounds to dismiss him. The duty extends to taking proper care of the employer's property (see *Superlux* v. *Plaistead* (1958)).

> ### *Lister* v. *Romford Ice and Cold Storage Co Ltd* (1957)
>
> Lister, a lorry driver employed by the company, negligently reversed his lorry, seriously injuring a fellow employee. The company claimed an indemnity from Lister, on the grounds that he had broken an implied term of his contract of employment.
>
> **Held:** The employer was entitled to an indemnity, because the employee had failed to use reasonable skill and care, as required by the implied terms. The driver was therefore liable for the damages awarded to his fellow employee.

4 Not to take bribes or make a secret profit

If an employee is in breach of his duty, he is abusing his position, and can be dismissed.

> ### *Reading* v. *Attorney-General* (1951)
>
> Reading, who was a sergeant in the British Army based in Egypt, used his position to accompany lorries containing illicit spirits, so that they would not be stopped by the police. Over a period of time Reading received £20 000 for his 'services'. When his role was finally discovered, he was arrested and the Army authorities confiscated his money. When he was released from prison he brought an action for the return of the money.
>
> **Held:** Reading was in breach of the implied duty not to take bribes or make secret profits. He had misused his position of trust and had therefore to account for those 'profits' to his employer. He was not entitled to have them returned to him.

> ### *British Siphon Co Ltd* v. *Homewood* (1956)
>
> Homewood was employed as chief technician by the plaintiff company in the design and development department. During his employment he designed a new

type of soda siphon. He did not disclose his invention to his employers. He then left his employment, and applied for letters patent in respect of his invention.

Held: The invention and the profits from it belonged to his employer. The invention was clearly related to his employer's business, and they were therefore entitled to the benefits from it.

The common law position regarding employees' inventions has been qualified by Sections 39-41 of the Patents Act, 1977.

14.7 Termination

14.7.1 Notice

If the employer wishes to terminate the employment of any employee, he must give the minimum period of notice required by the contract of employment, or if there is nothing stated in the contract, as laid down in Section 49 of the EPCA, 1978.

Section 49 states that where an employee has been continuously employed for between four weeks and two years, he shall be given one week's notice; or if he has been employed for more than two years, he is entitled to one week's notice for each year of employment, subject to a maximum of 12 weeks. The employer may give wages or salary in lieu of notice.

Where the employee wishes to terminate his contract of employment, he must give the minimum period of notice as stipulated in his contract. If there is nothing stated he must give a minimum of one week's notice – Section 49(2) of the EPCA, 1978.

14.7.2 Dismissal

There are various types of dismissal:

1 Lawful dismissal
This is where the employer gives the required period of notice and has a legitimate reason in the eyes of the law to terminate his employee's contract.

2 Summary dismissal
The employer may dismiss his employee without notice where the employee's conduct justifies such action. The employee's conduct must result in a serious breach of the contract of employment, e.g. theft. If the summary dismissal is not justified, the employee may bring an action for wrongful dismissal.

3 Wrongful dismissal
An action for wrongful dismissal at common law may be brought by an employee who is outside the unfair dismissal protection provided by the EPCA; or by an employee who has been dismissed unjustifiably without notice, or had not been given the required period of notice. Such an action will be commenced in the County Court, not in the industrial tribunal. Compensation in the form of wages and damages will be subject to the calculation of damages in contract.

4 Unfair dismissal
Employees who are protected by the EPCA have the right not to be unfairly dismissed, i.e. the employer must show that the reason for the dismissal was reasonable. See chapter 15.

Sample questions

1 (a) Explain the distinction between an employee and an independent contractor.

(b) You intend to renovate your workplace, which has an old wiring and plumbing system. This will involve a considerable amount of time and money. Consider the advantages and disadvantages of employing your own plumbers and electricians (of which there are three) to do the job, as opposed to engaging contractors.

Suggested answer

The following points should be considered:

(a) An employee is employed under a contract of service, i.e. he has a contract of employment, whereas an independent contractor is employed under a contract for services which only lasts as long as the particular job. Try to give an example, e.g. a cook is an employee under a contract of services, whereas a plumber is under a contract for services which will terminate when he has finished the required task.

You should refer to the importance of the distinction. An employee acquires certain statutory rights, e.g. protection against unfair dismissal as well as common law rights, e.g. implied duties are imposed on his employer. He will also be given protection where he is injured at work – employers' liability. An independent contractor acquires few statutory rights – see Section 3 of the Health and Safety at Work etc. Act, 1974 – and no special common law rights.

(b) Advantages:
Control over what they do and how they do it.
Cheapness, as employees will probably be paid less for the job.

Disadvantages:
Time – these employees will be tied to a demanding task for a lengthy period.
Liability for injuries to them – employers' liability.
Liability for injuries caused by them – vicarious liability.
Statutory protection rights if you wish to dismiss one of them for poor workmanship; independent contractors can be removed from the site without repercussions.
Common law protection – implied duties of the employer.
Liable for tax and National Insurance payments, sick pay, maternity pay, etc.

2 You are planning part of an induction session for new school-leaver recruits to your firm. Outline the common law duties imposed on an employee, which affect them.

BTEC HND, Staffordshire Polytechnic

Suggested answer

The following points should be considered:

You need to refer to each of the duties in detail and the relevant case law in turn. Duty to obey lawful and reasonable orders: *Pepper* v. *Webb*. Duty to act faithfully: *Hivac* v. *Park Royal Scientific Instruments Ltd*, *Home Counties Dairies* v. *Skelton*. Duty to exercise skill and care in carrying out one's job: *Lister* v. *Romford Ice & Cold Storage Co Ltd*. Duty not to take bribes or make a secret profit: *AG* v. *Reading*.

3 You work in a personnel department and have received a couple of requests for details of contracts of employment. When is an employee entitled to a written statement of the particulars of his contract of employment and what do these particulars have to contain?

BTEC HND, Staffordshire Polytechnic

Suggested answer

This should consider the following:

The written statement should be given to the employee by the thirteenth week of his commencing employment and it should contain all the main terms of his employment. You should refer to Section 1 of the EPCA, which lays down exactly what terms must be included. Reference should also be made to the additional terms concerning disciplinary and grievance procedures. The point should be made that the employer may refer the employee to a collective agreement rather than give him particulars if such an agreement is readily accessible.

4 Consider the following:

(a) Terry is employed as a fork-lift truck driver. Whilst manoeuvring crates around the warehouse, he injures Ben, a workmate, through his negligent driving and seriously damages the fork-lift truck.

(b) Gary works as a power press operator. He is paid on a piece-work rate. Some days there is very little work available and his pay is drastically reduced. As a result he supplements his income by working in a public house at night. His employer, on discovering this matter, says it will affect the quality of Gary's work and threatens to dismiss him unless he gives up his evening job.

Suggested answer

This should consider the following:

(a) The issue here, presuming Terry is employed under a contract of service, is whether he is in breach of the implied duty to exercise skill and care in the performance of his job. On the evidence he is clearly negligent, which indicates that he is in breach of his duty. As he was probably within the course of his employment when the accident occurred, his employer will be faced with legal action either under the heading of employers' liability or vicarious liability or both. As Terry is in breach of duty his employer can claim an indemnity from him and may take legal action for breach of duty – however, the employer will be protected by his compulsory liability insurance.

(b) The first issue is whether Gary's employer is under a duty to provide work. You need to consider whether employees on piece-work are to be regarded as a special case as he may not receive any pay if he is not producing any goods. If this is the case, his employer may be under a duty either to provide work or pay him a basic wage – *Devonald* v. *Rosser & Son*.

The second issue requires you to consider whether Gary is in breach of the implied duty to act faithfully. Does this situation come within *Hivac* v. *Park Royal Scientific Instruments*? This will be judged on the basis of whether there is a real conflict of interest.

Further reading

| For further reading on the topics covered in this chapter, see chapter 16.

15 Unfair dismissal

In this chapter we shall be considering the rules relating to unfair dismissal. As a general rule, employees, i.e. those employed under a contract of service are offered protection by the Employment Protection (Consolidation) Act, 1978 (EPCA) in the event of unfair dismissal by their employer. As we shall see, this protection is not confined to the payment of compensation, but may result in the employer having to reinstate or re-engage the employee. However, not all employees will necessarily qualify for the protection provided by EPCA.

15.1 Who qualifies under the EPCA?

The basic rule is that an employee who commenced work after 1st June 1985 must have worked at least 16 hours per week, and have at least two years' continuous employment in order to qualify. There is a presumption that continuity exists. The onus is therefore on the employer to show that it does not. After five years' continuous employment, provided the employee works eight hours per week, he will be regarded as continuously employed, and will therefore qualify.

Where the employee's hours of work are reduced from a minimum of 16 hours to eight hours or more per week and he has not worked for the same employer for five years, he will be entitled to count up to 26 weeks towards continuity.

The rules relating to the preservation of continuity, e.g. in the event of sick leave or a strike, are to be found in Schedule 13 to the EPCA and are considered in chapter 16 (16.1.2), to which you should refer. It is important to appreciate that in the event of continuity being broken, the employee has to commence his calculation of the qualifying period from the date of the break.

The following people are specifically excluded from the unfair dismissal provisions of the EPCA:

1 Registered dock workers.

2 Share fishermen.

3 Any employee who has reached the normal retirement age. (This is recognized as 65 for both men and women under the Sex Discrimination Act, 1986); or if relevant, the contractual retirement age.

4 Persons ordinarily employed outside Great Britain.

5 Persons employed under a fixed term contract of two years or more, who agree in writing to forgo their rights to claim compensation. Where the contract was made on or after 1st October 1980, the period of the fixed term is reduced to one year.

6 Where there is in existence a dismissal procedure agreement between the employer and an independent trade union which has been approved by the Secretary of State.

15.2 What is meant by dismissal?

The onus is on the employee to show that he has been dismissed within the meaning of the Act (Section 55 of the EPCA). There are three ways in which dismissal can take place (15.2.1–15.2.3):

15.2.1 Termination of the contract of employment by the employer

The employer may terminate the contract, with or without notice. Such a dismissal may be orally or in writing – if orally, the words should be unambiguous (see *Futty* v. *Brekkes Ltd* (1974)). One of the problems for the Courts has been deciding whether there has been a 'termination' within the meaning of the Act, i.e. by the employer.

1 Termination which is mutually agreed between the employer and employee is not a dismissal:

> *Harvey* v. *Yankee Traveller Restaurant* (1976)
>
> Harvey informed her employer that she was pregnant. As she was unable to do her normal job, they attempted to make other arrangements to allow her to continue work, all of which proved to be unsatisfactory. After discussion with her employer, it was agreed that she would resign.
>
> **Held:** There was no dismissal within the meaning of the Act, because the termination of the contract had arisen out of mutual agreement that she would resign.

2 Where the employee 'invites' a termination of his contract, either by his inaction or conduct, this may amount to dismissal.

> *Martin* v. *Yeoman Aggregates Ltd* (1983)
>
> Martin refused to get a spare part for the director's car; the director angrily told the employee to get out. Five minutes later the director took back what he had said and instead suspended Martin without pay until he could act more rationally. Martin insisted that he had been dismissed.
>
> **Held:** It was vital to industrial relations that both the employer and employee should have the opportunity to withdraw their words. It was up to a tribunal to decide whether the withdrawal had come too late to be effective.

3 Where the employer invites the employee to resign, this may amount to a dismissal.

> *Robertson* v. *Securicor Transport Ltd* (1972)
>
> Robertson had broken one of the works rules by signing for a load which had not actually been received. When his employer discovered what he had done, he was given the option of resignation or dismissal. He chose resignation.
>
> **Held:** Resignation in these circumstances amounted to dismissal by the employer because in effect there was no alternative action open to the employee. He would have been dismissed if he had not opted to resign on the invitation of his employer.

15.2.2 Expiration of a fixed-term contract

As you will recall, certain fixed-term contracts are excluded from the protection given by the Act, i.e. where the employee agrees, before the term expires, to forgo any claim for unfair dismissal. However, if a fixed-term contract is not renewed and it is not within the excluded category, the failure to renew amounts to a dismissal. One of the questions faced by the Courts has been the issue of what amounts to a fixed-term contract.

The EPCA (Section 2) requires that the duration of the contract must be certain, that is, there must be a date on which the contract expires. It follows, therefore, that a contract to do a specific job which does not refer to a completion date cannot be a fixed-term contract, as the duration of the contract is uncertain.

Furthermore, at one time it was thought that a fixed-term contract must run for the whole of the term, and must not be capable of termination before the term expired, e.g. by a clause giving either party the right to terminate (see *BBC* v. *Ioannou* (1974)). However, in *Dixon* v. *BBC* (1978) it was held that a fixed-term contract could exist even though it could be terminated by either party before it had run its full term.

15.2.3 Constructive dismissal

Constructive dismissal is an important concept, as the law recognizes that an employee may be entitled to protection, if he is put in a position where he is forced to resign. Constructive dismissal arises where the employee is forced to terminate his contract, with or without notice, due to the conduct of his employer. The main problem for the Courts is in deciding whether the employer's conduct warrants the action taken by the employee. It is now firmly decided that in order to permit the employee to constructively dismiss himself, the employer's actions must amount to a breach of contract, and must therefore be more than merely unreasonable conduct.

Western Excavating Ltd v. *Sharp* (1978)

Sharp took time off from work without permission. When his employer discovered this, he was dismissed. Sharp appealed to an internal disciplinary board which substituted a penalty of five days suspension without pay. He agreed to accept this decision, but asked his employer for an advance on his holiday pay, as he was short of money. This was refused. He then asked for a loan of £40, which was also refused. As a result he decided to resign, as this would at least mean that he would receive his holiday pay. At the same time, Sharp claimed unfair dismissal on the basis that he was forced to resign because of his employers' unreasonable conduct.

Held: Initially the tribunal found in Sharp's favour, i.e. the employers' conduct was so unreasonable that Sharp could not be expected to continue working there. However, the case eventually went to the Court of Appeal, where it was decided that, before a valid constructive dismissal can take place, the employers' conduct must amount to a breach of contract, such that it entitles the employee to resign. In this particular case there was no breach by the employer and therefore there was no constructive dismissal.

It would appear that if the breach by the employer is to allow the employee to resign, it must be a breach of some significance and must go to the root of the contract, e.g. a unilateral change in the employee's terms (express or implied) and conditions of employment (see *British Aircraft Corporation* v. *Austin* (1978).) If the employee does not resign in the event of a breach by his employer, he will be deemed to have accepted the breach and waived his rights. However, the law recognizes that he need not resign immediately but may, for example, wait until he has found another job(see *Cox Toner (International) Ltd* v. *Crook* (1981)).

Simmonds v. *Dowty Seals Ltd* (1978)

Simmonds was employed to work on the night shift. His employer attempted to force him to work on the day shift, by threatening to take action if he refused to be transferred from the night shift. Simmonds resigned.

Held: Simmonds was entitled to resign and could treat himself as constructively dismissed, because the employers' conduct amounted to an attempt to unilaterally change an express term of his contract, i.e. that he was employed to work nights.

The employee may also be able to claim, where he is forced to resign, when the employer is in breach of an implied term in the contract of employment. Although it must be stressed that the employee must not only be able to show the existence of the implied term, but also what is required by the implied term, i.e. its scope (see *Gardener Ltd* v. *Beresford* (1978)). As a result of the decision in *Western Excavating Ltd* v. *Sharp* it is clear that unreasonable conduct alone (which makes life difficult for the employee, so that he is put in a position where he is forced to resign) will not amount to constructive dismissal, unless it can be found to be a breach of the express or implied terms of the contract on the part of the employer. The employee may have to depend on the generosity of the Courts in establishing a breach of an implied term.

Pepper & Hope v. *Daish* (1980)

In December 1978 Pepper, who was employed by the defendants, negotiated for himself an hourly wage rate. In January 1979 his employers increased the hourly rate of all workers by 5 per cent, with the exception of Pepper. The employer would not increase Pepper's hourly rate. Accordingly, Pepper resigned. He claimed constructive dismissal.

Held: Pepper succeeded in his claim. The tribunal was prepared to imply a term into his contract that he would be given any wage increases received by the hourly rate workers. Such a term had therefore been broken by his employer, forcing him to resign. Whether the Courts will always be as generous in their interpretation is questionable.

15.3 Reasons for dismissal

An employee who is dismissed within the meaning of the Act is entitled to a written statement of the reasons for his dismissal (Section 53 of the EPCA). In order to be entitled to a written statement, however, he must have been continuously employed for 26 weeks. The employee must ask for the statement and it must be supplied within 14 days of this request. Failure of the employer to supply the statement will allow the employee to complain to the tribunal. He may also make a complaint to the tribunal where he has evidence that the statement is inadequate, i.e. the reasons are unclear. If the tribunal finds in favour of the employee, it may declare the real reasons for the dismissal and award the employee two weeks' pay.

15.4 Fair dismissals

Once the employee has established that he has been dismissed, be it by his employer or constructively, the onus moves to the employer to show that the dismissal was fair, i.e. that he had reasonable grounds for dismissing his employee. The grounds on which a dismissal is capable of being fair are laid down in Section 57 of the EPCA. These grounds are considered in turn below.

15.4.1 Capability or qualifications

Capability is defined in Section 57(4) as

> assessed by reference to skill, aptitude, health or any other physical or mental quality. . . . Whereas qualifications means any degree, diploma, or other academic, technical or professional qualification relevant to the position which the employee held.

Davison v. Kent Meters Ltd (1975)

Davison worked on an assembly line. She was dismissed as a result of assembling 500 components incorrectly. She alleged that she had merely followed the instructions of the chargehand. The chargehand maintained that he had not given her any instructions.

Held: The dismissal was unfair. Davison should have received supervision and training in the assembly of the components. It was clear from the evidence that she had not; therefore her employer had not acted reasonably in dismissing her.

Blackman v. Post Office (1974)

Blackman was a telegraph officer. He was required to pass an aptitude test. He was allowed the maximum number of attempts (three) and he still failed. He was then dismissed.

Held: As the taking of an aptitude test was a qualification requirement of that job, his dismissal was fair.

The employer must not only be able to show that, for example, the employee was incompetent or inadequately qualified, but that in the circumstances it was reasonable to dismiss him, i.e. what would the reasonable employer have done? The Court will have regard to all the surrounding circumstances such as training, supervision, the alternatives available, e.g. could the employee have been redeployed to another job? The employer may also have to show that he gave his employee a chance to improve his standing. If the employer is to be deemed to have acted reasonably, he must be able to show that dismissal was the last resort.

In deciding whether an employer has acted reasonably in dismissing someone, the Court may refer to the Code of Practice 'Disciplinary Practice and Procedures in Employment'. This is a set of guidelines which lay down a fair disciplinary procedure involving a system of warnings, oral and written, and where necessary the provision of a hearing, so that the employee may put his side of the case. This procedure ought to be followed by all employers. The Code may be used as evidence against an employer to show that he has not acted reasonably.

Lowndes v. *Specialist Engineering Ltd* (1977)

Lowndes made a series of errors in his job, which proved to be costly to his employer. He was therefore dismissed without being given any written warnings or a hearing by his employer. He brought an action for unfair dismissal and used as evidence the fact that the Code of Practice had not been followed.

Held: The dismissal was fair. On the evidence, even if the Code had been followed, the outcome would have been the same, i.e. the dismissal was a reasonable course of action. Furthermore, an unfair disciplinary procedure does not automatically make the dismissal unfair.

Polkey v. *A.E. Dayton Services Ltd* (1987)

Polkey was employed as a van driver. His employer, in order to avoid more financial losses, decided to make three van drivers redundant. There was no prior consultation; Polkey was merely handed a letter informing him that he was being made redundant. Polkey claimed that this amounted to unfair dismissal as the failure to consult showed that the employer had not acted reasonably in treating redundancy as a sufficient reason for dismissing him.

Held: In deciding whether the employer had acted reasonably, the tribunal should have regard to the facts at the time of the dismissal and should not base their judgment on facts brought to light after the dismissal, such as whether the failure to consult would have made any difference to the dismissal, or whether the employee had in practice suffered an injustice. The case has been remitted to the Industrial Tribunal for it to consider whether the employer acted reasonably in the light of the above criteria.

The importance of the decision in Polkey's case cannot be understated. As a result of this decision, procedural fairness is of paramount importance when considering the issue of unfair dismissal.

15.4.2 Conduct

In deciding whether a dismissal for misconduct is to be regarded as fair, attention must be paid to the nature of the offence and the disciplinary procedure. For example, gross or serious misconduct may justify instant dismissal, whereas a trivial act may only warrant a warning in line with the disciplinary procedure. The word 'misconduct' is not defined in the EPCA, but it is established that it covers assault, refusal to obey instructions, persistent lateness, moonlighting, drunkenness, dishonesty, failing to implement safety procedures and other similar situations.

Remember that reference must also be made to what the reasonable employer would have done, i.e. the test is objective.

Taylor v. *Parsons Peebles Ltd* (1981)

A works rule prohibited fighting. It was also the policy of the company to dismiss anyone caught fighting. The applicant had been employed by the company for 20 years without complaint. However, Taylor was caught fighting and was dismissed.

Held: The dismissal was unfair. Regard must be made to the previous 20 years of employment without incident. The tribunal decided that the reasonable employer would not have applied the sanction of instant dismissal as rigidly, because of the mitigating circumstances.

15.4.3 Redundancy

The employer must show that the reason for the dismissal was due to redundancy – Section 57(2) (c) of the EPCA. He must therefore be able to establish 'redundancy' within the meaning of the EPCA. A dismissal for reason of redundancy would be unfair if the employer had not acted as the reasonable employer would have acted in the circumstances. The following matters should be considered before the redundancies are put into effect:

1 Whether there is an alternative to making the employee redundant, e.g. redeployment.

> *Allwood* v. *William Hill Ltd* (1974)
>
> William Hill Ltd decided to close down 12 betting shops. Without any warning, they made all the managers redundant, offering no alternative employment. The managers, as employees, complained that this amounted to unfair dismissal.
>
> **Held:** In the circumstances, this amounted to unfair dismissal. The employer should have considered possible alternatives, such as transfer to other betting shops. Furthermore, the way in which the redundancies had taken place was not the way a reasonable employer would have acted. It is important to realize that, just because there is a redundancy provision within the meaning of the Act, it does not automatically follow that any dismissal due to redundancy will be fair.

2 Whether the criteria used for selection of those employees who are to be made redundant is fair, e.g. on a first in, first out basis, or last in first out, or part-time staff first.

> *Hammond-Scott* v. *Elizabeth Arden Ltd* (1976)
>
> The applicant was selected for redundancy because she was close to retirement age. She had been employed by the defendants for many years, but this was not taken into account when she was selected for redundancy.
>
> **Held:** Her selection for redundancy amounted to unfair dismissal, because the employer had not acted reasonably in the circumstances. In view of her age, length of service and the fact that she was close to retirement age, it would have had little financial effect on the company if they had continued to employ her until she retired.

3 Whether there has been any consultation with the relevant trade unions and whether the employer has discussed any representations made by the trade union. The employer should adhere to the Code of Practice on Redundancies.

4 Whether the employer has given adequate warning of the proposed redundancies to his employees – see *Kelly* v. *Upholstery & Cabinet Works Ltd* (1976).

There are **two** situations where selection for redundancy will automatically be deemed to be unfair: where employees in similar positions were not made redundant; and where a particular employee was selected for redundancy **either** because he was a member or non-member of a trade union, **or** contrary to an agreed custom, practice or procedure.

If the employer wishes to depart from an agreed procedure or practice, he must be able to justify such a departure as being fair in the circumstances – see *Vickers Ltd* v. *Smith* (1977).

15.4.4 Statutory restrictions (Section 57(2)(d))

If the dismissal is because the continued employment of the employee would result in a contravention of a statute or subordinate legislation, either on the part of the employer or employee, the dismissal will be *prima facie* fair. For example, if the employee has been banned from driving, yet his job requires him to hold a current driving licence, he would be in breach of the Road Traffic Acts if he continued to fulfil his job specification.

As with all cases of dismissal, the employer must act as the reasonable employer, and must therefore consider any possible alternatives, if the dismissal is to be regarded as fair.

15.4.5 Some other substantial reason

Where the employer is unable to show that the reason for the dismissal was one of those referred to above, he may show 'some other substantial reason' (Section 57(1)(*b*) the EPCA). There is no exhaustive list of what is recognized in law as 'some other substantial reason'. However, the following have been held to be valid reasons for dismissal, although it is important to appreciate that it is a question of fact in each case:

1 Conflict of personalities, primarily the fault of the employee: see *Treganowan* v. *Robert Knee & Co* (1975).

2 Failure to disclose material facts in obtaining employment, e.g. mental illness: see *O'Brien* v. *Prudential Assurance Co Ltd* (1979).

3 Commercial reasons, e.g. refusing to agree to a reduction in pay when other staff have agreed: see *Wilson* v. *Underhill House School Ltd* (1977).

4 A change in the terms of employment: see *Storey* v. *Allied Brewery* (1977).

15.5 Special situations

We shall now briefly consider the special provisions of the EPCA which refer to dismissal in relation to trade union membership (or non-membership) and trade union activities.

15.5.1 Trade Union membership or activities (Section 58)

Where the employee is dismissed because of his actual or proposed membership of an independent trade union, or because he is not a member of a trade union, or refuses to become a member, as a general rule the dismissal is automatically unfair. This is also the case where the employee has taken part or proposes to take part in any trade union activities. However, this rule is subject to the rules relating to dismissal in a closed shop, i.e. where employment is dependent on trade union membership. The employee need not have the required qualifying period of employment in order to bring an action for unfair dismissal under the Act.

15.5.2 Closed shop dismissals (Section 58, 3–8)

Any dismissal for failing to be a member of a specified independent trade union where there is in existence a union membership agreement between the trade union and the employer which requires membership for particular jobs or workers, will be regarded as fair where the employee refuses to become or remain a member. However, in the following situations, such a dismissal will be regarded as unfair:

1 Where the employee genuinely objects on grounds of conscience, or other deeply-held conviction, to being a member of any trade union.

2 Where, prior to the agreement, the employee was not a member of the union and has not been a member since (i.e. the agreement should not be allowed to apply retrospectively).

3 Where the agreement takes effect after 14th August 1980 and the agreement has not been approved in a secret ballot by at least 80 per cent of those covered by the agreement.

4 Where the employee is involved in legal proceedings relating to his expulsion or exclusion from the trade union, unless his non-membership is through his own fault.

5 Where the employee is a member of a professional body, and it would be a breach of its code of conduct to be a member of a trade union or to take part in a strike.

15.5.3 Dismissals in connection with industrial action

1 Lock-out by the employer (Section 62)
Where, at the date of the dismissal, the employer was conducting a lock-out, the tribunal is precluded from deciding whether the dismissal was fair or unfair, unless it can be shown that one or more of those employees involved were not dismissed, or if they were dismissed, they were re-engaged within three months of the date of the dismissal, but the applicant was not offered re-engagement; i.e. on the evidence, the applicant had been singled out by the employer.

2 Strike or other industrial action (Section 62)
Where the reason for the dismissal is that the employee is involved in a strike or other industrial action (e.g. sit-in), the tribunal is precluded from determining whether the dismissal is fair or unfair, unless it can be shown that one or more of those employees who worked at the same establishment as the applicant and were involved in the strike or industrial action were not dismissed, or that they were dismissed but were offered re-engagement within three months of the dismissal, but the applicant was not offered re-engagement. Remember the employer must show that he has acted

reasonably in his selection for dismissal. Protection is only afforded the employer where the dismissals take place during the industrial action, and not where they take place after the industrial action has ended – see *Midland Plastics Ltd* v. *Till* (1983).

15.5.4 Industrial pressure

Where an employer dismisses an employee because of industrial pressure brought to bear by other employees, the dismissal may be unfair. Section 63 provides that industrial pressure, such as the threat of a strike if the applicant continues to be employed by the employer, should be ignored by the tribunal, which must consider the dismissal on the basis of whether the employer had acted reasonably.

Where pressure is put on an employer to dismiss the applicant by a trade union because the applicant was not a member of a trade union, the trade union may be joined by the employer or applicant, as party to the proceedings. The tribunal may then make an award against the trade union if it finds that the dismissal was unfair.

15.6 Remedies

15.6.1 Reinstatement

Where the dismissal is found to be unfair, the tribunal has the power to make an order for reinstatement. The tribunal must ask the applicant if he wishes such an order to be made. The effect of an order for reinstatement is that the employer must treat the employee as if he had not been dismissed, i.e. his employment is on the same, or improved, terms and conditions as before.

15.6.2 Re-engagement

If the applicant so wishes, the tribunal may make an order for re-engagement. The effect of this is that the applicant should be re-engaged by the employer or an associated employer in a job which is comparable to his previous employment, or amounts to other suitable employment. The tribunal will specify the terms on which the applicant should be re-engaged, and this may make provision for arrears of pay.

The making of orders for reinstatement and re-engagement is at the discretion of the tribunal. Clearly, even if the applicant wishes to be reinstated or re-engaged, if it is not practicable, no order can be made.

15.6.3 Compensation

An award of compensation will be made where an order for reinstatement or re-engagement is not complied with, or it is not practicable to make such an order. There are various types of compensation:

1 Basic award
The calculation of the basic award is dependent upon the amount of continuous service, in years, which the applicant has attained.

Entitlement	Years	Weeks pay for each year of employment
Age	18–21	½
	22–40	1
	41–65	1½

The current maximum number of years which can be counted is 20, and the current maximum amount of weekly pay is £164. The maximum basic award is at present £4920. The basic award may be reduced by the tribunal on the grounds of contributory conduct on the part of the applicant. Where there is also an award of redundancy payments, the basic award will be reduced by the amount of redundancy payment, as long as it is established that the dismissal was for reason for redundancy.

In the following situations, the basic award will be two weeks' pay:

(a) Where the reason for the dismissal is redundancy, but the employee is not entitled to a redundancy payment because he unreasonably refused an offer of alternative employment within the four week trial period.

(b) Where the employee is not entitled to treat himself as dismissed for reasons of redundancy because his contract has been renewed or he has been re-engaged.

2 Compensatory award

This is in addition to the basic award, and is awarded at the discretion of the tribunal. The amount of the award is decided upon by the tribunal on the grounds of what is 'just and equitable in all the circumstances, having regard to the loss sustained by the applicant in consequence of the dismissal'.

At present the maximum amount of this award is £8000. The amount of the award may be reduced by failure on the part of the employee to mitigate his loss, contributory conduct and any *ex gratia* payment by the employer.

In making the award, the tribunal will take into account loss of wages, expenses incurred in taking legal action against the employer, loss of future earnings, loss of pension rights and other benefits, e.g. company car, the manner of the dismissal.

3 Additional award

An additional award can be made where the employer fails to comply with an order for reinstatement or re-engagement, and fails to show that it was not practicable to comply with such an order. The amount of this additional award will be between 13 and 26 weeks' pay; if the dismissal is unfair because it is based on sex or race discrimination, the additional award will be between 26 and 52 weeks' pay.

4 Special award

Where the dismissal is found to be unfair on the grounds of trade union membership or non-membership, and the applicant wants reinstatement or re-engagement, but the tribunal is unable to make such an order, or where it makes an order with which the employer fails to comply, a special award may be made. Such an award is subject to the following rules:

If no order in respect of reinstatement or re-engagement is made, the special award is one week's pay × 104 or £11 000, whichever is the greater, subject to a maximum of £22 000. The statutory maximum does not apply to the week's pay, in the case of the special award. If the employer fails to comply with the order and fails to show that it is not practicable to do so, the award is one week's pay × 156, or £25 584, whichever is the greater. Any special award may be reduced because of the contributory conduct on the part of the employee.

Sample questions

1 Outline the remedies available in an action for unfair dismissal.

Suggested answer

The following points should be considered:

An order for reinstatement – i.e. the employee should be reinstated in his former job on the same terms and conditions as before.

An order for re-engagement – the employee should be re-engaged by the employer on comparable terms and conditions as before.

Orders for reinstatement and re-engagement will only be made if the employee wants one of these remedies, and if it is practicable to make an order.

The alternative remedy is compensation, and you should refer to the different types of award and the grounds on which such compensation is awarded; i.e. basic award, computed on length of service and weekly wage; compensatory award, purely discretionary; additional award, awarded where the employer fails to comply with a reinstatement or re-engagement order; special award, where the dismissal was found to be on the grounds of trade union membership and the tribunal was unable to make an order for reinstatement or re-engagement.

2 When may an employee claim compensation for unfair dismissal?

CIMA

Suggested answer

The following points should be considered:

The employee must show that he has been dismissed within the meaning of the Act, and must include a reference to constructive dismissal. Once dismissal has been shown, the onus moves to the employer to show that the dismissal was fair and that he acted reasonably in dismissing the employee.

You must refer to the criteria on which it is decided whether the dismissal was fair and the relevant case law, i.e. capability/qualifications, conduct, redundancy, statutory restrictions, other reasons, trade union membership and activities.

In deciding whether the employer had acted as the reasonable employer, reference should be made to the method of dismissal and the Code of Practice 'Disciplinary Practice and Procedures in Employment'.

Whether there was an alternative to the dismissal should also be considered.

3 Explain whether the following dismissals are fair:

(a) David is dismissed when his employer discovers that he does not have the correct qualifications for the job.

(b) Lawrence is dismissed for allegedly spending too much time on trade union activities.

(c) Cyril is dismissed because he has been regularly late for work.

Suggested answer

The following points should be considered:

(a) The onus is on the employer to show that the reason for the dismissal was fair and that he acted reasonably in dismissing his employee (Section 57 of the EPCA). The reason for the dismissal here is on grounds of incorrect qualifications. You will need to consider whether this is a valid reason for dismissal under Section 57(4) – *Blackman* v. *Post Office*; the employer would have to show that particular qualifications were essential and that without them there was no alternative but to dismiss David.

(b) Dismissal for trade union activities is governed by Section 58 of the EPCA; such dismissals are automatically unfair. The main issue here is whether the activities in which Lawrence participated are to be regarded as trade union activities and whether the amount of time he spent on them was in reality excessive. This will depend on the nature of the activities as there is no guideline in the Act itself.

(c) It must be shown that the reason for the dismissal was fair and that the employer acted reasonably in dismissing Cyril. The employer may argue that the dismissal has arisen because of his employee's conduct. A dismissal for lateness may be fair where it can be shown that this had occurred regularly, but the employer must show that he acted reasonably. He may therefore be expected to show that he had given Cyril a chance to improve his position, which Cyril had failed to do. Reference should be made to the code of practice on disciplinary procedures as the employer would be expected to give Cyril appropriate warnings before dismissing him for this type of conduct.

4 Julian's life as foreman is made unbearable by the conduct of his immediate manager, who without justification constantly criticizes Julian's work and undermines his authority with his subordinates. After a particularly nasty episode where the manager swears at Julian in front of his colleagues, Julian hands in his notice. Advise Julian whether he has a claim for unfair dismissal.

Suggested answer

This should consider the following information:

The important issue here is to establish that Julian has been dismissed within the meaning of Section 55 of the EPCA. As Julian has handed in his notice, this has to be considered in the light of constructive dismissal, with reference to *Western Excavating Ltd* v. *Sharp*. There must therefore be a breach of an express or implied term of the contract on the part of the employer which is such that the employee can dismiss himself. It must be more than unreasonable conduct on the part of the employer. In this particular instance, you would need to consider whether the implied term of mutual respect had been broken, which on the evidence seems likely. This being the case, Julian can treat himself as dismissed and the onus moves to the employer to justify his conduct and show that he had acted reasonably.

Further reading

For further reading on the topics covered in this chapter, see chapter 16.

16 Redundancy

16.1 The EPCA

In this chapter we shall be considering the law relating to redundancy, and when an employee is entitled to redundancy pay. The law relating to redundancy can be found in the Employment Protection (Consolidation) Act, 1978 (EPCA). The Act provides for the payment of compensation based on an employee's service and wages, to tide the employee over the period in which he is without a job. However, as we shall see, the entitlement to redundancy payments only exists where it is established that the employee's dismissal was by reason of redundancy within the meaning of the Act.

The types of employee who qualify under the EPCA, and those who do not qualify, are set out at the beginning of chapter 15. You should note that different retirement ages for men and women (65 and 60 respectively) are maintained for redundancy.

As we have seen, the employee must have a minimum of two years' continuous employment with the same employer or with an associated employer. It is important to appreciate what this means – the rules can be found in Schedule 13 to the EPCA.

1 There is a presumption that employment is continuous, and the onus is on the employer to show that continuity has been broken, or that there are weeks which do not count towards continuity.

2 Any week in which an employee is employed for 16 hours a week counts towards continuity (excluding overtime).

3 Continuity is not broken by holidays, attending conferences, etc.

4 The first 26 weeks of sick leave, in addition to any contractual entitlement, counts towards continuity, as does maternity leave taken within the requirements of the EPCA.

5 Any week in which the employee is absent because of a temporary cessation of work, e.g. where there is no work available, counts towards continuity.

6 Where the employee is on strike or absent because of a lock-out, this period will not break continuity but neither will it count towards it.

7 In any week in which an employee is absent by arrangement or custom, continuity is to be maintained (e.g. time off for family bereavements).

Continuity is not only important for qualification purposes, but also because the longer the period of continuity with the same employer or an associated employer, the greater the amount of redundancy payment. If continuity is broken, the employee has to start building up his continuity from the break.

16.2 Dismissal

Where an employee meets the basic qualification requirements, he then has to show that he has been dismissed within the meaning of Section 83 of the EPCA. An employee shall be treated as dismissed by his employer if, but only if:

1 the contract of employment is terminated by the employer with or without notice; or

2 it is a fixed term contract which has expired without being renewed; or

3 the employee terminates the contract, with or without notice, in circumstances which are such that he is entitled to terminate it without notice by reason of the employer's conduct;

4 the contract is terminated by the death of the employer, or the dissolution or liquidation of the firm (Section 93).

Whether a dismissal is within Section 83 or 93 is a question of fact in each case. For example, a variation in the terms of the employee's contract will amount to a dismissal if he does not agree to the new terms. If, however, the employee accepts the new terms, there can be no dismissal, and continuity is preserved.

> *Marriot v. Oxford & District Co-operative Society Ltd* (1970)
>
> Marriot was employed as a foreman by the defendants. He was informed that from a certain date he would be employed on a lower grade and his rate of pay would be reduced accordingly.
>
> **Held:** This variation in the terms of the existing contract amounted to termination by the employer, which Marriot could treat as dismissal.

Clearly there may be a clause in the contract which allows the employer to vary the terms. If the employee in this situation does not like the new terms, and chooses to leave his employment, this will not amount to a dismissal for the purposes of the Act.

One type of contentious term has proved to be the 'mobility clause', which many executive contracts contain.

> *McCaffrey v. Jeavons & Co Ltd* (1967)
>
> McCaffrey's contract of employment contained a term that he would work anywhere in the UK. His employer asked him to move from Bristol to Reading. He refused, and tendered his resignation.
>
> **Held:** McCaffrey was bound by the 'mobility clause', which was clearly part of his contract; he could not therefore regard himself as dismissed.

However, it is important that the employee does not anticipate the employer's actions, as his subsequent resignation may not amount to a dismissal.

> *Morton Sundour Fabrics v. Shaw* (1966)
>
> Shaw was employed as a foreman by Morton. He was informed that there might be some redundancies in the near future, but nothing specific had been decided. In the light of what he had been told, he decided to leave the firm in order to take another job.
>
> **Held:** Shaw had not been dismissed, and therefore was not entitled to redundancy payments. His precipitous action could not be shown to relate to the subsequent redundancies made by his employer.
>
> Obviously he would have succeeded with his claim had he waited until he had received his notice of redundancy. However, when he resigned there was no way of knowing exactly who would be made redundant.

16.3 Redundancy

In order for the employee to be entitled to redundancy payments he must have been dismissed 'for reason of redundancy'. There is a presumption that once the employee has shown that he has been dismissed, the reason for the dismissal was redundancy (Section 91(2)). The onus is on the employer to show that the dismissal was for some reason other than redundancy.

The EPCA provides this definition of 'redundancy' (Section 81(2)):

> [This is where] . . . dismissal is attributable wholly or mainly to *either* (a) the fact that his employer has ceased, or intends to cease, to carry on the business for the purposes of which the employee was employed by him, or has ceased, or intends to cease, to carry on that business in the place where the employee was so employed, *or* (b) the fact that the requirements of that business for employees to carry out work of a particular kind, or for employees to carry out work of a particular kind in the place where they were so employed have ceased or diminished or are expected to cease or diminish.

In effect, there are three situations in which the dismissal can be said to be for redundancy. These are as follows:

16.3.1 Cessation of the employer's business

This covers both temporary and permanent closures of the employer's business in respect of the type of work carried on at the premises.

> *Gemmel* v. *Darngavil Brickworks Ltd* (1967)
>
> The brickworks closed for a period of 13 weeks for substantial repairs to be carried out. Some of the employees were dismissed.
>
> **Held:** The dismissal was for reason of redundancy even though part of the premises was still in use.

16.3.2 Closure of the place of work

Where the employer ceases to trade at a particular place, as opposed to the cessation of the type of work, the dismissal of his employees will usually be for reason of redundancy. This is subject to any contract of employment which contains a 'mobility clause'.

> *O'Brien* v. *Associated Fire Alarms Ltd* (1969)
>
> O'Brien was employed by the defendants at their Liverpool branch. There was a shortage of work and he was asked to work in Barrow-in-Furness. He refused, and was dismissed by his employer. He contended that the dismissal amounted to redundancy.
>
> **Held:** As there was no clause in O'Brien's contract of employment which would have allowed his employer to move him to a different location, the dismissal was for reason of redundancy.

Where the employer only moves his place of work a short distance, and/or remains within the same town or conurbation, any offer of work at the new place of employment to his existing employees may prevent any dismissal from being for reason of redundancy. Obviously it will depend on accessibility to the new premises, as well as the terms on which the offer is made – remember the terms must not be worse than existing terms. It can therefore be within the employer's expectations that his employees will move to different premises without there being a redundancy situation, if it is reasonable in all the circumstances of the case.

> *Managers (Holborn) Ltd* v. *Hohne* (1977)
>
> The defendants occupied premises in Holborn in which Hohne was a manageress. They decided to move their business to Regent Street, which was only a short distance away. Hohne refused to move there and claimed redundancy on the basis that there was no term in her contract which required her to move.
>
> **Held:** The new premises were just as accessible as the old ones and therefore it was reasonable for her employer to expect her to move without there being any issue of redundancy. There was no evidence of any additional inconvenience to Hohne if she agreed to move to the new premises. Therefore she did not succeed in her action.

16.3.3 Reduction in the type of work carried on by the employer

As a general rule, where the employer is forced to dismiss employees because of a reduction in the work available, such employees are surplus to the requirements of the business, and any dismissal is for reason of redundancy. Furthermore where there is a change in systems of work so that fewer employees are actually needed to do the job, this too can amount to redundancy. From time to time the Courts are faced with the difficult task of deciding whether dismissal for failure to keep up with modern working practices amounts to redundancy.

> *North Riding Garages* v. *Butterwick* (1967)
>
> Butterwick had been employed at the same garage for 30 years and had risen to the position of workshop manager. The garage was taken over by the appellants and Butterwick was dismissed for inefficiency on the grounds that he was unable, or

unwilling, to accept new methods of work which would involve him in some administrative work.

Held: The dismissal was not for reason of redundancy because the employee was still expected to do the same type of work, subject to new working practices. As far as the Court was concerned, employees who remain in the same employment for many years are expected to adapt to new techniques and methods of work and even to higher standards of efficiency. It is only when the new practices affect the nature of the work, so that in effect there is no longer any requirement to do a particular kind of work, that a redundancy situation may arise.

Chapman v. *Goonvean & Rostowrack China Clay Co* (1973)

The defendants provided free transport to and from work for many of their employees. They then decided to withdraw this benefit, because it was no longer an economic proposition. Chapman was forced to resign because it was now too difficult for him to get to work.

Held: The applicant was not redundant within the meaning of the Act. His job still existed – it was merely inconvenient for him to continue working at that particular place of work.

Hindle v. *Percival Boats Ltd* (1969)

Hindle was employed in the repair of wooden boats, and had been so for many years. This type of work was in decline because of the increasing use of glass-fibre. He was dismissed because he was 'too good and too slow' and it was uneconomical to keep him on. He was not replaced; his work was merely absorbed by existing staff.

Held: Hindle's dismissal was not for reason of redundancy. The Court felt that the employer was merely shedding surplus labour, and that this was not within the Act. Clearly there are situations where 'shedding surplus labour' will amount to redundancy; each case must be considered on its merits.

Haden Ltd v. *Cowen* (1982)

Cowen was employed as a regional supervisor. He was based in Southampton and had to cover a large part of southern England as part of his job. He suffered a mild heart attack. He was then promoted to divisional contracts surveyor by his employer, as it was thought that this would make his life less stressful. One of the terms of his contract required him to undertake, at the discretion of the company, any duties which reasonably fell within the scope of his capabilities. The company was later forced to reduce the number of employees at staff level. Cowen was not prepared to accept demotion and was dismissed. He claimed both redundancy and unfair dismissal.

Held: Cowen was dismissed for reason of redundancy because there was no other work available within the terms of his contract, i.e. as divisional contracts manager.

It is suggested that the true test of redundancy is to be found in this case, and the issue to be considered is 'whether the business needs as much work of the kind which the employee could, by his contract, lawfully be required to do'. This is not a question of the day-to-day function of the employee, but what he could be expected to do under his contract of employment: see *Pink* v. *White* (1985).

16.3.4 Lay-off and short time (Sections 87–89 of the EPCA)

In certain circumstances, lay-off and short time may give rise to redundancy. If there is a term in the contract of employment which allows the employer to put his employees on short time, i.e. where they receive less than half of their normal weekly wage, or to lay them off, such action will not amount to redundancy unless the employee is laid-off or on short time for four consecutive weeks, or six out of the previous 13 weeks. In these circumstances, the employee may give written notice to his employer of his intention to claim redundancy payment, i.e. he can treat himself as dismissed subject to notice being given to his employer.

Following this action by the employee, the employer may serve a counter-notice within seven days of the employee's notice contesting the claim and stating that there is a reasonable chance that, within four weeks of the counter-notice, the employee will commence a period of 13 weeks consecutive employment. This then becomes a matter for the tribunal.

If the employer withdraws the counter-notice or fails to employ the employee for 13 consecutive weeks, the employee is entitled to the redundancy payment.

16.3.5   Change in ownership and transfer of undertakings

Where there is a change in the ownership of a business, and existing employees either have their contract renewed or are re-engaged by the new employer, this does not amount to redundancy, and continuity is preserved (Section 94), e.g. where the business is sold as a going concern, rather than a transfer of the assets. However, if the employee has reasonable grounds for refusing the offer of renewal, he may be treated as redundant (Section 82(6)).

Section 94 is subject to the Transfer of Undertakings (Protection of Employment) Regulations, 1981. Where the transfer of a business is within the Regulations, the contracts of employment of the employees are also transferred, as if they had been made by the transferee. If there is a subsequent dismissal, the employee may claim unfair dismissal, or if it is for an economic, technical or organizational reason, redundancy payments may be claimed. Where there is a dual claim and the employee has received redundancy compensation, this amount is subtracted from the basic award payable to the employee for his unfair dismissal. The compensatory award is not affected.

16.4   Burden of proof

The burden of proof in the initial stages of any claim for redundancy is on the employee to show that he was dismissed. There is then a presumption that the dismissal was for reason of redundancy, and the burden then moves to the employer to show that redundancy was not the reason for the dismissal.

16.5   Offer of alternative employment

This is covered by Section 82 of the EPCA 1978. The general rule is that where the employer makes an offer of suitable alternative employment, which is unreasonably refused by the employee, the employee will be unable to claim redundancy. This contract, which is either a renewal or a re-engagement, must take effect on the expiry of the old contract, or within four weeks. Clearly the main issue is what amounts to 'suitable'.

Consideration must be taken of the old terms and conditions compared with the new ones, i.e. the nature of the work, remuneration, hours, location, skills and experience including qualifications etc. Where the conditions of the new contract do not differ materially from the old contract regarding place, nature of the work, pay etc. then the question of suitability does not arise.

It is a question of fact in each case as to whether an offer can be deemed 'suitable'. However, the facts must be considered objectively.

> *Taylor v. Kent CC* (1969)
>
> Taylor was made redundant from his post as headmaster of a school. He was offered a place in the pool of supply teachers from which temporary absences were filled in schools. There was no loss of salary or other rights other than status. Taylor refused the offer.
>
> **Held:** His refusal was reasonable. The offer was not suitable because of the loss of status as he was being removed from a position as head of a school to that of an ordinary teacher.

> *Sheppard* v. *NCB* (1966)
>
> Sheppard was employed as a carpenter. He was offered another job as a carpenter, but on different terms and conditions which meant more travel, no overtime and the loss of certain fringe benefits. He refused this job.
>
> **Held:** Although the extra travel was not excessive, nor the loss of overtime too detrimental, coupled with the loss of fringe benefits the offer was deemed to be unsuitable.

In considering whether a refusal by the employee is reasonable, regard must be given to the personal circumstances of the employee, such as housing and domestic problems. It may be reasonable for an employee to refuse a job offer which involves a move to London when he lives in the Midlands, because of the associated housing problems. However, a refusal based upon a personal whim would be unreasonable (see *Fuller* v. *Stephanie Bowman* (*Sales*) *Ltd* (1977)). Remember, the onus is on the employer to show that the employee's rejection of the offer is unreasonable.

In *Rawe* v. *Power Gas Corporation* (1966) it was held to be reasonable to refuse a move from the south-east of England to Teesside, because of marital difficulties.

> *Souter* v. *Henry Balfour & Co Ltd* (1966)
>
> Souter, a pattern-maker, was offered a job as a progress clerk. This resulted in a drop in salary, although he was given staff status and a review of his pay after six months.
>
> **Held:** Even though the offer was suitable, it was a reasonable refusal by the employee as he had been a craftsman all his life and wished to continue doing the same work as before; this new job would have entailed doing different work.

16.5.1 Effect of acceptance

Where the offer of alternative employment is accepted by the employee, there is deemed to be continuity of employment between the former contract and the new contract.

16.5.2 Trial period (Section 84 of the EPCA)

The employee is entitled to a trial period of four weeks (or longer, if agreed with the employer) if his contract is renewed on different terms and conditions. If the employee terminates his employment during the trial period for a reason connected with the new contract, he will be treated as having been dismissed on the date his previous contract was terminated. Whether he will be entitled to redundancy will depend on whether it was a suitable offer of alternative employment and whether his refusal to accept it was reasonable (see *Meek* v. *J. Allen Rubber Co Ltd & Secretary of State for Employment* (1980)).

16.6 Calculation of redundancy payment

16.6.1 Claim

The employee must inform his employer in writing of his intention to claim a redundancy payment from him. If the employer does not make the payment, or there is a dispute over entitlement, the matter is referred to an industrial tribunal. As a general rule the claim must be made within six months of the date of termination of the contract of employment. This period can be extended at the discretion of the industrial tribunal, but cannot exceed 12 months.

16.6.2 Method of calculation

This is outlined in chapter 15 (see section 15.6.3).

There are certain factors which may affect the award of redundancy payment and result either in its reduction or loss. These are as follows:

1 Misconduct by the employee during the period of notice; depending upon the severity of the misconduct, the tribunal may decide that the employee is no longer entitled to his redundancy payment, or that it should be reduced.

2 Strike action; if the employee is involved in a strike during his period of notice he will still be entitled to redundancy payment. However, if he receives his notice of dismissal while on strike he will not be entitled to claim redundancy payment.

16.7   Procedure for handling redundancies

This is governed by Section 99–107 of the Employment Protection Act, 1975, which introduces the principle of consultation with trade unions if redundancy is proposed. The rules are as follows.

Where an independent trade union is recognized for collective bargaining purposes by the employer, the employer must consult with the representatives of the trade union:

1 At the earliest opportunity about the proposed redundancies.

2 At least 90 days before the first dismissal takes effect, when he proposes to make 100 or more employees redundant at one establishment within a period of 90 days or less.

3 At least 30 days before the first redundancy takes effect, where he proposes to make 10 or more employees redundant at one establishment within a 30-day period.

The employer must disclose the following information during the consultations:

1 The reasons for the proposed redundancies.

2 The number and description of the employees whom it is proposed to make redundant.

3 The total number of employees of that description employed at that establishment.

4 The method of selection, e.g. last in, first out (LIFO), or part-timers first.

5 The method of carrying out the redundancies, having regard to any procedure agreed with the trade union.

During these consultations the trade union may make any representation which it sees fit. The employer may not ignore these representations, and must give his reasons if he chooses to reject them. Where there are special circumstances such as insolvency, the employer need only do what is reasonably practicable to comply with the consultation requirements.

16.7.1   Effect of non-compliance with the procedure

Where the employer fails to comply with the consultation procedure, in circumstances where it was reasonably practicable to expect him to do so, the trade union can complain to the industrial tribunal. If the tribunal finds in favour of the trade union it must make a declaration to this effect, and it may make a **protective award** to those employees who are affected. This award takes the form of remuneration for a protected period and is purely discretionary. The length of the protected period usually reflects the severity of the breach by the employer. However the protected period:

1 must not exceed 90 days where it is proposed to make 100 or more redundant within 90 days;

2 is 30 days where it is proposed to make 10 or more redundant;

3 is 28 days if the redundancies did not fall within 1 and 2 above.

All employees covered by the protective award are entitled to one week's pay for each week of the protected period.

16.7.2   Notification of redundancies to the Secretary of State

By virtue of Section 100 of the EPA 1975, an employer must notify the Secretary of State of his intentions where he proposes:

1 To make 100 or more employees redundant at one establishment within a 90 day period; the notification must take place within 90 days.

2 Where he proposes to make 10 or more employees redundant within a 30 day period; the notification must take place within 30 days.

Failure to meet these requirements may result in prosecution or a reduction in the employer's rebate from the redundancy fund.

Sample questions

1 Brian is a senior safety officer with Pan-Technic Engineering. The company is taken over by another firm. Brian is offered a job with the new firm based at the same place as security and safety officer. This involves greater responsibility at the same rate of pay. Brian takes up the new post and works for two weeks whilst looking for a new job. In this time he is able to find a job he thinks is more suitable, and he hands in his notice.

Discuss Brian's legal position.

Suggested answer

The following points should be considered:

If Brian wants to bring an action for redundancy under the EPCA he must show firstly that he qualifies, i.e. that he has been continuously employed for two years or more, with an explanation of what this means (Schedule 13) and that he does not fall within one of the excluded categories of employee.

If Brian initially qualifies, it must then be shown that he has been dismissed within the meaning of Section 83 of the EPCA. The issue here is whether he will be deemed to have accepted a variation in the terms of his contract in which case he will not have been dismissed for the purposes of the Act. However reference should be made to *Marriot* v. *Oxford & District Co-operative Society Ltd* and the Transfer of Undertakings (Protection of Employment) Regulations, 1981.

If dismissal can be shown, it must then be established that the dismissal was for reason of redundancy. Reference should be made to the presumption in Section 91(2) and to the fact that the onus is on the employer to show that the dismissal was for some other reason. The offer of suitable alternative employment must be considered in the light of Section 82; and the effect of rejection within the trial period.

2 Outline the situations when an employee may claim redundancy payment.

Suggested answer

The following points should be considered:

Firstly you must refer to the fact that the employee must show that he qualifies for redundancy within the EPCA and that he has been dismissed. As there is then a presumption that the dismissal was for reasons of redundancy, the onus is now on the employer to show that there was some other reason. The EPCA (Section 81(2)) lays down three situations where the dismissal is deemed to be for reason of redundancy and you would need to consider these in some detail including reference to the case law.

You must therefore look at cessation of the employer's business, e.g. *Gemmell* v. *Darngavil Brickworks Ltd*; closure of the place of work – *O'Brian* v. *Associated Fire Alarms*; or reduction in the type of work – *North Riding Garages* v. *Butterwick*. The effect of the provisions relating to lay-off and short-time (Sections 87-89) also need to be considered.

3 Graham has been employed for 30 years by Hand-Crafted Cabinet Makers. He has always used traditional working methods. These methods are now changing, as many of the tasks previously done by hand can be done by machine. Graham has found it difficult to keep up with these changes. His employer informs him that his services are no longer required and he is given two weeks' notice. Graham seeks your advice, and asks you to list important items. Advise Graham of his rights against his employer.

BTEC HND, Staffordshire Polytechnic

Suggested answer

The following points should be considered:
It would have to be established that Graham qualified, i.e. that he had two or more

years continuous employment (Schedule 13) and that he had been dismissed – these points should not pose a problem on the evidence as he has 30 years' service and two weeks' notice of the termination of his employment.

The employer would then have to show that the dismissal was not for reason of redundancy. In this case he could argue that Graham had failed to keep up with modern working methods although the essence of his job remained the same – *North Riding Garages* v. *Butterwick*; *Hindle* v. *Percival Boats* – in neither of these cases was the dismissal for reason of redundancy.

The length of notice given to Graham must be considered. This does not comply with the statutory minimum laid down in Section 49 of the EPCA, which is based on the period of continuous employment. Graham may have a case for wrongful dismissal on the grounds that he has not been given the correct period of notice.

4 (a) Which persons qualify for redundancy payments under the EPCA 1978?

(b) Outline the rules relating to offers of alternative employment.

Suggested answer

(a) The following points should be considered:

The general rule is that the employee should have two years' continuous employment, i.e. he should have worked 16 hours a week for the same employer; reference should be made to Schedule 13 regarding the rules for assessing continuous employment. The excluded categories of occupations should then be referred to, e.g. dock workers, crown employees.

(b) The rules relating to an offer of alternative employment can be found in Section 82 of the EPCA. The main issues are whether the employment offered is suitable and whether if it was refused the refusal was unreasonable. This is a question of fact in each case with reference to existing terms and conditions – *Taylor* v. *Kent CC*.

An employee will only be allowed to proceed with his claim for redundancy if the refusal is found to be reasonable; reference should be made to the four week trial period.

Further reading

Selwyn, N. *Employment Law* (Butterworths)
Holmes, A. E. M. and Painter, R. *Employment Law* (*SWOT*) (Blackstone Press)

17 Health and safety at work

Health and Safety at work is a wide topic, as it covers the obligations imposed on an employer by both the criminal and civil law; although, as we shall see, criminal law applies not only to employers but also to occupiers of factories, self-employed persons etc. The topic of employer's liability under civil law has already been dealt with in chapter 12. This chapter is therefore restricted to an outline of the main statutes and numerous regulations. In a course on business law it is likely that reference will only be made to the main statutes and their effect.

17.1 Control by statute

Protection for employees in respect of health and safety matters is a recent innovation, having been in existence for just over a hundred years. The need for such protection arose out of the effects of the Industrial Revolution, as this brought with it a substantial increase in death and serious injury to employees. Furthermore, appalling working conditions had come to be accepted by the employees, who included many women and young children. Protection was gradually introduced in the form of statutes and the Factory Inspectorate was set up to enforce the statutory provisions. The three statutes which now govern health and safety in the workplace are:

1 the Factories Act, 1961;

2 the Offices, Shops and Railway Premises Act, 1963;

3 the Health and Safety at Work etc. Act, 1974.

A change in approach by the legislature has come about with the passing of the Health and Safety at Work etc. Act., 1974 (HASAWA 1974) and the regulations made under it. It is now felt that self-regulation on the part of the employer, rather than 'policing' by the Factory Inspectorate, is the best way to encourage long-term improvement in health and safety; whether this will be effective remains to be seen.

17.2 Factories Act, 1961

A breach of this Act is a breach of the criminal law, although not every breach will result in prosecution. Whether a firm or company will be prosecuted is at the discretion of the factory inspector.

The nature of the statute is important, as many of the sections impose strict liability on the occupier of a factory – that is, liability does not rest on proof of negligence, recklessness or intentional acts and therefore the occupier cannot plead that it was not his fault that a breach occurred, i.e. he has no defence.

17.2.1 Premises covered by the Act

The Factories Act, 1961 only applies in 'factories' as defined in Section 175. Although this may sound logical, the word 'factory' actually encompasses much more than one might imagine. As a general guideline, a factory is a place where people are employed in manual labour in the process of manufacturing or doing anything incidental to any article, including such things as alteration, repair and adapting for sale, e.g. packing goods.

The word 'factory' also includes such places as slaughter houses, dry docks, printing works, laundries etc. – see Section 175(2).

In real terms, a certain amount of logical reasoning has to be applied if there is any doubt as to whether particular premises are in fact a 'factory' within the meaning of the Factories Act; i.e. is the main activity connected with a manufacturing process?

17.2.2 Scope of the duties imposed by the Factories Act

The first point to note is that the Act imposes duties on the 'occupier' of a factory; at no time does the Act refer to the employer, although in the majority of cases the occupier and the employer will be the same person. The person who is to be regarded in law as the occupier is bound to inform the Health and Safety Executive of his intended occupation of a factory (Section 137).

The Factories Act divides the duties into three main areas, headed 'health', 'safety' and 'welfare' – safety being the largest section. These duties are owed to all the people who work in the factory, as opposed to visitors (see *Hartley* v. *Mayoh & Co* (1954)). The duties are many and varied; they are also very specific in nature and the Act quite literally spells out what the occupier must do in order to comply. As the duties are so extensive, it is not possible to consider most of them in detail here – however, one duty from each area is covered, so that a 'feel' for the Act can be gained.

1 Health

This covers such diverse matters as the painting of walls, the question of overcrowding, toilet facilities, ventilation etc. Specifically, part of Section 3 provides that 'effective provision shall be made for securing and maintaining a reasonable temperature in each workroom. . .'. What is 'reasonable' is a question of fact in each case, and reference must be made to the type of activity being carried out in the factory. For example, if the work is arduous, as in some areas of a foundry, a 'reasonable' temperature will be lower than in a light engineering workshop. The section further provides that the method of heating the workroom should not be such that fumes, e.g. gas or vapour, are allowed to escape into the workroom, which are likely to be injurious or offensive to persons employed there.

The specific nature of this duty gives the occupier guidelines within which he has to work. Although the method in which he heats the workroom is not spelt out, he knows what is not acceptable under the Act.

2 Safety

The provisions in this area range from the guarding and use of machinery, to the safe use of lifts, cranes, boilers, and the maintenance of a safe place of work. One of the most important sections relates to the guarding of machinery. Section 14 stipulates that 'every dangerous part of any machinery shall be securely fenced . . .'. This section only applies to machinery which is installed in the factory, and not to machinery which is being manufactured. The occupier need only fence the 'dangerous part'. Whether a part of a machine is dangerous or not is judged on the basis of the test in *John Summers & Sons Ltd* v. *Frost* (1955). A part is dangerous if it is:

> . . . a reasonably foreseeable cause of injury to anybody acting in a way in which a human being may be reasonably expected to act in circumstances which may be reasonably expected to occur.

It follows therefore that the occupier does not have to guard against extremes of behaviour or unusual occurrences, unless he has had prior warning in the past. However, he may have to guard against the stupidity of the machine operator.

Uddin v. *Associated Portland Cement Manufacturers Ltd* (1965)

Uddin was employed as a machine minder. One day he climbed a ladder in order to retrieve a pigeon. As he leant across a revolving shaft which was not guarded, he was injured, losing the use of his arm.

Held: The employer was in breach of Section 14. It was foreseeable that an employee might climb the ladder, and as a result might come into contact with the unfenced shaft.

The accepted standard of fencing is that which prevents the workman coming into contact with the dangerous part, even if this means that the machine can no longer be used – remember there is an absolute duty.

John Summers & Sons Ltd v. *Frost* (1955)

The occupier failed to guard adequately the abrasive wheel on a grinding machine.

The machine operator was injured when he came into contact with the exposed part of the wheel.

Held: The duty to fence is absolute. A dangerous part therefore is only adequately fenced when the workman is effectively prevented from coming into contact with it. This is the case even if it means that the machine can no longer be used if guarded effectively.

'Secure fencing' must be capable of protecting other workmen, as well as the operator of the machine. If the duty was confined to the protection of the operator, the occupier would be able to guard the front and sides of the machine and leave the rear of the machine unfenced, even though there may be access to the dangerous part. The foreseeable behaviour of all the persons employed is relevant in judging the standard of fencing required on a particular machine.

There is, however, no need to guard against fragments of the machine, or of the material being machined, from flying out of the machine.

Close v. *Steel Co of Wales Ltd* (1962)

The drill bit of a portable drilling machine shattered and injured the operator's eye. The drill bit on such machines had shattered before, but no one had ever been injured.

Held: The employer was not liable, as the duty to fence did not extend to guarding against bits flying off the machine.

Nicholls v. *Austin (Leyton) Ltd* (1946)

A piece of wood which was being machined flew out of the machine and struck the operator. The blade, which was the 'dangerous part' of the machine, was securely fenced.

Held: The fence was intended to keep the worker out, not to keep the machine or its products in. The occupier was not therefore in breach of his duty.

In deciding whether the fencing provided is 'secure', regard must be had to the requirements of Section 16. Section 16 states that all fencing must be of substantial construction, constantly maintained and kept in position while the dangerous part is in motion or use, i.e. the machine does not have to be doing its usual work to be covered by the Act. Furthermore, the occupier does not fulfil his obligations by merely providing the correct standard of fencing, he must do more. This should take the form of planned preventative maintenance which involves regular checks of the guards.

3 Welfare

The Factories Act gives little attention to the welfare of workmen. The welfare provisions are therefore very sparse, and to some extent are out of keeping with modern expectations. They range from the provision of drinking water, to the removal of dust and fumes and in part have been superseded by regulations, e.g. First Aid Act Regulations, 1980 and the Control of Lead at Work Regulations 1982. For example, Section 57 of the Factories Act, 1961 requires that:

> . . . there shall be provided and maintained at suitable points conveniently accessible to all persons employed an adequate supply of wholesome drinking water from a public main or from some other source approved in writing by the district council.

As a general rule drinking water should be supplied directly from a rising main, and should not come from a storage tank. The tap or vessel should be clearly marked 'drinking water'. The obligation on the occupier is to maintain, as well as provide, the supply. He must therefore keep the supply in a good state of repair in order to prevent contamination.

17.2.3 Civil remedy

Although the Factories Act creates a criminal offence, an injured workman may bring a civil action in tort for breach of statutory duty. It is recognized that at the very least the safety provisions of this Act provide such a remedy which, should the workman succeed, will mean that he receives some compensation for his injuries without having to prove negligence. However, he must show that there has been a breach of the Act and that he and the damage done to him come within the wording of the section pleaded.

17.3 Offices, Shops and Railway Premises Act, 1963

There is little to be said about this Act. In nature and approach it is the same as the Factories Act. Indeed, it is the equivalent of the Factories Act as it applies to offices, shops and railway premises. The duties, while similar, are not as extensive as those contained in the Factories Act. The reason for this is that there are not as many hazards to cater for in offices, etc. as in factories. The interpretation of the wording of the sections is the same as in the Factories Act – for example, Section 17 which deals with the fencing of machinery, is subject to the same tests as Section 14 of the Factories Act.

17.4 Health and Safety at Work etc. Act, 1974

17.4.1 Origin

This Act is regarded as the watershed for the current legislative approach towards health and safety at work. The 1974 Act arose out of the 1972 Report of the Committee on Health and Safety at Work. This is known more familiarly as the Robens Report. In this report criticism was made of the existing legislation, on the grounds that it was restrictive in application, i.e. it applied only in specific types of premises, such as factories, mines and quarries. Indeed, at the time of the report a million people had no protection at all, as they worked in premises not covered by any legislation, e.g. health service staff, local government, telephone engineers; there was too much legislation for the occupier to remember and some of it was obsolete – there were over 500 pieces of legislation, many of which were rarely enforced; there was evidence that the legislation was no longer effective as the rate of reduction in accidents at work had become static; the existing strict liability approach had come to rely on 'policing' by the Factory Inspectorate and there was a shortage of inspectors.

The Robens Report recommended new legislation, which would apply to everyone at work and also offer protection to the public. This new statute would encourage a positive approach on the part of management towards health and safety in the workplace. Also, participation by trade unions and employees was to be encouraged. The 1974 Act fulfils many of the recommendations made by the Committee.

17.4.2 Premises

Unlike the Factories Act, the Health and Safety at Work Act does not use terms such as 'premises' or 'occupier'. The duties imposed by the 1974 Act are imposed on the employer, and therefore protection is afforded to everyone employed. As we shall see, the Act goes even further than this by placing duties on the self-employed, employees and manufacturers and suppliers of articles and substances. Protection is also given to members of the public.

17.4.3 Scope of duty

Duties imposed on employers in respect of their employees

These duties are of a general nature, in that Section 2 requires the employer 'to ensure so far as is reasonably practicable the health, safety, and welfare at work of all his employees'. The section then refers to particular matters which are covered by the duties. These are as follows:

1 The provision and maintenance of plant and systems of work that are safe and without risks to health. This covers such things as the guarding of machinery, planned preventative maintenance on lifting tackle etc.

2 Arrangements for ensuring the safe use, handling, storage and transport of articles and substances. This covers, for example, the use of acids or toxic substances, such as cadmium or mercury.

3 The provision of such information, instruction, training and supervision as is necessary to ensure the health and safety at work of his employees. This recognizes the need to assess the risks and to provide the workforce with the necessary training etc., so that they are informed of the dangers, and know how to avoid accidents arising from these dangers.

For example, special training may have to be given to inexperienced employees using dangerous machinery, and they will have to undergo a period of supervision. It would not satisfy the requirements of the Act if they were merely told about the risks, but not told how to guard against them.

In *R* v. *Swan Hunter Shipbuilders Ltd* (1981), it was held that this duty extends to the instruction and training of contractors if it is necessary in order to protect employees.

4 The maintenance of any place of work under the employer's control in a condition which is safe and without risks to health. Also, the provision and maintenance of a safe means of access to and from the place of work.

It does not satisfy the requirements of the Act merely to provide a safe place of work without any thought as to the access to and from such a place. For example, proper crawling boards may have been provided for roof work. However, if a ladder with a broken rung is the only means of access and egress to and from the roof, then the employer is in breach of his duty.

5 The provision and maintenance of a working environment that is safe, without risks to health, and adequate as regards facilities and arrangements for their welfare at work.

This requirement gives much greater scope than the requirements of the Factories Act. It is not confined to the provision of toilets or drinking water, but can be used in relation to no smoking areas, eating areas etc.

Whilst the HASAWA appears to be much wider in scope than the Factories Act, all of the requirements considered above are subject to the term 'so far as is reasonably practicable'. This clearly lessens the burden on the employer, as the following interpretation of this term by Asquith L. J. in *Edwards* v. *NCB* (1949) illustrates:

> 'Reasonably practicable' is a narrower term than 'physically possible', and seems to me to imply that a computation must be made by the owner in which the quantum or risk is placed on one scale and the sacrifice involved in the measures necessary for averting the risk (whether in money, time or trouble) is placed in the other, and that, if it be shown that there is a gross disproportion between them — the risk being insignificant in relation to the sacrifice — the defendants discharge the onus on them. Moreover this computation falls to be made by the owner at a point of time anterior to the accident.

Although this interpretation was made prior to the passing of the 1974 Act, it is the accepted interpretation of the words 'reasonably practicable'. It serves to illustrate the difficulties faced by the enforcement agencies in enforcing the 1974 Act or indeed any requirement which uses the words 'reasonably practicable', as the employer is allowed to introduce factors such as finance and time — if these outweigh the risk, the employer need not reduce or eliminate the 'danger' to his employees. Whether such factors should be taken into account where there is a risk of injury is open to debate.

In order to assist the employer in fulfilling his duties under Section 2 and to ensure that he adopts a positive approach to health and safety, Section 2(3) requires him to prepare a written safety policy; (note, this is confined to establishments with 20 or more employees). This safety policy should show the employer's commitment to the health and safety of his employees, and should lay down the arrangements made and the organization for carrying out the policy. All employees must have notice of the policy, and it must be revised as often as necessary.

Duties owed to persons other than employees

Section 3 places a further duty on the employer to conduct his undertaking in such a way as to ensure that persons not in his employment who may be affected are not exposed to risks to their health and safety. This duty does not extend to welfare. There is a corresponding duty on self-employed persons.

Self-employed persons are also obliged not to expose themselves to unnecessary risks. This section is also subject to the term 'so far as is reasonably practicable'.

For example, demolition work may be taking place in a busy high street and if a passer-by is injured by falling masonry, this would be a breach of Section 3.

Section 4 places a duty on persons in control of premises to ensure that the access and egress and any plant or substances in the premises are safe and without risks to the health of persons using the premises, who are not employees.

This section is intended to protect contractors, such as window cleaners or plumbers etc. who are not employed on the premises but have access to them on certain occasions.

Duties owed by designers, manufacturers, suppliers etc. in respect of articles and substances for use at work

Section 6 imposes a duty on any person who designs, manufactures, imports or supplies any article or substance for use at work:

1 To ensure that it is safe and without risks to health when properly used.

2 To carry out any tests or examination as may be necessary in order to comply with 1 above.

3 To make available adequate information about the use of the product to ensure it will be safe and without risks to health. The designer or manufacturer is under a duty to carry out research in order to eliminate or minimize any risks to health and safety to which the design of the article or substance may give rise.

There is also a duty on the person who erects or installs the article to ensure that there is nothing in the way it is installed or erected, which makes it unsafe, or a risk to health, when properly used.

All of the duties referred to here are subject to the term 'so far as is reasonably practicable'. This section recognizes that health and safety begin with design and manufacture. Obviously if an article is designed or manufactured outside the UK, the onus moves to the importer or supplier to comply with current UK standards. In theory, if Section 6 is complied with, the responsibilities on the employer become less onerous. To be covered by Section 6 the article or substance need not be used exclusively at work, e.g. some agricultural chemicals can be obtained in small quantities for use by householders. However, the duty does not cater for their improper use, i.e. used without regard to any relevant information or advice relating to its use which has been made available by the designer, manufacturer, importer or supplier.

Duties of employees

By virtue of Section 7 every employee must:

1 Take reasonable care of his own health and safety and that of persons who may be affected by his acts or omissions.

2 Cooperate with his employer or any other person on whom there is a duty or requirement imposed by statute, to enable such a person to comply with the duty or requirement.

This recognizes that safety is also the responsibility of the employee, and it serves to increase his awareness with respect to health and safety at work. However, in practice the onus does not move to the employee until the employer has fulfilled his obligations. For example, the employer cannot succeed in arguing that the employee should not have put his hand in the machine, if the machine was not provided with the correct standard of guarding. Cooperation is an essential element in establishing good safety practices; so, if the employer is obliged to provide eye protection, there is a corresponding obligation on the employee to wear it.

Finally, Section 8 places a duty on all persons, including employers and employees. Section 8 makes it unlawful for a person to intentionally or recklessly interfere with or misuse anything provided in the interests of health, safety or welfare under the statutory provisions. For example, if someone took the guard off a machine, this would be a breach of Section 8.

17.4.4 Civil remedy

Unlike the Factories Act, there is no civil remedy for breach of statutory duty for breaches of Sections 2–7; this is expressly excluded by Section 47. However, there may be an action for damages arising out of a breach of regulations made under the 1974 Act, unless the regulations specifically exclude it.

17.5 Enforcement

Although the enforcement provisions are contained in the HASAWA, they apply equally to the Factories Act and any regulations made under it. The 1974 Act gives wider powers of enforcement than were available under the Factories Act, and sets up the Health and Safety Commission and Health and Safety Executive.

Enforcement of the statutory provisions is carried out by the Health and Safety Executive (HSE), which is divided into various Inspectorates, e.g. Factory Inspectorate, Agricultural Inspectorate, Nuclear Installations Inspectorate, etc. The HSE is answerable to the Commission. It is the duty of the Commission to promote health and safety at work, carry out research, publish information, carry out investigations, inquiries and so on.

The following diagram illustrates the organization for the enforcement of health and safety matters:

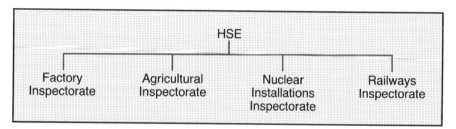

17.5.1 Powers

Inspectors appointed by the HSE are given specific powers under Section 20 of the 1974 Act. These powers are extensive, in order to enable inspectors to carry out their jobs properly. Inspectors have a right of entry into premises covered by the Acts. Whilst on those premises, they can, for example, take with them any persons or equipment as is necessary to enable them to carry out their investigations. They can take photographs, measurements, samples and recordings and require persons to answer any questions they think fit to ask.

17.5.2 Enforcement action

Where a breach of the statutory provisions is found, the inspector may take various actions:

1 If the breach is regarded as minor in nature, he may give verbal instructions, or more likely he will write, informing the employer of the breach and perhaps suggesting how it may be remedied.

2 If the breach is more serious, he may issue an improvement notice which stipulates the breach, and gives the person contravening the Act a certain time by which the improvement must be carried out. The notice may suggest various ways in which compliance can take place. If there is a breach which involves, or may involve, a risk of serious personal injury, a prohibition notice may be served prohibiting the activity. The activity must cease until the contravention has been remedied. The notice may specify how this should be done. There is a right of appeal to an industrial tribunal for the person on whom the notice is served.

3 Finally, the inspector may bring a prosecution for any breach of the statutory provisions. However, in practice, a prosecution is only likely where there has been an accident or where there have been continuous breaches of the law. Prosecution is automatic for failing to comply with an improvement or prohibition notice.

17.6 Safety regulations

The safety regulations are too numerous to mention in specific detail. However, there are in existence regulations made under the Factories Act and the HASAWA, although regulations made after 1974 are made under the HASAWA. The plan for the future is to repeal the Factories Act and the regulations made under it, and to use the powers in the HASAWA to make regulations which are more general in scope.

This is illustrated by noting that regulations made under the Factories Act are very specific and are intended to supplement the provision of that Act, e.g. Power Press Regulations 1965, Woodworking Machines Regulations 1974; whereas regulations made under the HASAWA are intended to compliment the provisions of that Act, e.g. Packaging and Labelling of Dangerous Substances Regulations, Manual Handling Regulations 1985 etc.

Two sets of regulations need to be mentioned in a little more detail:

17.6.1 The Safety Representatives and Safety Committees Regulations 1977

These regulations were made under Section 2(3) of the HASAWA and are recognition of the importance of trade union and employee participation in promoting health and safety at work. The regulations encourage the appointment of safety representatives by trade unions from the employees at a given establishment; these appointed representatives take part in consultations with the employer. The regulations also provide for the setting up of safety committees. Safety representatives are allowed time off to carry out their duties under the regulations.

17.6.2 The Health and Safety (Enforcing Authority) Regulations 1977, & 1982

These make provision for the local authority to be the enforcing authority in certain cases – generally in respect of lower risk activities, e.g. office activities, warehouses, laundrettes. These activities are kept under review and from time to time other activities are transferred to the local authority, e.g. zoos, motor vehicle repair workshops.

Sample questions

1 Outline the statutory provisions relating to the fencing of the dangerous parts of machinery, with reference to the ways in which the Courts have interpreted these provisions.

Suggested answer

The following points should be considered:

The main area to be considered is Section 14 of the Factories Act 1961, although you may also wish to refer to any regulations relating to specific machinery, such as the Woodworking Machines Regulations 1974. Before considering Section 14 you should make the point that the Factories Act imposes an absolute duty on the occupier of a factory, in respect of Section 14, and no proof of negligence is required before an offence is committed.

In referring to Section 14 itself you need to consider the test formulated in *John Summers & Sons Ltd* v. *Frost* for establishing what amounts to a dangerous part, i.e. a reasonably foreseeable cause of injury to anybody acting in a way in which a human being may be reasonably expected to act in circumstances which may be reasonably expected to occur (*Uddin* v. *Associated Portland Cement Manufacturers Ltd*).

You should also refer to the standard of fencing required under Sections 14 and 16, in the light of *John Summers Ltd* v. *Frost*, and *Close* v. *Steel Co of Wales*.

2 Explain how the health and safety legislation is enforced and what action can be taken by the enforcement officers.

Suggested answer

The following points should be considered:

The easiest way of illustrating enforcement is through the use of a flow-chart. You can then offer a further explanation of the enforcement authority.

The main enforcement agency is the Health and Safety Executive (HSE) and inspectors appointed by HSE, known as Factory Inspectors, carry out the day-to-day enforcement work, i.e. inspections, accident investigations and the investigation of complaints. Some enforcement work, e.g. in offices and shops is carried out by Environmental Health Officers who work for the local authorities.

The HASAWA, 1974 gives specific powers to Inspectors to enable them to carry out their duties, e.g. a right of entry, a power to take samples etc. You need to consider the action which can be taken by an inspector if there is a breach of the law or one is about to be committed. If there is a breach of the law the inspector may prosecute, or he may issue an improvement notice or a prohibition notice; if a breach of the law is imminent he may issue a prohibition notice; you would need to explain when notices may be issued and their effect.

3 An accident occurs in your workshop when one of your employees is injured on the unguarded cutter of a horizontal milling machine. A guard has been provided in the past but it was damaged as it was in constant use; it was then removed from the machine by an unknown person and you have never bothered to check that it had been replaced. Discuss the possible breaches of the criminal law.

Suggested answer

The following points should be considered:
You need to consider whether there has been a breach of Section 14 of the Factories Act 1961 and Section 2 of the HASAWA, 1974. Remember that the Factories Act imposes an absolute duty on the occupier of a factory so it would be no defence to argue that one had been provided and it was not the occupiers' fault that it had been removed – see also Section 16 regarding maintenance. You would have to consider the wording of Section 14 and its interpretation in order to establish that the cutters on a horizontal milling machine could be classified as a dangerous part.

In considering Section 2 of the HASAWA you would need to point out that this is a lesser standard than Section 14 of the FA because of the words 'so far as is reasonably practicable'; however, what is required of the employer under Section 2 would be the same standard of guarding unless it could be shown that the cost of guarding outweighed the risk, which is unlikely where the part of a machine is regarded as dangerous under Section 14. In considering whether the employer has a defence under Section 2 it is unlikely that he would be able to succeed on the basis that he had provided a guard once but this had been removed by persons unknown. The duty under Section 2 would require the employer to check that guards were maintained and replaced as necessary.

4 Explain the significance and scope of the Health and Safety at Work etc. Act, 1974 and its relationship with the Factories Act 1961.

Suggested answer

The following points should be considered:
You should explain why the HASAWA, 1974 came about, i.e. reference should be made to the Robens Report and its criticism of the existing legislation and the fact that over eight million people had no protection under the existing legislation while they were at work because it only applied to factories, construction sites etc.

Further reading

Selwyn, N. *The Law of Health and Safety at Work* (Butterworths)
Holmes, A. G. M. and Painter, R. W. *Employment Law* (Blackstone Press)

18 Partnership law

This chapter deals with one of the most common forms of business organization, the partnership. Existing commercial practice, as recognized by the common law, was codified in the Partnership Act, 1890, and where the Act is silent it is still common law principles which apply. Many of the provisions of that Act may be modified by agreement between the partners. The Limited Partnership Act of 1907 permits the formation of limited partnerships. These are not very common, but their key features are:

1 They must be registered with the Companies Registry.

2 A limited partner is not liable for partnership debts beyond the extent of his capital contribution, which he is not permitted to remove.

3 A limited partner is not permitted to take part in the management of the partnership, and cannot bind it to any transaction.

18.1 Definition of partnership

Section 1 of the Partnership Act (PA) states that 'partnership is the relation which subsists between persons carrying on a business in common with a view to profit'. It should be noted with regard to this definition that:

1 Companies are expressly excluded by the section.

2 A business must be carried on. Business includes any trade, occupation, or profession. The mere fact that people jointly own property does not necessarily mean that they are partners.

3 Partnerships usually continue over an extended period of time, but they can be formed for a single business venture.

4 The business must be carried on with a view to profit, therefore neither charitable, nor mutual benefit endeavours constitute partnerships.

5 Although the receipt of a share of profits is *prima facie* evidence of a partnership relationship, it is not conclusive. For example, a person is not treated as a partner in the following cases:

(a) where he receives payment of a debt by installments from business profits;

(b) where he receives his wages in the form of a share of profit;

(c) where he receives interest on a loan to a business which varies in relation to profits.

18.2 The legal status of a partnership

A partnership is simply a group of individuals collectively involved in a business activity. It has no separate personality distinct from the persons who together form it. (As will be seen, the law does distinguish between companies and their members.) Section 4 of the PA, however, does recognize an element of unity. It provides for the partnership being known collectively as a firm, and permits the business to be carried out under the firm's name. Legal action may be taken by and against the partners in the firm's name.

18.3 Formation of a partnership

18.3.1 The partnership agreement

Partnerships arise from the agreement of two or more persons to carry on a business enterprise together. The rules relating to the contents of any such agreement are those of general contract law. There are no specific legal requirements governing the formation of a partnership. The agreement may be made by deed, in writing, or by word of mouth. Agreement may even be implied from conduct. It is usual, however, for the agreement to be set out in written form. In such circumstances, this document is known as the 'Articles of Partnership'. The parties involved decide what should be included in the Articles. Any gaps are filled in by the Partnership Acts or the common law. Provisions in Articles of Partnership usually relate to the matters such as the nature of the business to be transacted, the name of the firm, the capital contributions made by the individual partners, the drawing up of the business accounts, the method of determining and sharing profits, the dissolution of the partnership.

18.3.2   Illegal partnership and the number of partners

A partnership is illegal if it is formed **either** to carry out an illegal purpose, **or** to carry out a legal purpose in an illegal manner. In such cases, the Court will not recognize any partnership rights between the persons involved, but it will permit innocent third parties, who have no knowledge of any illegality, to recover against them.

Partnerships are generally not lawful if they consist of more than 20 persons (Companies Act, 1985, Section 716). However, certain professional partnerships, such as solicitors, accountants, surveyors, etc., are exempt from this maximum limit.

18.3.3   Capacity

The common law rules generally relating to capacity to enter into contracts are equally applicable in regard to the membership of partnerships. Thus, any partnership agreement entered into by a minor is voidable during his minority, and for a reasonable time after the attainment of his majority. Third parties cannot recover against partners who are minors, but they can recover against the other, adult, partners. If the former minor has not repudiated the partnership agreement within a reasonable time of majority, then he will be liable for any debts as a *de facto* partner.

Mental incapacity does not necessarily prevent a person from entering into a partnership, but subsequent mental incapacity is grounds for having the partnership dissolved.

18.3.4   The firm's name

Partnerships can use the words '& Company' in their names, but are prohibited from using the word 'limited' or any related abbreviation. The partnership can use the names of the partners, or it may trade under a collective firm name. Any name must comply with both the Business Names Act, 1985, and the common law provisions relating to the tort of 'passing off'.

1 Business Names Act, 1985

This requires that, where the firm does not carry out its business under the surnames of all the partners, then the names of those partners must be displayed on the business premises and on the stationery. In addition, the Act requires the approval of the Secretary of State before certain names can be used. There is no longer any need to register business names.

2 'Passing off'

The law does not permit anyone to use a name which is likely to divert business to him by suggesting that the business is actually that of some other person, or is connected with that of another person. See *Ewing* v. *Buttercup Margarine Company Ltd* (1917).

18.4   The relation of partners one to another

18.4.1   Content and variation of the partnership agreement

Partners are free to make and change the rules concerning their internal affairs as they see fit; provided there is unanimous agreement (Section 19 of the PA). Consent does not have to be expressed, but may be inferred from conduct.

Pilling v. Pilling (1887)

The articles of partnership entered into between a father and his two sons stated, amongst other things, that the business was to be financed with the father's capital, which was to remain his personal property, rather than partnership property. It also stated that the father was to receive interest on the capital. In practice, the sons as well as the father received interest on capital.

Held: The capital supplied by the father was to be treated as partnership property, as the conduct of the parties had amounted to a valid alteration of the written agreement.

18.4.2 Partnership property

Property may be used by the partnership as a whole, yet remain the personal property of only one of the partners. During the continuation of the firm, partnership property constitutes a joint estate: i.e. partners are joint owners of the property as a whole. The distinction between partnership property and personal property is important for a number of reasons:

1 Section 20 of the PA states that partnership property must be dealt with exclusively for partnership purposes.

2 Any increase in value of partnership property belongs to the firm, whereas any increase in the value of personal property belongs to the person who owns the property.

3 On the dissolution of the firm, partnership property is applied in the payment of debts before personal property.

4 Partnership property and personal property are treated differently in the satisfaction of claims made by partnership creditors, as opposed to personal creditors. A writ can only be executed against partnership property in respect of a judgment against the partnership (Section 23 of the PA). The personal creditor may, however, apply for a charging order against the partner's share in the partnership.

The other partners may redeem the charge at any time by paying off the debt, in which case the charge becomes vested in them.

5 On the death of a partner, any interest in partnership land will pass as personalty, whereas any land owned personally will pass as realty. The effect of this may be that the interest will pass to different persons.

Section 20 of the PA states that partnership property consists of all property brought into the partnership stock or acquired on account or for the purposes of the firm. Any property bought with money belonging to the firm is deemed to have been bought on account of the firm (Section 21). Whether any particular property belongs to the firm or not is always a matter of fact, depending on the circumstances of the case in question. If there is no express agreement that property is to be brought into the firm as partnership property, the Court will only imply such a term to the extent required to make the partnership agreement effective.

Miles v. Clarke (1953)

Clarke had carried on a photography business for some time before taking Miles into partnership. The partnership agreement merely provided that the profits were to be divided equally. When the partners quarrelled, a dispute arose with regard to the assets used by the partnership.

Held: Only the consumable stock-in-trade could be considered as partnership property. The lease of the business premises and other plant and equipment remained the personal property of the partner who introduced them into the business.

18.4.3 Assignment of a share in a partnership

Unless the partnership agreement states otherwise, a partner is at liberty to mortgage or assign absolutely his share in the partnership to an outsider. The assignee is only entitled to the share of profits due to the assigning partner, or, on dissolution, to the appropriate share of partnership assets. He does not become a partner and has no right to involve himself in the management of the business. (Section 31 of the PA.)

> *Garwood v. Paynter* (1903)
>
> Garwood charged his share of a partnership to a trust, of which his wife was one of the beneficiaries. When the partners later began to pay themselves salaries, Mrs Garwood objected, on the basis that such payment reduced the income of the trust.
>
> **Held:** The payment of salaries was a management matter, and therefore the trustees, who were assignees under Section 31, could not interfere, in the absence of fraud.

The assignee does not take over responsibility for partnership debts. These remain the liability of the assignor. Where, however, the assignment is absolute, the assignee must indemnify the assignor.

18.4.4 Rights of partners

Unless the partnership agreement provides otherwise, partners may exercise the following rights under Section 24 of the PA:

1 To share equally in the capital and profits of the business, and to contribute equally to any losses.

2 To be indemnified by the firm for any liabilities incurred or payments made in the course of the firm's business.

3 To receive interest at the rate of 5 per cent on any payment made on behalf of the firm, or advance to the firm beyond his agreed capital contribution. No interest is payable on capital, unless the partnership agreement so provides.

4 To take part in the management of the business. A partner is not entitled to remuneration for acting in the partnership business unless so provided. It is common for partnership agreements to contain such provisions.

5 To have access to the firm's books, which are to be kept at the firm's principal place of business.

6 To prevent the admission of a new partner, or prevent any change in the nature of the partnership business. Such changes require unanimous consent. Other differences may be decided by a majority.

Section 25 provides that no majority of partners can expel any partner, unless such a power is contained in the partnership agreement. Even where there is such a power, it must be exercised in good faith.

18.4.5 Duties of partners

Partners are under an implied general duty to deal with fellow partners in utmost good faith. In addition, the Partnership Act lays down specific duties, as follows:

1 The duty of disclosure (Section 28). Partners must render true accounts and full information of all things affecting the partnership to any partner or their legal representative.

> *Law v. Law* (1905)
>
> One partner accepted an offer from the other to buy his share of the firm. He discovered only later that certain partnership assets had not been disclosed to him, and sought to have the contract set aside.
>
> **Held:** The purchasing partner had breached the duty of disclosure, and the agreement could have been set aside. In fact, there had been a settlement of the dispute, so no such order was granted.

2 The duty to account to the firm for any benefit obtained, without consent, from any transaction concerning the partnership, or its property, name, or business connection (Section 29).

> *Bentley v. Craven* (1953)
>
> Craven was in partnership with the plaintiff in a sugar refinery business. He bought sugar on his own account and sold it to the partnership at a profit, without informing the other partners.
>
> **Held:** That the partnership was entitled to recover the profit.

3 The duty not to compete with the partnership business (Section 30). Any profits made through competition must be paid over to the partnership.

18.5 Relation of partners to persons dealing with them

18.5.1 The authority of partners to bind the firm

Every partner is an agent of the firm and of his other partners for the purpose of the business (Section 5 of the PA). Each partner, therefore, has the power to bind, and make his co-partners liable on partnership business transaction by him. A partnership agreement may, however, expressly limit the powers of any partner. The effect of such limitations with regard to outsiders is as follows.

If the other partners have given their prior approval for a partner to exceed his powers, then the partner in question has express actual authority, and the firm is bound by his action. If they approve the action after it has been done they are also liable. In this case they are said to have ratified the transaction. The firm may still be bound even where the other partners have not approved the excess of authority, as long as the partner has acted within his implied powers, i.e. within the usual scope of authority of a partner.

> *Mercantile Credit v. Garrod* (1962)
>
> Parkin and Garrod were partners in a garage business mainly concerned with letting garages and repairing cars. The partnership agreement expressly excluded the sale of cars. After Parkin had sold a car (to which he had no title) to the plaintiffs, they claimed back the money paid from Garrod.
>
> **Held:** The selling of cars was, from the point of view of an outsider, within the usual course of business of a garage. Parkin, therefore, had acted within his implied authority and the firm was liable to repay the money.

If the outsider is aware that the partner has no authority to act, then the firm is not bound by the transaction.

18.5.2 The extent of a partner's implied authority

Every partner (other than a limited partner) is presumed to have the implied authority to enter into the following transactions:

1 selling goods of the firm;

2 purchasing goods of a kind normally required by the firm;

3 receiving payments and giving receipts for debts due to the firm;

4 engaging employees for the purposes of the firm's business;

5 employing a solicitor to act for the firm, either in defending an action or pursuing an action for debt.

The above implied powers apply equally to trading and non-trading partnerships. Partners in trading firms, those which essentially buy and sell goods, have the following additional implied powers;

6 accepting, drawing, issuing, transferring or endorsing bills of exchange or other negotiable instruments on behalf of the firm. Partners in non-trading firms only have powers in relation to ordinary cheques;

7 borrowing money on the credit of the firm;

8 pledging the firm's goods, or making an equitable mortgage for the purpose of borrowing.

18.6 The nature of partners' liability

Every partner is responsible for the full amount of his firm's liability. Outsiders have the choice of taking action against the firm collectively, or against the individual partners. Where damages are recovered from one partner only, the other partners are under a duty to contribute equally to the amount paid.

18.6.1 Liability on debts and contracts

The liability of partners in regard to debts or contracts is joint (Section 9 of the PA). The effect of joint liability used to be that, although the partners were collectively responsible, a person who took action against one of the partners could take no further action against the other partners, even if he had not recovered all that was owing to him.

This situation was remedied by the Civil Liability (Contributions) Act, 1978. This effectively provides that a judgment against one partner does not prevent a subsequent action against the other partners, even where the liability is said to be a joint one.

18.6.2 Liability for torts

The liability of partners in regard to torts or other wrongs committed in the ordinary course of the firm's business is joint and several (see Section 10 of the PA). Where liability is joint and several, there is no bar on taking successive actions against partners in order to recover all that is due.

The wrong sued on must have been committed in the ordinary course of partnership business, or with the express approval of all of the partners. If a tort is committed outside this scope, then the partner responsible is personally liable.

> *Hamlyn* v. *Houston & Co* (1905)
>
> One partner in Houston & Co bribed a clerk employed by the plaintiff to gain information about their rival's business. Hamlyn sued the partnership to recover the loss he had sustained as a consequence.
>
> **Held:** The firm was liable in damages for the wrongful act of the one partner, as he had acted within the usual scope of his authority, although he had used illegal methods in so doing.

> *Arbuckle* v. *Taylor* (1815)
>
> A partner in a firm instituted criminal proceedings against Arbuckle for the alleged theft of partnership property. Arbuckle sued for malicious prosecution and wrongful imprisonment.
>
> **Held:** It was not within the general scope of the firm's business to institute criminal proceedings, and therefore the partner who did so was solely liable.

18.6.3 The liability of incoming and outgoing partners

A person who is admitted into an existing firm is not liable to creditors of the firm for anything done before he became a partner (Section 17 of the PA, 1890). The new partner can, however, assume such responsibility by way of novation. (This is the process whereby a retiring partner is discharged from existing liability, and the newly constituted partnership takes the liability on themselves.)

Novation is a tripartite contract involving the retiring partner; the new firm; and the existing creditors. As creditors are effectively giving up rights against the retiring partner, their approval is required. This approval can be express or may be inferred from the course of dealing between the creditor and the firm.

> *Thompson* v. *Percival* (1834)
>
> Charles and James Percival had been in partnership, until Charles retired. The plaintiff creditors, on applying for payment, were informed that James alone would be responsible for payment as Charles had retired. They therefore drew a bill for payment against James alone.
>
> **Held:** It was implied from Thompson's conduct that they had accepted the discharge of Charles from his liability.

Creditors do not have to accept a novation. A creditor may still hold the retired partner responsible for any liabilities due at the time of his retirement. The newly-constituted firm may, however, agree to indemnify the retiring partner against any such claims.

Apart from novation, a retired partner remains liable for any debts or obligations incurred by the partnership prior to his retirement (Section 17 of the PA, 1890). The date when the contract was made decides the question of liability. If the person was a partner when the contract was entered into, then he is responsible, even if the goods are delivered after he has left the firm. The estate of a deceased partner is only liable for those debts or obligations arising before his death.

Where a person deals with a firm after a change in its membership, he is entitled to treat all the apparent members of the old firm as still being members until he receives notice of the change (see Section 36 of the PA 1890). In order to avoid liability for future contracts a retiring partner must:

1 ensure that individual notice of his retirement is given to existing customers of the firm; and

2 advertise his retirement in *The London Gazette*. This serves as general notice to persons who were not customers of the firm prior to the partner's retirement, but were aware that he had been a partner. This is effective whether it is actually read or not. (This is known as constructive notice.)

Failure to advertise in the *Gazette* does not make a retired partner responsible to persons who had no previous dealings with the firm, and did not know that he had ever been a partner.

> *Tower Cabinet Co Ltd* v. *Ingram* (1949)
>
> Ingram and Christmas had been partners in a firm known as Merry's. After it was dissolved by mutual agreement, Christmas carried on trading under the firm's name. Notice was given to those dealing with the firm that Ingram was no longer connected with the business, but no notice was placed in *The London Gazette*. New notepaper was printed without Ingram's name. However, when the plaintiffs, who had had no previous dealings with the firm received an order, it was written on old paper bearing Ingram's name. Ingram had no knowledge of this. When the Tower Cabinet company obtained a judgment for the price of the goods supplied, they sought to enforce it against Ingram.
>
> **Held:** Ingram was not liable, as he had not represented himself to be a partner, nor had the plaintiffs been aware of his membership prior to the dissolution.

18.6.4 Partnership by estoppel

Failure to give notice of retirement is one way in which liability arises on the basis of estoppel, or 'holding out'.

Any person who represents himself, or knowingly permits himself to be represented, as a partner is liable to any person who gives the firm credit on the basis of that representation (Section 14 of the PA). Such a person does not actually become a partner, although he is treated as if he were a partner by third parties.

In *Tower Cabinet Co Ltd* v. *Ingram*, the defendant was not affected by Section 14 as he was not aware that he had been represented as a partner.

18.7 Dissolution of a partnership

18.7.1 Grounds for dissolution

Subject to any provisions in the partnership agreement, the PA provides that a partnership is dissolved:

1 By the expiry of a fixed term or the completion of a specified enterprise (Section 32). If a partnership continues after the preset limit it is known as a partnership at will, and it can be ended at any time thereafter, at the wish of any partner.

2 By notice if the partnership is of indefinite duration (Section 32).

3 By mutual consent.

4 By the death or bankruptcy of any partner (Section 33).

5 By the occurrence of events making the continuation of the partnership illegal. An example would be where a firm contained an enemy alien in wartime.

In addition the Court may, by virtue of Section 35, order the dissolution of the partnership under the following circumstances:

1 A partner suffers from mental disorders.

2 A partner suffers from some other permanent incapacity.

3 A partner conducts himself in a way prejudicial to the carrying on of the business.

4 A partner persistently commits a breach of the partnership agreement, or so conducts himself as to make it unreasonable for the other partners to carry on in business with him.

5 Where the business can only be carried on at a loss.

6 Where any circumstances have arisen which, in the opinion of the Court, make it just and equitable to dissolve the partnership.

After dissolution, the authority of each partner to bind the firm continues, so far as is necessary to wind up the firm's affairs, and complete transactions begun but unfinished at the time of dissolution (Section 38). They cannot enter into new contracts.

18.7.2   Treatment of assets on dissolution

On dissolution, the value of the partnership property is realized and the proceeds are applied in the following order:

1 In paying debts to outsiders.

2 In paying each partner any advance made to the firm beyond his capital.

3 In paying partnership capital.

4 Any residue is divided between the partners in the same proportion as they shared in profits (see Section 44 of the PA).

If the assets are insufficient to meet debts, partners' advances, and capital, then the deficiency has to be made good out of any profits held back from previous years, **or** out of partners' capital, **or** by the partners individually in the proportion in which they were entitled to profits.

An example will clarify this procedure. Partners A, B and C contributed £5000, £3000 and £1000 respectively. A made an advance of £1000. On dissolution, the assets realized £8000, and the firm had outstanding debts amounting to £2500. The procedure was as follows:

1 the creditors were paid off from the sum realized: (£8000 − £2500; leaving £5500).

2 A's advance of £1000 was paid back; leaving £4500;

3 assuming no agreement to the contrary, profits and losses were shared equally. The actual loss on capital is as follows:

Original capital	£9000
Minus money left	£4500
	= £4500

This loss of £4500 has to be shared equally in this case; each has to provide £1500 to make good the shortfall in capital.

In the case of A and B, this is a paper transaction, as the payment due is simply subtracted from their original capital contribution.

However, C actually has to make a contribution of £500 from his personal wealth, as his due payment exceeds his original capital. Thus:

A's share of net assets is £5000 less £1500 = £3500

B's share of net assets is £3000 less £1500 = £1500

C's share of net assets is £1000 less £1500 = −£500

A provision in the partnership agreement for profits to be shared in proportion to capital contribution would have the following effect: As capital was contributed in the ratio of 5:3:1, this would be the ratio in which the capital loss would be apportioned:

A would contribute $\frac{5}{9}$th of the £4500, i.e. £2500.

B would contribute $\frac{3}{9}$th of the £4500, i.e. £1500.

C would contribute $\frac{1}{9}$th of the £4500, i.e. £500.

Their shares in net assets would therefore be as follows:

A: (£5000 − £2500) = £2500,

B: (£3000 − £1500) = £1500.

C: (£1000 − £500) = £500.

18.7.3 Bankruptcy of partners

When a partner is bankrupt on the dissolution of a firm, the partnership assets are still used to pay partnership debts. It is only after the payment of partnership debts that any residue due to that partner is made available for the payment of the partner's personal creditors.

Where one partner is insolvent and there is a deficiency of partnership assets to repay the firm's creditors and any advances, the burden of making good the shortfall has to be borne by the solvent partners in proportion to their share in profits. If, however, the deficiency relates only to capital, the procedure is governed by the rule in *Garner* v. *Murray* (1904). This states that in such a situation the solvent partners are not required to make good the capital deficiency, due to the insolvency of their co-partner. As a consequence, there will be a shortfall in the capital fund, which has to be made good by the solvent partners in proportion to their capitals.

To return to the original example:

The net assets were £4500 and the capital deficiency was £4500. All three partners were to contribute £1500. In effect, C was the only one to actually pay out any money, the others merely suffering an abatement in the capital returned to them. However, the assumption now is that C is insolvent and can make no contribution. He loses his right to repayment, and this reduces the fund required from £9000 to £8000.

As previously, A and B contribute their portion of the total loss, taking the capital fund up to £7500.

There still remains a shortfall of £500. This is borne by A and B in proportion of their capital. Thus, A suffers a loss of $\frac{5}{8}$th of £500; and B a loss of $\frac{3}{8}$th of £500.

So, from the capital fund of £7500:

A receives £5000 − ($\frac{5}{8}$ × £500) = £4687.50 (in reality he simply receives £3187.50).

B receives £3000 − ($\frac{3}{8}$ × £500) = £2812.50 (in reality he simply receives £1312.50).

Sample questions

1 F, G and H decided to develop a new business as partners. They all agree to supply starting capital, but it was agreed that H's liability was to be limited to £1000, which he duly paid to the partnership. Since the partnership started, F borrowed £5000 from the partnership's bank account and, without the knowledge of G and H, he used it on his house. G subsequently ordered a large quantity of raw materials for the business, but the bank has advised him that there are insufficient funds in the account to pay for them.

Further, the partnership is being sued by a customer for alleged personal injury after using a product made by the partnership. *ACCA*

Suggested answer

This question can be split into four parts:

The first part relates to H and requires consideration of the provisions of the Limited Partnership Act, 1907, in particular, how limited partnerships are formed, the restricted powers of the limited partner, and the extent of his liability.

The second part concerns the partners' implied authority, and specifically to F's borrowing. As a trading firm, the partners have the implied authority to borrow money on the firm's credit. Unless the bank is aware that F is acting outside his authority, the partnership is liable on the debt. If the firm has insufficient funds to pay, then F and G are liable to repay the money individually out of their personal assets. H's liability is fixed at his £1000 capital.

In the third part, similarly, G has the authority to order goods for use in the course of the firm's business. It should be noted that although liability is joint in regard to debts and contracts, this no longer means that judgment against one partner bars action against others (Civil Liability (Contribution) Act.)

In the fourth part, partners are liable, jointly and severally, for torts committed in the course of the partnership business, and again if the partnership assets are not sufficient to pay any damages awarded in negligence, recourse will be made to the personal assets of the unlimited partners.

2 Alan and Bob are partners in a building company. Colin was a partner, who recently retired from the firm, but has not as yet had his name removed from the firm's notepaper and signs. The running of the day-to-day business is left to an employee, Dave. When Edward, a builders' merchant, visits the firm, Dave, in order to impress him tells him that he (Dave) has just become a partner in the business.

Edward is impressed by Dave and supplies £10 000 of material to the firm on favourable credit terms. Now payment is due, but the firm does not have sufficient assets to clear the debt. Advise the partners concerned.

BA, Business Studies

Suggested answer

This problem can also be split into four parts:

The first part relates to the authority of Dave to enter into the contract on behalf of the firm. If Dave is employed in the capacity of manager, then he has the usual authority of such a person and the firm is bound by his action. Even if he is not formally appointed as the firm's agent they would be estopped from denying his authority, on the basis that they permitted him to conduct the partnership business. (See chapter 9 on Agency.)

The second part is related to Dave's claim that he was a partner in the firm. This is an example of partnership by estoppel. Although Dave does not actually become a partner, he is not permitted to deny the truth of the statement, and is liable to outsiders, such as Edward, who act on the basis of the representation. So Dave is liable to Edward to make good any shortfall that cannot be recovered by the firm.

The third part relates to the liability of Colin as a retiring partner. Colin's name still appears on the firm's documents and he is therefore apparently still a partner. As such, he is liable to pay any shortfall that cannot be recovered from the firm. In order to avoid liability, a retiring partner should inform all existing clients of his withdrawal. An advertisement in *The London Gazette* counts as notice to people who have had no previous dealings with the firm.

If his name was used without his knowledge or permission, then he might not be liable (*Tower Cabinet Co* v. *Ingram*). This does not appear to be the case with Colin.

The fourth part relates to the liability of Alan and Bob and is simply an application of the normal rules that partners are personally liable if the funds of the firm are insufficient to meet outstanding payments.

Further reading

Hardy Ivamy, E. *Underhill's Principles of the Law of Partnership* (Butterworths)
Morse, G. *An Introduction to Partnership Law* (Financial Training Publications)

19 Company law

This chapter deals with the formation and regulation of a common alternative form of business association to the partnership, namely the registered company. The flexibility of the company form of organization is shown in the fact that it is utilized by businesses of widely different sizes and needs; from the one-man business to the multinational company.

Company law, although it has many doctrines and principles which are the product of the common law, is essentially the creation of statute law. The most important piece of legislation in this field is the Companies Act, 1985, and references to Sections numbered in the main text will refer to that Act, unless otherwise stated. Other Acts will be referred to by title.

19.1 Corporations and their legal characteristics

19.1.1 Definition of corporation

Companies differ from partnerships in that they are bodies corporate, or corporations. Corporations can be created in one of three ways:

1 By grant of royal charter. Such corporations are governed by the common law. Nowadays this method of incorporation tends to be restricted to professional, educational and charitable institutions, and trading companies are no longer formed in this way.

2 By virtue of a special Act of Parliament. Such bodies are known as statutory corporations. Although this method of incorporation was common during the 19th century, particularly with regard to railway and public utility companies, it is not greatly used nowadays, certainly not by trading companies.

3 By registration under the Companies Acts. The Companies Act, 1985 sets out the procedure by which businesses can be incorporated. This is the method by which the great majority of trading businesses are incorporated.

19.1.2 Effect of incorporation

The effect of incorporation is that, whereas the law treats a partnership as simply a group of individuals trading collectively, a company, once formed, possesses its own legal personality, completely distinct and separate from the persons who are its members.

> *Salomon* v. *Salomon & Co* (1897)
>
> Salomon had been in the boot and leather trade. Together with other members of his family he formed a limited company, and sold his previous business to it. Payment was in the form of cash, shares and debentures (the latter is loan stock which gives the holder priority over non-secured creditors in regard to payment if the company is wound up.) When the company was eventually wound up, it was argued that Salomon and the company were the same, and as he could not be his own creditor, his debentures should have no effect.
>
> **Held:** His debentures were valid. In the absence of any suggestion of fraud, the company had been validly constituted and as a consequence it was, in law, a distinct legal person, completely separate from Salomon.

A number of consequences flow from the fact that corporations are treated as persons in their own right.

1 Limited liability

No person is responsible for anyone else's debts without agreement to be so bound. Similarly, at common law, members of a corporation are not responsible for its debts without agreement. Registered companies, those formed under the Companies Acts, are not permitted unless the shareholders agree to accept liability for their company's debts. In return for this agreement the extent of their liability is set at a fixed sum – either, in the case of a company limited by shares, the amount left unpaid on the shares they hold, or, in the case of a company limited by guarantee, the amount they have agreed to guarantee (Section 1).

2 Perpetual succession

The corporation exists in its own right. Changes in membership have no effect on the status of the company. It is this attribute that, in theory, permits the free transfer of shares in companies, although in practice, many companies do restrict share transfers.

3 Property

Any assets are owned by the corporation itself. They are not the property of the members. This can cause unforeseen problems.

> *Macaura* v. *Northern Assurance Co* (1925)
>
> Macaura had owned a timber estate. He later formed a 'one-man company' and sold the estate to it. He continued to insure the estate in his own name, rather than in the name of the company. When the timber was lost in a fire, the plaintiff claimed under the insurance policy.
>
> **Held:** Macaura had no personal interest in the timber, which belonged to the company. He had, therefore, no right to insure it, and could not claim for its loss.

4 The rule in *Foss* v. *Harbottle*

This states that, where the company suffers an injury, it is for the company to take the appropriate remedial action. The corollary of this rule is that the individual shareholder cannot raise an action in response to a wrong suffered by the company.

> *Foss* v. *Harbottle* (1843)
>
> Two individual shareholders tried to take action against the directors on the grounds that they had sold assets to the company at over-value.
>
> **Held:** The alleged wrong had been suffered by the company, not the individual members. As there was nothing to prevent the company from taking action, the individual shareholders could not assume this power.

There are a number of occasions, both statutory and at common law, when the doctrine of separate personality will not be followed. On these occasions the 'veil of incorporation' is said to be pierced, lifted or drawn aside. Examples are as follows:

1 Under the Companies Act:

(a) Section 24 provides for personal liability if the company carries on business with less than two members.

(b) Section 229 requires consolidated accounts to be prepared by a related group of companies.

2 To prevent fraud or the evasion of a legal duty:

> *Gilford Motor Co Ltd* v. *Horne* (1933)
>
> An employee had covenanted not to solicit his former employer's customers. After he left their employment, he formed a company to solicit those customers.
>
> **Held:** The company was a mere sham and the Court would not permit it to be used to evade the covenant.

If a business has been carried on with intent to defraud creditors, then the persons responsible may be held personally liable to contribute to the assets of the company on winding up (Section 213 of the Insolvency Act 1986).

19.2 Types of companies

Companies can be classified in a number of ways:

19.2.1 Limited and unlimited companies

One of the major advantages of forming a company is limited liability, but companies can be formed without limited liability. Such companies have the advantage that their annual accounts need not be available for public inspection. The great majority of companies, however, are limited liability companies. This means that the maximum liability of shareholders is fixed, and cannot be increased without their agreement. The liability of the company itself cannot be limited. It must pay its debts, as long as it has available assets.

There are two ways of establishing limited liability:

1 **By shares** This is the most common type of limited liability. It limits liability to the amount remaining unpaid on shares held. If the shares are fully paid up, then no liability remains.

2 **By guarantee** This type of limited liability is usually restricted to non-trading enterprises, such as charities and professional bodies. It limits liability to an agreed amount, which is only called on if the company cannot pay its debts on being wound up.

19.2.2 Public and private companies

The essential difference between these two forms is an economic one. Private companies tend to be small enterprises, owned and operated by small numbers of individuals. Many such companies are sole traders, or partnerships which have incorporated in order to secure the benefit of limited liability. Outsiders do not invest in this type of company. Their shares tend not to be freely transferable, and they are not quoted on any share market.

Public companies, on the other hand, tend to be large, and to be controlled by managers rather than owners. They are a source of investment and have freely transferable shares which can be sold on the Stock Exchange.

The law reflects these economic differences. Whereas the public company can offer its shares and debentures to the public, the private company is prohibited from so doing (Section 81).

As a consequence of the difference in regard to ownership and control many of the provisions in the Companies Act, designed to safeguard the interests of shareholders in public companies, are not applicable to private companies.

19.2.3 Holding and subsidiary companies

According to Section 736, such a relationship exists between two companies, H and S, in any of the following circumstances:

1 H is a shareholder in S and controls the composition of its board of directors;

2 H owns more than half of the equity share capital of S;

3 S is a subsidiary of a company which is in turn a subsidiary of H.

19.3 Formation of companies

19.3.1 Procedure

A registered company is incorporated when particular documents are delivered to the registrar of companies (Section 10), who then issues a certificate of incorporation (Section 13).

The documents required under Section 10 are:

1 memorandum of association;

2 articles of association (unless Table A articles are to apply);

3 a statement detailing the first directors and secretary of the company with their signed consent, and the address of its registered office;

4 a statutory declaration that the relevant requirements of the Companies Act have been complied with;

5 a statement of the nominal capital of the company for the purposes of assessing duty payable.

On the registration of these documents, together with the appropriate fee, the registrar issues a certificate of incorporation. This is the 'birth certificate' of the company. Its issue is conclusive evidence that the formalities of registration have been complied with, even if this is not in fact the case. It does not guarantee the legality of the company's objects.

19.3.2 Commencement of business

A private company may commence its business and use its borrowing powers as soon as the certificate of incorporation has been issued. A public company, however, cannot commence business or borrow until it has obtained an additional certificate from the registrar (see Section 117). This confirms that the company has met the requirements relating to minimum allocated capital, i.e. it has issued shares of a nominal value of at least £50 000 (see Section 118), which must be at least one quarter paid up (Section 101).

19.4 Memorandum and articles of association

These are the constitutional documents of a company. The memorandum governs the company's external affairs. It represents the company to the outside world, stating its capital structure, its powers and objects. The articles primarily regulate the internal working of the company. They are public documents, available for inspection, and as a consequence outsiders are held to have constructive notice of their content. This means that they are deemed to know their contents, even if they have no actual knowledge of what they contain.

If there is any conflict between the provisions of the two documents then the memorandum prevails over the articles.

These important documents will be considered in turn:

19.4.1 Memorandum of association

This document must be signed by at least two subscribers from amongst the company's first shareholders. The memorandum of every company must contain the six clauses relating to:

1 the name of the company;

2 the registered office;

3 the objects of the company;

4 the limitation on liability;

5 the authorized share capital;

6 the wish to form an incorporated association.

In addition, the memorandum of every public company must state that it is to be such. These clauses should be considered in detail.

1 The name of the company
The name must end with either the word 'limited', in the case of a private limited company, or 'public limited company' (Section 25). The appropriate abbreviations – 'Ltd' and 'plc' – can be used (Section 27). The name must not be the same as a name already registered, nor should it constitute a criminal offence, nor be offensive, nor suggest unauthorized connection with the Government or any local authority (Section 26).

A 'passing off' action can be taken against a company, as previously considered in partnership law.

Companies are required to display their name outside their business premises, on business documents, and on their seal. In addition to committing a criminal offence, any person who fails to use a company's full name on any documents will be personally responsible for any default.

> *Penrose* v. *Martyr* (1858)
>
> A bill of exchange drawn on a company failed to state that it was a limited company. The company secretary accepted the bill in that state.
>
> **Held:** The company secretary was personally liable when the company defaulted.

The name of a company can be changed by a special resolution of the company (Section 28).

2 The registered office

The registered office is the company's legal address. It is the place where legal documents such as writs or summons can be served on the company. It is also the place where particular documents and registers, such as the register of members, are required to be kept available for public inspection.

The memorandum of association does not state the actual address, but only the country in which the company is registered, whether Scotland or England and Wales. The precise location of the registered office, however, has to be stated on all business correspondence (Section 351).

3 The objects of the company

Companies registered under the Companies Acts are corporations only for limited purposes. The objects clause states the purposes for which corporations are formed and sets the limit of their authority. They are only able to contract within the scope of the purposes set out in that clause. Any attempt to act outside that limited authority is said to be *ultra vires* and is void.

> *Ashbury Railway Carriage & Iron Co Ltd* v. *Riche* (1875)
>
> The objects of the company authorized it to make railway carriages. It undertook to finance the construction of a railway line in Belgium, and entered into a contract with Riche to that end. When the company repudiated the contract Riche sued for breach of contract.
>
> **Held:** A company could only do what was authorized by its objects clause. The contract was outside the stated objects of the company. It was *ultra vires* and void. It could not be ratified, even by the unanimous consent of the shareholders. Riche's action, therefore, failed.

The *Ashbury* case states the *ultra vires* principle in stark terms, but a number of later developments have lessened its harshness.

Objects clauses are now drafted in such a way as to give companies maximum scope, either by setting out a wide range of independent objects, or giving directors the power to carry on any business they consider to be of benefit to the company.

Companies can alter their objects clause to cover new areas of business by a special resolution (see Section 4). This power is subject to the right of appeal to the Court by the holders of 15 per cent of the issued capital, within 21 days.

A third party who deals with the directors of a company in good faith, without knowledge as to the company's limited powers is now protected by Section 35 of the Companies Act. Such a person can enforce an *ultra vires* contract against the company, but Section 35 does not permit the company to enforce the contract against the third party.

The memorandum and articles of association are public documents available for inspection at the Companies Registry. As a consequence of this fact, outsiders are deemed to know the contents of these documents, whether they actually know them or not. This is a form of constructive notice. Section 35 effectively removes the doctrine of constructive notice as it applies to companies' documents.

4 The limitation on liability

This clause simply states that the liability of the members is limited. It must be included even where the company has permission not to use the word 'limited' in its name. This privilege may be granted to charitable, educational and professional bodies which have incorporated (see Section 25).

5 The authorized share capital

This states the maximum capital which the company is authorized to issue. The capital has to be divided into shares of a fixed amount.

6 The association clause

This provides that the subscribers to the memorandum wish to form a company and agree to take the number of shares placed opposite their names.

It should be recalled that the memorandum of public companies must contain a clause stating that they are public companies.

19.4.2 Articles of association

The articles of association are the internal regulations of the company. They govern the rights and relations of the members to the company, and vice versa, and the relations of the members between themselves. They constitute an enforceable contract in regard to those rights and relationships (Section 14).

The articles deal with such matters as the allotment and transfer of shares, the rights attaching to particular shares, the rules relating to the conduct of meetings, and the powers of directors.

A company may draw up its own set of articles but regulations made under the Companies Act provide a set of model articles, known as Table A. Companies do not have to submit articles of association, but if they do not, then Table A applies automatically. Usually companies adopt Table A articles with appropriate modifications.

Articles can be altered by the passing of a special resolution. The alteration has to be made in good faith and be in the interest of the company as a whole.

> *Brown* v. *British Abrasive Wheel Co* (1919)
>
> An alteration to the articles of the company was proposed to give the majority shareholders the right to buy the shares of the minority.
>
> **Held:** The alteration was invalid, as the alteration would benefit the majority, not the company as a whole.

> *Sidebottom* v. *Kershaw Leese & Co* (1920)
>
> Here the alteration to the articles gave the directors the power to require any shareholder who competed with the company to transfer their shares to nominees of the directors at a fair price.
>
> **Held:** This alteration was valid, as being in the interest of the company as a whole.

19.5 Share capital

19.5.1 The share

A share is 'the interest of the shareholder in the company measured by a sum of money, for the purposes of liability in the first place and of interest in the second, but also consisting of a series of mutual covenants entered into by all the shareholders' (*Borland's Trustees* v. *Steel* (1901)).

It follows from this definition that:

1 The nominal value of the share normally fixes the amount which the shareholder is required to contribute to the assets of the company.

2 The share represents a proportionate interest in the business. This interest takes the form of a right to receive divided payments. The assets are the property of the company, and shareholders only have a claim against them after the company is wound up.

3 The share gives the holder contractual rights to participate in the operation of the company, such as attending and voting at meetings.

19.5.2 Share capital

The word 'capital' is used in a number of different ways in relation to shares:

1 Nominal or authorized capital

This is the figure stated in the company's memorandum of association. It sets the maximum number of shares that the company can issue, and the nominal, or face value, of each share. There is no requirement that companies issue shares to the full extent of their authorized capital.

2 Issued or alloted capital

This represents the nominal value of the shares actually issued by the company. It is more important than authorized capital as a true measure of the substance of the company. Public companies must have a minimum issued capital of £50 000 (Section 11).

3 Paid-up capital

This is the proportion of the nominal value of the issued capital actually paid by the shareholders. It may be the full nominal value, or merely a part of it. Shares in public companies must be paid-up to the extent of at least a quarter of their nominal value (Section 101).

4 Called and uncalled capital

Where a company has issued shares as not fully paid up, it can at a later time 'make a call' upon the shareholders. This means that the shareholders have to provide more capital, up to the amount remaining unpaid on the nominal value of their shares. Called capital should equal paid up capital; uncalled capital is the amount remaining unpaid on issued capital.

5 Reserve capital

This arises when a company passes a special resolution that it will not 'make a call' on any unpaid capital. This then becomes a reserve, only to be called on if required when the company is wound up.

19.5.3 Types of shares

Companies can issue shares of different value, and with different rights attached to them. Classes of shares can be separated into the following types:

1 Ordinary shares

These are sometimes referred to as the 'equity' of the company. They carry the greatest risk, but in recompense receive the greatest return. They receive dividends after preference shares, but are entitled to any remaining profit.

They usually have full voting rights, and thus control the company.

2 Preference shares

These shares may have priority over ordinary shares in two respects; dividends and capital repayment.

They carry a fixed rate of dividend which has to be paid before the ordinary shares receive any return.

They are cumulative unless otherwise provided. This means that a failure to pay a dividend in one year has to be made good in subsequent years.

As regards repayment of capital, preference shares do not have priority unless, as is usually the case, this is specifically provided for. Without specific provision, preference shares have the same rights as ordinary shares, but it is usual for their voting rights to be restricted. They are entitled to vote at class meetings convened to consider the alteration of their rights, but usually they only have rights to vote at general meetings when their dividends are in arrears.

3 Deferred shares

These shares postpone the rights of their holders to dividends until after the ordinary shares have received a fixed return.

4 Redeemable shares

These are shares issued on the understanding that they may be bought back by the company (Section 159). Redemption may be at the option of either the company or the shareholder depending on the terms of issue.

Most companies now have the power to purchase their own shares and are not restricted to buying redeemable shares (Section 162).

19.6 Loan capital

19.6.1 The borrowing powers of companies

Trading companies have an implied power to borrow money for business purposes, and they also have the implied power to give security for any loans undertaken. Non-trading companies require the power to borrow to be expressly stated in the objects clause of their memorandum of association.

19.6.2 Debentures

A debenture is a document which acknowledges the fact that a company has borrowed money. The use of the term debenture, however, is extended to cover the loan itself. Debentures usually provide security for the loan. Debentures with no security are referred to as 'unsecured loan stock'.

A debenture may be issued to a single creditor, or it may signify the company's indebtedness to a large number of people. Each of these has a proportionate claim against the total 'debenture stock'. Debentures differ from shares in the following respects:

1 Debenture holders are creditors of the company. Unlike shareholders, they are not members of the company.

2 As creditors, debenture holders receive interest, not dividends. They are entitled to receive payment whether the company has made a profit or not; even if it comes from capital. Shareholders must not receive any payment from capital.

3 Debentures may be issued at a discount. Shares may not be.

19.6.3 Charges

There are two types of security for company loans:

1 A fixed charge
This is where a specific asset of the company is made subject to a charge in order to secure a debt. The company cannot thereafter dispose of the property without the consent of the debenture holders. If the company fails to honour it commitments, then the debenture holders can sell the asset to recover the money owed.

2 A floating charge
This charge does not attach to any specific property of the company until it crystallizes by the company committing some act or default. This permits the company to deal with its property without the need to seek the approval of the debenture holders.

The most common floating charge is over the 'undertaking and assets' of a company. The security is provided by all the property owned by the company, some of which may be constantly changing, such as its stock-in-trade. A fixed charge has priority over a floating charge in respect to the paying off of company debts.

All charges, both fixed and floating, have to be registered with the Companies Registry within 21 days of their creation. If they are not registered, they are void against any other creditor, or the liquidator, but not against the company.

In addition to registration at the Registry, companies are required to keep a register of all charges on their property. Failure to comply, although an offence, does not invalidate the charge (Section 407).

19.7 Directors

19.7.1 Position of directors

Directors are the persons to whom the management of the company is given by its members. Their position can be described in a number of ways:

1 Directors are officers of the company (Section 744).

2 Directors are agents of the company. They are not, however, the agents of the shareholders. They are therefore able to bind the company without incurring personal liability.

3 Directors are in a fiduciary relationship with their company. This means that they are in a position similar to trustees. The importance of this fact lies in the nature of the duties imposed on directors.

4 Directors are not employees of their company *per se*. They will not be entitled to any remuneration unless the articles provide for their payment, or they have a service contract with the company.

19.7.2　Number of directors

Public companies require a minimum of two directors. Private companies only require one. There is no statutory maximum number.

19.7.3　Appointment of directors

The first directors are usually named in the articles or memorandum. Subsequent directors are appointed under the procedure stated in the articles. The usual procedure is for the company in general meeting to elect the directors by an ordinary resolution.

Casual vacancies are usually filled by the board of directors co-opting someone to act as director. That person then serves until the next AGM, when they must resign and stand for election in the usual manner.

19.7.4　Removal of directors

1 Rotation

Table A provides that one third of the directors shall retire at each AGM, being those with longest service. They may be re-elected.

2 Retirement

Directors of public companies must retire at the first AGM after they reach the age of 70.

3 Disqualification

The articles usually provide for the disqualification of directors on the occurrence of certain circumstances: bankruptcy, insanity, or prolonged absence from board meetings.

In addition to the above, individuals can be disqualified from acting as directors under the provisions of the Company Directors Disqualification Act, 1986. Grounds for such disqualification include:

1 Persistent breaches of the Companies Act.

2 Committing offences in relation to companies.

3 Fraudulent trading.

4 General unfitness.

4 Removal

A director can be removed at any time, by an ordinary resolution of the company (Section 303). The company must receive special notice (28 days) of the intention to propose such a resolution.

This power cannot be restricted by any provision in the company's documents or any external contract. The director may, however, have a right to sue for breach of his service contract.

19.7.5　Powers of directors

Article 70 provides that the directors may exercise all the powers of the company. This power is given to the board as a whole, but article 72 permits the delegation of their power to committees made up of one or more directors.

Limitations on directors' powers

Article 70 gives the board of directors general power, but the articles may endeavour to restrict the authority of the directors within particular limits. The effectiveness of such restrictions were considered in the following case:

> *Royal British Bank* v. *Turquand* (1856)
> The constitutional documents of a company stated that directors only had the power to borrow money after a resolution of the company. The directors borrowed from the bank without first seeking the approval of the company. It was argued for the company that the bank had constructive notice of the limitation, and were bound by it.

> **Held:** The company was bound by the transaction. An outsider had no way of knowing if the appropriate resolution had been passed, and was entitled to assume that it had been.

This common law rule is of less importance than previously, as such transactions are now governed by Section 35 of the Companies Act. This section effectively disposes of constructive notice as it affects the authority of not just directors but the company itself.

19.7.6 The managing director

Article 84 provides that the board of directors may appoint one or more of their number to be managing director (MD). The board of directors may confer any of their powers on the managing director as they see fit. The mere fact of appointment, however, means that he has the implied authority to bind the company in the same way as the board, whose delegate he is. Outsiders can assume that the MD has all the powers usual for someone in his position. Any limitations are ineffective on outsiders without knowledge (Section 35).

Problems tend to arise where someone acts as a managing director without having been properly appointed to that position. In this situation, the person has no actual authority to bind the company. They may, however, have apparent authority, and the company may be estopped from denying that authority.

> *Freeman & Lockyer v. Buckhurst Park Properties (Mangal) Ltd (1964)*
>
> Although a director had never been appointed as managing director, he acted as such with the knowledge of the other directors. He entered into a contract with the plaintiffs on behalf of the company. The plaintiffs took action to recover fees due on the contract.
>
> **Held:** The company was liable on the contract. A properly appointed MD would have been able to enter into such a contract. Outsiders were entitled to rely on the representation of the other directors that the person in question had been properly appointed.

19.7.7 Directors' duties

Directors' duties are essentially fiduciary in nature, and are owed to the company rather than the individual shareholders. They comprise:

1 the duty to act *bona fides* for the benefit of the company as a whole;

2 the duty not to act for any collateral purpose;

3 the duty not to permit a conflict of interest and duty to arise.

In addition, directors are under a duty to exercise due care and skill in the performance of their duties.

19.8 Company meetings

19.8.1 Powers of general meeting

In theory, the ultimate control over a company lies with the members in general meeting. Some powers are reserved to the members by statute, such as the right to petition for voluntary winding up. In practice, however, the residual power of the members is restricted to their ultimate control over the company's memorandum and articles of association, together with the composition of the board of directors. They can also instruct the directors to act by passing a special resolution (Table A, article 70).

19.8.2 Types of meeting

There are three types of membership meeting:

1 The annual general meeting
Every company is required to hold an annual general meeting (AGM) every calendar year. Members are required to be given 21 days' notice of the AGM, which normally

deals with such matters as considering the accounts, declaring dividends, and electing directors.

2 Extraordinary general meeting

An EGM is any meeting other than the AGM. EGMs are usually called by the directors, although members holding 10 per cent of the voting shares may requisition one.

The notice period depends on the type of resolution to be considered, and is usually either 14 or 21 days.

3 Class meeting

This meeting is restricted to the holders of shares of a particular class, such as preference shares. They are called when it is proposed to vary their rights.

19.8.3 Types of resolution

1 Ordinary resolution

This requires a simple majority of those voting. Members who do not attend or who do not vote are disregarded. Notice depends on the type of meeting at which it is proposed (AGM 21 days; EGM 14 days).

2 Extraordinary resolution

This requires a majority of not less than three-quarters of those voting. Again notice depends on the type of meeting being held.

3 Special resolution

This also requires a majority of not less than three quarters, but notice of 21 days must be given to the members.

19.8.4 Voting

This may be carried out in person or by proxy, where a member appoints someone else to vote on his behalf. Voting rights are set out in the company's articles and takes place by either a show of hands (each member has one vote, regardless of the number of shares held) or a poll. The number of votes depends on the number of shares held; usually one vote per share.

19.9 Minority protection

19.9.1 At common law

The rule in *Foss* v. *Harbottle* prevents individual shareholders from taking action to remedy any wrong suffered by their company. It is for the company acting through the majority to decide to start proceedings.

Problems arise when the wrongdoers have a majority of the voting shares. The law does not permit them to use this voting power to commit a fraud on the minority. In such circumstances, the individual shareholder can take action.

> *Cook* v. *Deeks* (1916)
>
> The directors, who were also the majority shareholders of a company, negotiated a contract on its behalf. They took the contract for themselves, and used their voting power to pass a resolution declaring that the company had no interest in the contract.
>
> **Held:** The majority could not use their votes to ratify what was a fraud on the minority. The contract belonged to the company in equity, and the directors had to account to it for the profits made on the contract.

19.9.2 Statutory protection

By virtue of Section 459, any member may petition the Court for an order on the grounds that the affairs of the company are being conducted in a way which is unfairly prejudicial to the interests of some of the members. The Court has general discretion in regard to the content of any order it grants (Section 461).

> *Re London School of Electronics* (1986)
>
> The petitioner held 25 per cent of the shares in the company LSE. The remaining 75 per cent were held by another company, CTC. Two directors of LSE, who were also directors and principal shareholders in CTC, diverted students from LSE to CTC. The petitioner claimed that such action deprived him of his share in the potential profit to be derived from those students.
>
> **Held:** The action was unfairly prejudicial, and the Court instructed the CTC to purchase the petitioners' shares in LSE at a value which was to be calculated as if the students had never been transferred.

By virtue of Section 122 of the Insolvency Act, 1986, a company may be wound up by the Court if it thinks it is just and equitable to do so. This section may be used to provide a remedy in small private companies where there is either deadlock on the board, or a member is removed from the board.

> *Re Yenidje Tobacco Co Ltd* (1916)
>
> The company had two shareholders who were also directors. They fell out and refused to talk to one another.
>
> **Held:** Under the circumstances, it was justified to wind up the company.

> *Re Westbourne Galleries* (1973)
>
> A business which two people had carried on as a partnership was transformed into a private company. After a time, one of the original two partners was removed from the board of directors of the company.
>
> **Held:** The removal from the board, together with the loss in management, was grounds for winding up the company.

It should be noted that the above cases involve small private companies which the Courts recognize as 'quasi-partnerships'. The same outcome would not be forthcoming with regard to public companies.

19.9.3 Investigations

By virtue of Section 431, the Secretary of State may appoint inspectors to investigate the affairs of a company on application by:

1 the company itself, after passing an ordinary resolution; or

2 members holding 10 per cent of the company's issued share capital; or

3 200 or more members.

Under Section 432, the Secretary of State may order such an investigation where:

1 the company's affairs have been conducted with intent to defraud creditors, or for an unlawful or fraudulent purpose; or

2 the company's affairs have been conducted in a manner unfairly prejudicial to some part of the members; or

3 the promoters or managers have been found guilty of fraud; or

4 the shareholders have not been supplied with proper information.

Under Section 442, the Secretary of State has power to appoint inspectors to investigate the ownership and control of companies.

19.10 Winding-up

Winding-up, or liquidation, is the process whereby the life of that particular type of legal person, the company, is terminated. It is the formal and strictly regulated procedure whereby the business is brought to an end, and the company's assets are realized and distributed to its creditors and members. The procedure is governed by the Insolvency Act, 1986.

There are three types of winding-up:

1 A members' voluntary winding-up

This requires that the company be solvent, i.e. able to pay off its creditors when wound-up. The directors must make a declaration to that effect. The liquidation is initiated by a special resolution.

2 A creditors' voluntary winding-up

This occurs when the directors of the company do not believe that it will be able to pay off its creditors. The creditors may form a committee of inspection which oversees the actions of the liquidator. The liquidation is initiated by an extraordinary resolution.

3 A compulsory winding-up

This is a winding-up ordered by the Court under Section 122 of the Insolvency Act, 1986. The most common reason for the compulsory winding-up of a company is its inability to pay its debts. If a company with a debt exceeding £750 fails to pay it within three weeks of receiving a written demand, then it is deemed unable to pay its debts (Section 123).

19.11 Insider dealing

One of the most important attributes of a share is the right it grants to participate in the profit generated by a company. For the purposes of company law, the value of a share is fixed at its nominal value.

The economic value of the share, essentially reflecting the value of the share as a source of income, changes in line with the profitability of the company. Thus, the economic value of the share will fluctuate in line with the performance of the company. This fluctuation in the value of shares is readily apparent in respect of companies which are listed on the Stock Exchange. The prices of such shares are continually in a state of flux.

It is the fact that share prices fluctuate in this way that permits the possibility of people making large profits, or losses, in speculating in shares. It also affords some people the opportunity to take advantage of their relationship with a company in order to make profits from illegal share dealing. Such illegal trading in shares is known as insider dealing, and is governed by the Company Securities (Insider Dealing) Act, 1985 (CSIDA).

Any individual who is, or who in the previous six months has been, connected with a company is prohibited from dealing on a stock exchange in securities of that company on the basis of confidential, unpublished price-sensitive information (Section 1 of the CSIDA).

Confidential, unpublished price-sensitive information is specific information which is not generally known, but which if it were generally known would affect the price of the securities to which it relates (Section 10 of the CSIDA). It is also an offence to pass on this information to someone who is likely to make use of it in share dealing (Section 1).

Any person who receives unpublished price-sensitive information is also prohibited from dealing on it (he is known as a 'knowing tippee') (Section 1 of the CSIDA).

Insider dealing is a criminal offence, and on indictment it carries a maximum penalty of two years in prison and/or an unlimited fine (Section 8).

Sample questions

1 Bill and Ben trade in partnership as garage mechanics. They are considering changing their form of business association and trading as a private registered company limited by shares.

Explain to them the legal procedure that they must follow in order to form such a company, and advise them on the advantages of trading as a private company, as opposed to a partnership.

ACCA

Suggested answer

This is a very popular type of question for all levels of study. The procedure requires that various documents be submitted to the Registrar of Companies as follows:

(a) Memorandum of association.

(b) Articles of association, unless Table A is to apply.

(c) A statement of who the first directors and company secretary are to be.

(d) A statement of shares allotted.

(e) A statutory declaration, signed by a director, secretary, or company solicitor, that the requirements for forming a company have been complied with.

A certificate of incorporation is then issued and the private company can legally begin trading.

The advantages of the company form tend to flow from the fact that the company constitutes a distinct legal personality in its own right. Amongst them are the following:

(a) The shareholders in the company may have limited liability, whereas partners are personally liable for the debts of the partnership to the full extent of their personal wealth.

(b) Shares may be freely transferable, if the articles so permit.

(c) Although partners have a right to be involved in the management of the firm, company members may involve themselves in the management of the company in the capacity of directors.

(d) Companies can create floating charges over their undertakings, but partnerships cannot.

(e) Companies have perpetual succession and the death of any of the members does not affect the company as it would a partnership.

The main disadvantages in regard to companies are the expenses and formality involved in setting them up, and the continued formality involved in operating them. They are also subject to the doctrine of *ultra vires*, whereas partnerships are not.

2 Ever since the calamitous decision in *Salomon* v. *Salomon and Co* (1897) a single group of traders are almost tempted by law to conduct their business in the form of a limited liability company . . . Khan Freund (7 MLR). Consider this statement.

CIMA

Suggested answer

This question involves a critical consideration of the doctrine of separate personality, particularly as it applies to 'one-man' companies. The key issue is the desire to limit liability, and although this advantage is not immediately available to sole traders or partnerships, they can avail themselves of it, by simply registering as a company under the Companies Acts. This practice becomes even more problematic when the persons forming the company receive debentures and thus get priority over unsecured creditors if the company is wound up.

Although *Salomon* v. *Salomon* decided that such a procedure was legal, Khan Freund is questioning its legitimacy. You are being invited to express your opinion in this matter. You should point out that separate personality is not always an advantage, as in *Macaura* v. *Northern Assurance Co*. It should also be pointed out that the law has recognized that separate personality can be abused, and has taken action to lift the veil of incorporation on a number of occasions, as in *Gilford Motor Co Ltd* v. *Horne*.

3 (a) To what extent is it accurate to regard a company's articles of association as constituting a contract between the company and its members?

(b) David Bay is a director of Bay Ltd and owns 25 per cent of the ordinary shares in the company which carry voting rights. The articles of association of Bay Ltd appointed him as managing director for life. His fellow directors have recently discovered that David Bay is acting as financial consultant to other companies which are in competition with Bay Ltd. The other directors of Bay Ltd's board wish to propose an alteration of the companies articles to restrict the powers of the managing director by requiring him to seek the approval of the rest of the board for certain major policy decisions. Advise the directors whether they may so alter the articles and the possible effects of the proposed alteration.   *ACCA*

Suggested answer

(a) Section 14 of the Companies Act specifically provides that the memorandum and articles of a company bind the company and the members as if they had been signed and sealed by every member. The rights and obligations imposed by Section 14 refer only to membership rights and not to rights which affect a member in some other, non-membership, capacity. Thus although a member can rely on Section 14 to insist on his right to vote at meetings (*Pender* v. *Lushington* (1877)), he cannot enforce a promise to employ him in some capacity which is contained in the articles (*Eley* v. *Positive Government Security Life Assurance Co* (1876)).

(b) The articles of a company can be altered by passing a special resolution (Section 9). As this requires a 75 per cent majority the other directors have the power to pass it in spite of David's opposition. He might argue that such a resolution would be invalid on the basis of its not being bona fide, but he would be unlikely to succeed. The purpose is to protect the company from the effects of his connections with rival businesses, and would be valid in those circumstances (*Shuttleworth* v. *Cox Bros & Co* (*Maidenhead*) (1927)).

It is also unlikely that David would be able to argue for constructive dismissal and seek damages, on the basis of the reduction in his powers; but even if he did succeed he cannot rely on the articles as forming a contract of employment for life on the basis of the *Eley* case.

4 (a) Why does the law prohibit 'insider dealing'?

(b) To what extent is 'insider dealing' now regulated by statute?

(c) Explain why the current regulation of 'insider dealing' has been criticised as 'ineffectual'.   *ILE*

Suggested answer

This question is interesting in that it requires not simply an exposition of the law relating to insider dealing; but also looks for some understanding of the social context of the law, as well as a knowledge of its shortcomings.

(a) The answer should start by stating precisely what insider dealing is: the use of unpublished price sensitive information, by either an insider (i.e. a person connected to a company) or a someone to whom an insider has passed on such information. Insider dealing is prohibited for the simple reason that it is seen as an abuse of the market in shares. Insiders have an unfair advantage over outsiders and should not be able to benefit from that advantage. It could be stated that such behaviour questions the integrity of the whole share market.

(b) Insider dealing, as defined above, is now regulated by the Company Securities (Insider Dealing) Act 1985. This Act makes it an offence for an insider to deal in the shares on the basis of his inside information. It is also an offence for him to pass on the information, or to advise others to buy shares on the basis of such information. People who receive unpublished price sensitive information from insiders are known as 'knowing tippees', and are subject to the same restrictions, and can commit the same offences as the original insider.

(c) The Act itself is one source of difficulty in controlling insider dealing, in that Section 3 provides a potential loophole, if the insider shows that he dealt in the shares in question for some other reason than to make a profit or avoid a loss. The main problem area, however, is simply in finding out who is behind insider transaction. The use of foreign registered companies assists in such cover ups. The Financial Services Act 1986 gives the Secretary of State for Trade and Industry wide powers to investigate insider dealing. It remains to see how successful this will prove.

Further reading

Abbot, K. R. *Company Law* (DPP Publications)

Farrar, J. H. *Company Law* (Butterworths)

20 Sale of goods I

20.1 The contract of sale

Sale of goods is a basic transaction in our society, and the law relating to it was codified in statute form in the Sale of Goods Act, 1893. This Act has now been re-enacted, with a few amendments, in the Sale of Goods Act, 1979. These statutes describe a sale as a contract through which a seller agrees to transfer property in goods for a money consideration, called the price.

This transaction is dependent on the general rules of contract, but there are other terms, about quality, for example, which are implied into the contract by the Sale of Goods Act, 1979. Thus, in every sale of goods contract, there are express terms, agreed upon by the buyer and seller (e.g. the amount to be paid) and implied terms according to the Act (e.g. that the goods must be of merchantable quality).

The Sale of Goods Act, 1979 is concerned with the relationship between the **buyer** and the **seller**, and these are the important parties. In the next chapter it will be possible to consider other interests, such as those of the manufacturer or producer of the goods. It is important to consider various aspects of the contract of sale.

Questions on this chapter normally relate to faulty goods, or implied terms that relate to faulty goods, but there are also questions relating to the passing of property, or the definition of 'goods'. Problem questions may be about the perishing of goods or sale by sample.

20.1.1 What are 'goods' under the Sale of Goods Act, 1979?

The Sale of Goods Act, Section 61(1), defines the type of goods covered by the Act. The Act covers personal property of a moveable type. Some of the rules are as follows:

Real property: land or buildings are excluded.

Chattels real: e.g. leaseholds are excluded.

Choses in action: e.g. debts, cheques etc. are excluded, and so is money in current circulation.

The personal property which is left is basically that which can be physically possessed in some way and is not attached to land. Crops become 'goods' within the meaning of the Act if they are about to be harvested. Money may become 'goods' when it becomes 'antique' or 'collectable'. Services are separate from goods, but the same implied terms now largely apply to them after recent legislation, i.e. the Supply of Goods and Services Act, 1982.

20.2 Transfer of property in goods

This is an important feature of the contract. It is important to determine when property passes, because this usually determines where the risk lies, if anything should go wrong, e.g. if goods are destroyed by fire, when it may be important to determine who bears the financial risk of loss of the goods, the seller or the buyer. Various possibilities can complicate the situation. It is possible that the title to the goods has passed to the buyer, and yet he still does not have possession. Similarly, it is possible that the buyer has the goods in his possession, but the title to the goods, and the risk, has not yet passed.

There are three types of goods that need to be considered separately:

1 Specific goods – goods identified and agreed upon at the time of the contract of sale: e.g. I purchase the bar of chocolate that I pick up.

2 Ascertained goods – goods identified and agreed upon after the making of the contract, e.g. I asked to buy 20 sacks of flour and paid, and some time later I agreed to have those 20 sacks in the corner of the warehouse, which are then labelled as mine. The goods are now ascertained.

3 Unascertained goods – these are goods which have not been specified, e.g. the goods which I have agreed to purchase are still part of a larger bulk.

4 Future goods – these are goods to be manufactured or acquired by the seller after making the contract of sale.

20.2.1   The passing of property in specific goods

The general rule is that, if a contract of sale is unconditional, the property passes to the buyer when the contract is made. This can be affected by the intention of the parties.

> *Re Anchor Line (Henderson Bros Ltd)* (1937)
> A crane was 'sold' to buyers who agreed to pay annual sums for 'depreciation'.
> **Held:** The buyers would not have paid depreciation on their own goods, so the intention must be inferred that the property in the goods remained with the sellers, until the price was fully paid.

> *Dennant v. Skinner* (1948)
> A gentleman bought a car at an auction, and afterwards he signed a form to the effect that the ownership of the vehicle would not pass to him until the cheque had been cleared. He sold the car to a third person, and there was some dispute about the ownership of the car.
> **Held:** The contract was complete, and ownership passed as the auctioneer's hammer fell. Therefore, the third party had a good title to the car.

If the contract is for the sale of specific goods, but the owner is bound to do something to them to put them into a deliverable state, then ownership does not pass until that thing is done, and the buyer has notice that it is done. If the goods are to be weighed, tested or measured, the property will not pass until the process is complete, and the buyer is informed of that, unless there is a specific agreement to the contrary.

20.2.2   The passing of property in ascertained goods

The general rule is that the property passes to the buyer when the goods are specified, and the buyer is informed of this. This general rule can be contradicted by the particular circumstances of the case.

20.2.3   The passing of property in unascertained goods

No property can be transferred unless and until the goods are ascertained.

> *McDougall v. Aeromarine of Emsworth Ltd* (1958)
> S (seller) agreed to build a pleasure yacht for B (buyer), and after the first instalment was paid, the yacht and all the materials were meant to become the 'absolute property' of B.
> **Held:** No property could pass to the buyer, as it was not physically in existence at that time.

> *Healy v. Howlett* (1917)
> 190 boxes of fish were carried by rail. The buyer was to purchase 20 boxes, and S directed the railway to set aside 20 boxes, but before they did so, the fish went bad. S had sent B an invoice saying that the fish were carried at the buyer's 'sole risk' (in rather bad taste!).
> **Held:** The fish had gone bad before the goods were 'ascertained' so the buyer could reject them.

NB It seems reasonable that, whilst the buyer's goods could not be identified as his when they deteriorated, he should not be asked to pay for the consequences of deterioration.

20.3   The perishing of goods

In a case in which goods have perished because delivery has been delayed, through the fault of either the buyer or the seller, then the loss falls on the party at fault.

> *Demby Hamilton Co* v. *Barden Ltd* (1949)
>
> S agreed to sell B 30 tons of crushed apple, and B wrongly failed to give proper delivery instructions. The crushed apple went bad before it could be delivered.
>
> **Held:** The loss would fall on B.

20.3.1   Definition of 'perish'

There has been some confusion about the meaning of 'perish'. Goods must become unrecognizable before they can be held to have 'perished'. Goods that never existed cannot perish. If a portion of a consignment of goods is destroyed, then the goods have been described as having 'perished' under the Act.

> *Barrow Lane & Ballard* v. *Phillips* (1929)
>
> About one seventh of the goods disappeared, presumed stolen.
>
> **Held:** The goods had 'perished' within the meaning of the Act.

20.3.2   Perishing of specific goods

If the specific goods perished before the contract was made, then the contract can be avoided.

> *McRae* v. *Commonwealth Disposals Commission* (1951)
>
> S agreed to sell B a specific shipwrecked oil tanker that did not exist.
>
> **Held:** S was liable to B because he had impliedly warranted that it did exist.

> *Couturier* v. *Hastie* (1856)
>
> There was a contract to sell a cargo of corn, but, unknown to the seller, the ship's master had already sold it in Tunisia because it had begun to ferment.
>
> **Held:** The contract was void.

If goods perish after the contract, the contract can be avoided if the risk has not yet passed to the buyer. If the risk has passed, then the buyer must bear the loss.

> *Asfar* v. *Blundell* (1896)
>
> There was a sale of dates, which had been impregnated by sewage.
>
> **Held:** The contract was void. The goods had 'perished', within the meaning of the Act.

20.3.3   Perishing of unascertained goods

A contract for unascertained goods may be void, if it is established that some goods have perished and it is therefore impossible to carry out the contract. This depends upon whether the unascertained goods are to be ascertained from a specific bulk, or there was simply a general description of a type of goods; e.g. the buyer may ask for 12 jars of honey from Mr Hayes' clover-fed bees, or just 12 jars of honey! In the latter case, the contract is not void, because the goods can be obtained from another source.

20.3.4   Frustration of contract

When it becomes impossible to carry out a contract as originally conceived, through the fault of neither party, a wider principle of common law can be applied, that of frustration of contract. This can occur because goods perish, or because the contract becomes impossible to carry out legally:

> *Avery* v. *Bowden* (1855)
>
> There was a contract to bring goods from Russia. The Crimean war broke out, and it became illegal to trade with Russia.
>
> **Held:** No claim could be brought against the defendant for failure to load the goods, because the contract had been frustrated by illegality.

If the contract is frustrated, under the Law Reform (Frustrated Contracts) Act, 1943, then the buyer can recover his money, but the Court can deduct expenses incurred by the seller in performance of the contract. The law puts into effect what it assumes the parties would have intended, had they considered the circumstances.

> *Sainsbury* v. *Street* (1972)
> There was a contract for 275 tons of barley, to be grown by the seller on his farm. The crop was only 140 tons. The buyer argued that the seller should not be excused performance.
> **Held:** There was an implied term that the buyer had an option of accepting reduced quantities at pro rata rates. Hence the seller was liable for non-delivery of the 140 tons.

20.4   Nemo dat quod non habet rule

There is an implied condition, in Section 12 of the Sale of Goods Act, that the seller has a right to pass on a good title to the goods. The rule *nemo dat quod non habet* means that a person cannot give what he has not got, so that, in general, ownership is protected. The law may often have to choose between the rights of two innocent parties, however, the innocent purchaser and the real owner of the goods.

Although the general rule is that ownership will be protected, there are several exceptions to this general rule, and in these cases a non-owner can pass title in the goods.

1 Estoppel

If the seller or buyer, by their conduct, make the other party believe that a certain fact is true, and the other party alters his position, then that same party will later be estopped (or prevented) from saying that the fact is untrue. This has arisen where a party has, for complicated reasons, signed a statement that their own property belongs to someone else, and, in two known cases, ended up 'buying' back their own property. They may be estopped from denying the statement they made falsely about the ownership of the property.

2 Agency

If P (principal) appoints A (agent) to sell his goods to T (third party), then any sale by A, in accordance with instructions given, will pass on a good title to T. If, however, A had exceeded his instructions in some way, then no title would pass to T unless A had 'apparent authority'.

3 Mercantile agency

T has even stronger grounds to claim a title if A is a mercantile agent, e.g. T, as a consumer buys a car from A who is in the car trade. A mercantile agent is one 'having in the customary course of business as such agent, authority either to sell goods or to consign goods for the purposes of sale, or to buy goods or to raise money on the security of goods' (Factors Act, 1889, Section 1(1)).

> *Pearson* v. *Rose and Young* (1950)
> The owner of a car took it to the dealer and asked him to obtain offers. He did not intend to hand over the registration book, but left it with the dealer by mistake. The dealer sold the car, with the book, to an innocent buyer. The question of the true ownership of the car was raised.
> **Held:** The dealer had obtained the car 'with the consent of the owner' but this consent did not extend to the registration book. Hence the sale must be treated as a sale without registration book, and the buyer could not get a good title to the car.

4 Sales authorized by law

There are cases in which the title does not pass directly from the owner, because the sale is authorized by a Court, e.g. the sale of goods which are the subject-matter of legal proceedings.

Similarly, in common law or statute, it is sometimes declared that a non-owner is entitled to sell goods e.g. as an agent of necessity, or an unpaid seller.

5 Sale in market overt

This is an old rule relating to well-established open public markets in England, and shops within the City of London. These rules do not apply in Scotland and Wales. When goods are sold in these places, at business premises in the normal hours of business between sunrise and sunset, the buyer always gets a good title.

> *Reid v. Metropolitan Police Commissioner* (1974)
> A pair of glass candelabra were stolen from Reid. Subsequently, an art dealer bought them in the New Caledonian Market for £200. The market normally commenced business at seven, but it was normal for dealers to buy earlier, and the candelabra had been purchased in half light. The goods were seized by the police.
> **Held:** Reid could recover the goods, The sale must take place within the usual hours of the market, but it must also be 'between the rising of the sun and the going down of the same'. Thus the dealer did not acquire a good title because of the half-light, since the sale has to take place between sunrise and sunset, and within the usual hours of the market.

6 Sale under a voidable title

In this case the sale by the original owner is fully binding, until the seller takes steps to have it set aside.

> *Car and Universal Finance Co v. Caldwell* (1965)
> A car was sold to a rogue by cheque, and the cheque was dishonoured. The owner went to the police.
> **Held:** By this action, the owner had avoided his contract with the rogue.

Clearly, the situation before an owner takes steps to avoid the contract, is that someone who does not have a good title (e.g. the rogue) can pass on a good title to the innocent third party who pays good value for the goods.

7 Disposition by a seller in possession

A contract of sale can be complete and valid, but the goods are still in the possession of the seller, e.g. awaiting delivery. Suppose that the seller sells the goods to a second buyer: the second buyer will get a good title to those goods, if he takes delivery of them.

8 Disposition by a buyer in possession

This is the corresponding situation, where the buyer possesses the goods but the seller has retained the property in them. Then, if the buyer has the goods and any necessary documents of title, and he transfers these to an innocent transferee (second buyer), that transferee will obtain a good title to the goods.

9 Sale of motor vehicles which are the subject of a hire-purchase agreement

The law changed in 1964 to protect 'private purchasers' of motor vehicles that were subject to a hire-purchase agreement. The original hirer will still have the same obligation to the finance company. The final purchaser should have taken the car in good faith, without notice of the hire purchase agreement.

These nine exceptions summarize the cases in which the private purchaser may get a good title to goods, from someone who is not the owner of those goods. In all other cases, the title remains with the true owner, who can sue in tort for the conversion of the goods. He can sue the person who possesses the goods currently, and all those who have possessed those goods before that person.

20.5   Implied terms

There are some terms which are implied into a sale of goods contract by the Sale of Goods Act 1979. The most fundamental terms are as follows:

1 The seller must give a good title to the goods (Section 12).

2 The goods must accord with any description applied to them in the contract (Section 13).

3 The goods must be of merchantable quality (which can be roughly translated as 'saleable') (Section 14).

4 The goods must be reasonably fit for their normal purpose, or for a purpose which was specified by the buyer (Section 14).

5 If the sale is a 'sale by sample', the goods must correspond with the sample shown (Section 15).

20.5.1 Title

There is an implied condition that the seller has a right to sell the goods, and the ability to transfer a good title to the buyer.

> *Niblett Ltd* v. *Confectioners' Materials Co* (1921)
>
> The labels on some tins of milk infringed Nestlé's trademark. These tins were being imported from America and were seized by customs, and not released to the buyer.
>
> **Held:** Although the American company had a right to transfer title in these goods, the goods were not what they purported to be. The buyer could, therefore, claim damages and breach of condition, as he would not get a trouble-free title to the goods i.e. what the law calls 'quiet enjoyment' of the goods. His title would clearly be challenged as sale of the goods infringed Nestlé's trademark.

In cases brought under Section 12, the buyer can recover the full purchase price, even though he may have used the goods for some time – if he does not receive a good title to the goods, there is total failure of consideration.

> *Rowland* v. *Divall* (1923)
>
> The buyer had used a car for four months. The title to the car had not been transferred to him.
>
> **Held:** He had not received all he bargained for and he could therefore recover the full price paid.

20.5.2 Description

The goods must accord with any description applied (Section 13). It must be proved that there was such a description, and determined whether the goods complied with it. A contractual description consists of any words, oral or written, which can be relied upon as identification of the goods that are being bought.

> *Beale* v. *Taylor* (1967)
>
> The buyer read an advertisement offering for sale a 'Herald convertible 1961' and when he went to see the car, it had a disk stating '1200' on the back of the car. He bought the car, and later discovered that it was the back half of a 1961 model welded to the front half of an earlier model.
>
> **Held:** Since the buyer bought the car with reference to the description, he was entitled to damages under Section 13.

The description may be very simple, as in the case of *Grant* v. *Australian Knitting Mills*, where 'underpants' was held to be a contractual description, as it was the way in which the buyer identified the item he was purchasing. Not all the words used by the buyer will be part of the contractual description.

> *Ashington Piggeries* v. *Christopher Hill Ltd* (1972)
>
> There was a written contract which stated that the sellers would make 'a vitamin-fortified mink food to be called King Size'. The food was made up to a formula specified by the buyers, which was also in the contract. It was stated that the formula was the description which specified what the buyers wanted. One of the

> ingredients was herring meal, which was contaminated, but it was still identifiable as herring meal.
>
> **Held:** The sellers had made the food up correctly, so that there was no breach of description (Section 13).

20.5.3 Merchantable quality

There is an implied condition that the goods shall be of merchantable quality according to Section 14(2) of the Sale of Goods Act, 1979.

Once the seller has sold the goods in the normal course of business, the law inserts an implied term that the goods are of merchantable quality, with two exceptions:

1 There is no claim for a defect in the goods under this section if the defect is specifically brought to the buyer's attention at the time of the contract of sale.

2 There can be no claim when the buyer has examined the goods, and any defects should have been revealed by that examination.

The goods which come into this category include not only goods sold in the normal course of business, but also, goods sold as a business proposition to the consumer, e.g. the sale of a car that has been used in a grocery business.

The Sale of Goods Act defines merchantable quality as 'fit for the purpose for which goods of that kind are commonly bought as it is reasonable to expect having regard to any description applied to them, the price (if relevant) and all other relevant circumstances'.

> *Kendall (Henry) & Sons* v. *William Lillico & Sons Ltd* (1968)
>
> This case concerned a sale of groundnut extract for feeding to cattle and poultry. It contained a poison which killed the poultry (clearly contrary to the purpose the buyers had in mind) but did not affect the cattle. The buyer's pheasants were killed.
>
> **Held:** The goods were of merchantable quality, because the test to be applied was 'goods are of merchantable quality if they are fit for one of their normal purposes (regardless of whether they are fit for the buyer's particular purpose) and are saleable under their contractual description for one of their normal purposes without reduction in price'.
>
> Thus, in this case, the goods were of merchantable quality because they were fit for cattle, as there was evidence that buyers of the goods for cattle would have been willing to buy the goods as groundnut extract, without any reduction in price.

There was a loophole in this last case, however, because buyers who made a bad bargain, and paid too much for their goods, would be able to claim that they were not of merchantable quality.

The buyers should have made their particular purpose known to the seller, and if they had done so, they would have had a successful case under Sections 13 and 14 (description and fitness for purpose).

> *Brown (BS) & Sons Ltd* v. *Craiks Ltd* (1970)
>
> The buyers supplied specifications for cloth to be made for use in dressmaking. The sellers did not know that it was to be used for dressmaking, and the specifications were more like those for industrial cloth. The sellers complied with the instructions, and the cloth was suitable only for industrial purposes. The buyers tried to reject the goods on the grounds that they were not of merchantable quality, as the price was too expensive for industrial cloth. They argued that no one would be willing to buy the cloth, except with a reduction in price.
>
> **Held:** The cloth was of merchantable quality, as it complied with the specifications given, and goods would only be held to be not of merchantable quality if the reduction in price was really substantial.

The 1979 Act gives the Court discretionary powers to reach a fair decision in cases of 'reduction in price' (Section 14(b)). This discretion would formerly have been used in the case of *Kendall* v. *Lillico*, but not in a case such as *Brown* v. *Craiks*, where specifications had been supplied.

20.5.4 Reasonable fitness for purpose

There is an implied condition in a contract for sale of goods that the goods supplied are reasonably fit for any purpose expressly or impliedly made known to the seller under Section 14(3) of the Sale of Goods Act, 1979. Where goods have a normal purpose, the law implies that you buy those goods for that purpose, e.g. in the case of *Grant* v. *Australian Knitting Mills* where the purpose of underpants was to be worn. If the purpose of use is unusual, however, or the goods have several normal, but distinct uses, e.g. timber for paper, or for furniture; then the purpose must be made known expressly, i.e. spelt out clearly – verbally or in writing, to the seller, before the buyer can rely on this section. An example of this is in *Ashington Piggeries* v. *Hill* (above) when the buyers made it clear that the end product would be fed to mink, even though they supplied the formula.

The question of whether goods are reasonably fit for the purpose is a question of fact.

> *Griffiths* v. *Peter Conway Ltd* (1939)
> The buyer bought a tweed coat. She was allergic to it.
> **Held:** She had no claim under Section 14 that the coat was not reasonably fit for the purpose, because the coat was fit for wear by any normal person. She had not made any reference to her condition.

This condition does not apply where the buyer does not rely on the seller's skill and judgment, e.g. chooses a brand other than that recommended by the seller; or where it is unreasonable for him to have relied on that skill and judgment.

20.5.5 Sale by sample

This section applies only if there is a term of the contract which states that it is a contract of sale by sample. This could be an oral contract, but if it is in writing, then the term about sale by sample must be in the written contract. The mere act of showing a sample of the goods during negotiations does not make the 'sale by sample' unless the parties agree to do so.

In a case last century, Lord MacNaghten explained the function of a sample (*Drummond* v. *Van Ingen*, 1887).

> The office of a sample is to present to the eye the real meaning and intention of the parties with regard to the subject matter of the contract, which, owing to the imperfection of language, it may be difficult or impossible to express in words. The sample speaks for itself.

It is no defence under Section 15(2) to say that the bulk can easily be made to correspond with the sample.

> *E. & S. Ruben Ltd* v. *Faire Bros & Co Ltd* (1949)
> Linatex was sold which was crinkly, whereas the sample had been soft and smooth. The seller argued that by the simple process of warming, the bulk could have been made as soft as the sample.
> **Held:** The sellers were liable to pay damages to the buyers.

A buyer may well not be able to claim damages under Section 15(2) for defects he could reasonably have discovered upon examination of the goods. He may still have an action under Section 14(2) or 14(3). It is important to remember that the implied conditions under Section 15 are:

1 that the bulk shall correspond with the sample;

2 that the buyer shall have reasonable opportunity to compare the goods with the sample;

3 that the goods will be free from any defect rendering them unmerchantable which would not be apparent on reasonable examination of the sample.

20.6 Exclusion clauses

The effect of exclusion clauses on the operation of this Act is limited by the Unfair

Faulty goods (not sale by sample)
Have you a remedy?

Were the goods faulty when you bought them?

No → How soon did the fault develop?

- After a lot of use → Probably no claim
- In a short time → Were you using the goods for the ordinary purpose?
  - **No** → Did you explain your purpose for buying the goods to the salesman?
    - **No** → You probably have no claim
    - **Yes** → You probably have a claim under Section 14(3), Sale of Goods Act, 1979
  - **Yes** → You probably have a claim for damages under Section 14(3) and 14(2), Sale of Goods Act, 1979

Yes → Did you pay a reasonable price for the goods?

- **Yes** → Have you accepted the goods?
  - **Yes** → (to: Were you using the goods for the ordinary purpose?)
  - **No** → You can refuse to accept them
- **No** → Was the fault fundamental, e.g. a cup that was impossible to drink out of?
  - **No** → You will find it difficult to claim damages if the defect was obvious
  - **Yes** → You probably have a claim under Sections 13 or 14. You can reject goods

Flow chart setting out consumers' rights concerning faulty goods

1 It is impossible to exclude liability under Section 12 of the Sale of Goods Act, i.e. the seller must pass on a good title.

2 In the case of a consumer purchaser (i.e. private individual as purchaser dealing with a trader, e.g. an individual in a shop) it is impossible to exclude liability under Sections 13-15 of the Act.

3 In the case of a non-consumer contract (i.e. the buyer is not a private individual and/or the seller is not acting in the course of business, e.g. as in a private sale) it is possible to restrict liability under Sections 13-15, only to the extent that the exclusion clause is considered 'reasonable'.

4 Any other liability for breach of contract can be excluded or restricted only to the extent that it is 'reasonable'.

5 It is impossible to exclude liability for death or personal injury.

6 It is possible to exclude liability from loss or damage arising from negligence or misrepresentation only to the extent that the clause is 'reasonable'.

NB The requirement of 'reasonableness' means that the exclusion clause 'shall have been a fair and reasonable one to be included, having regard to the circumstances which were, or ought to have been known to or in the contemplation of the parties when the contract was made' (see Schedule 2 to the Unfair Contract Terms Act, 1977).

Sample questions

1 (a) In a sale of goods, why is it important to determine the precise point at which the property passes?

(b) When does the buyer become owner of the goods in the following transactions:

(i) David supplies Enid with jewellery on approval, on condition that property passes when the goods are paid for. Enid gives the jewellery to Frank.

(ii) Gloria orders a washing machine from Hampton Stores, who have a number in stock. *IPS*

Suggested answer

(a) The transfer of property is important because it is usually the moment of transfer of risk. It is also possibly the time when payment is due (depending on the contract). This is particularly important in cases where goods have perished. If the goods perished before the passing of property, then the contract may well be frustrated.

It may be important to determine whether the goods are specific, ascertained, or unascertained goods because property can only pass in goods which have been specified – the seller's duty to provide the goods may well still remain, even if certain goods have perished if the goods are unascertained and not to be obtained from a specific bulk of these goods. The transfer of property and risk may well determine the nature of the claim if goods are lost, e.g. to the seller or to an insurance company.

(b) (i) When Enid gives jewellery to Frank, she is acting with proprietary rights. Normally the property would pass on such an act, but since David has reserved the property rights until payment has been made, this will override her title.

(ii) When the washing machine is identified for Gloria and she is informed, the property has become ascertained, and property will normally pass except if there is a separate condition that property will not pass until a certain date. The question does not state anything about payment for the machine. If Gloria has paid already, the property will certainly pass when the goods are ascertained. If she has not paid, then property may well pass on payment.

2 Consider the following:

(a) Give a short account of the implied terms as to the quality of goods contained in the Sale of Goods Act, 1979.

(b) E ordered from F 100 sacks of potatoes. F delivered the potatoes to E in half-sacks. E had contracted to sell the potatoes to Y by the sack, so, notwithstanding to have the trouble of repacking them, he rejects F's consignment. *CIS*

Suggested answer

(a) The following points should be considered:

Goods must accord with their description (Section 13 of the Sale of Goods Act, 1979)

Goods must be of merchantable quality, i.e. suitable for their normal purpose and saleable.

Goods should be reasonably fit for the purpose sold, that is the normal purpose for which those goods are used, or any particular purpose specified in the contract.

(b) The Sale of Goods Act regards packaging as part of the product. 'One hundred sacks' was specified as a term of the contract, and this is not satisfied if the wrong quantities are delivered in the packs. The case of *Niblett* v. *Confectioners' Materials Co* held that the packaging was to be regarded as part of the product. E is entitled to reject the consignment.

3 You are working in the Consumer Services Department of Spoulton Pottery. Recently you have received several complaints about cracks in china which has been made by Spoultons, all of which have been purchased from the same place, the Superfine Pottery Warehouse. Your employer suspects that Superfine have been mishandling the pottery, and potentially obtaining 'seconds' from somewhere between the production line and the factory shop, selling them as 'first quality'. Spoulton therefore wishes to ensure that claims are made against Superfine, so that the blame can be fairly apportioned on further investigation. Draft a letter to these customers, explaining what remedy they have for their faulty china and against whom.

BTEC HND, Staffordshire Polytechnic

Suggested answer

The following points should be considered:

The letter must be formally drafted and contain the following points. The Sale of Goods Act provides for a contract between the buyer and the seller and it offers certain protection from faulty goods, i.e. that goods should correspond to their description, that they should be of merchantable quality, and should be reasonably fit for their purpose. If the goods are described as 'fine bone china' and not as 'seconds' they should be perfect and without fault. They should also be suitable for serving food upon and they are certainly not suitable for this purpose if there are cracks in the pottery. The goods are not of merchantable quality because they would not fetch a reasonable price in that condition. It is therefore suggested that the pottery is returned to Superfine Pottery Warehouse and the money claimed back.

4 *Nemo dat quod non habet* is an important rule about the transfer of property. Explain its significance.

BA, Business Studies

Suggested answer

The following points should be considered:

The *nemo dat* rule means that a person cannot normally pass on a good title to something he does not have a good title to himself. However, there are various exceptions to this rule:

(a) Estoppel. In this case the owner acts as if someone else owns the goods, or had authority to pass title, and he is estopped from denying that.

(b) Agency. In this case, the agent is authorized to act for the owner.

(c) Mercantile agent. In this case the public are protected in that they will usually receive a good title from such an agent if he has authority to sell (see *Pearson* v. *Rose and Young* as an exceptional case.)

(d) Sales authorized by law, by Court or statute.

(e) Sale in market overt. Sales are protected in open publically constituted markets and the city of London. Consider the case of *Reid* v. *Metropolitan Police Commissioner.*

(f) Sale under a voidable title. This is the case in which the passing of title could be avoided but has not been done so, e.g. *Car and Universal Finance Ltd* v. *Caldwell.*

(g) Disposition by the seller in possession. He can pass on a good title to a second buyer, but must compensate the first one.

(h) Disposition by the buyer in possession. He can also pass on a good title even if the title has not passed to him.

(i) Sale of motor vehicles on hire-purchase. This caused so many problems in the past, the law now states that the purchaser will get a good title, although the seller/hirer may have to pay damages according to his agreement.

In all other cases the title remains with the true owner, who can sue in tort for conversion of the goods. He can sue the person who possesses the goods currently, and he has the right to sue all those who have possessed the goods without his permission before that.

This does not mean that the owner claims damages several times over, but that the damages, that he is entitled to, can come from any of these sources.

Further reading

Harvey, Brian W. *The Law of Consumer Protection and Fair Trading* (Butterworths)
Marsh and Soulsby *Business Law* (McGraw-Hill)

21 Sale of goods II

The previous chapter dealt with issues relating to the initial contract. This chapter follows up those points by examining issues relating to the performance of a contract, once it is established. These are not always two distinct phases of contract, and they are only divided here for convenience of presentation. Questions for assessment of this area may be based on delivery, acceptance or payment for the goods, or statutory remedies for breach of the contract.

21.1 Performance of the contract

Normally, it is the duty of the seller to deliver the goods, and the duty of the buyer to accept the goods and pay the agreed price for them. Disputes arise most frequently at significant times in the performance of the contract, such as the time of delivery of the goods, and the acceptance of those goods or the time of payment.

21.1.1 Delivery and acceptance of goods

Delivery is 'the voluntary transfer of possession from one person to another', according to the Act. Delivery by instalment is not acceptable, unless the contract specifically states that delivery is going to take place by this method.

If delivery is late, the buyer may reject or accept the goods – in the latter case, the buyer cannot repudiate the contract. The buyer loses the right to reject the goods if he accepts delivery late, but he is still able to claim damages. He cannot usually accept or reject a part of the goods unless the contract is severable into instalments.

The buyer may also lose the right to reject goods by waiver of that right. This could happen where the seller is in breach of condition before the goods are delivered, and the buyer has knowledge of this. If the buyer then indicates that, under the new circumstances, he would still accept the goods, that could amount to a waiver of his right to reject.

Acceptance occurs when either:

1 The buyer states to the seller that he has accepted the goods, e.g. he signs an acceptance note; or

2 The goods are delivered and the buyer either retains the goods for a reasonable length of time without rejecting them, or he does an act inconsistent with the seller's ownership such as sell the goods or process them (Section 35, Sale of Goods Act, 1979).

Section 34 of the Act states that the buyer is not deemed to have accepted the goods until he has examined them or has had reasonable opportunity to do so. Section 35 follows this by stating that the buyer must have reasonable opportunity to examine the goods even if he does an act inconsistent with the ownership of the seller, or keeps the goods a reasonable length of time.

21.1.2 Price

The price is usually considered to be a basic part of the contract for the sale of goods, and so it is normally expressly agreed.

Section 8 of the Act states that the price may be fixed or determined by an agreed procedure. If not, then the buyer must pay a reasonable price, which will be a question of fact depending on the circumstances of the case.

May v. *Butcher* (1934)
There was an agreement for the purchase of government tentage which provided that the price, manner of delivery and dates of payment were to be agreed upon

> from time to time. If the contract had failed to mention those items the matter
> could have been resolved by applying the provisions of the Sale of Goods
> Act, 1893, but the contract expressly stated that the items were to be the subject
> of a later agreement.
>
> **Held:** The parties had not intended to make a contract. The House of Lords stated
> that the parties simply had an agreement to agree—there was no contract.

It is interesting to note that if there had been no mention of the price, the contract
may well have been valid under the Sale of Goods Act 1893, and the price could have
been a 'reasonable' price.

Consider another case in contrast to this, where the price was a less important
element of the contract and provision was made for determining the sum in the event
of controversy.

> *Foley* v. *Classique Coaches Ltd* (1934)
>
> The defendants bought some land from the plaintiffs, and it was a condition of the
> contract that the defendants agreed to purchase petrol from the plaintiffs, for the
> coach business, at a price 'to be agreed by the parties from time to time'; and failing
> agreement the price was to be settled by arbitration. It was argued that there was
> not sufficient basis for a contract.
>
> **Held:** The parties still had a binding contract. The price to be paid was a
> 'reasonable' price.

Valuation by a third party is one method that the parties can stipulate for
ascertainment of the price. The Act stresses that where he cannot or does not make
that valuation, the contract is avoided. If, however, the buyer has already
appropriated some of the goods, or if lack of valuation is caused by the fault of either
party, then damages are payable.

21.1.3   Time of payment and delivery

There is a presumption that time of payment is not a fundamental condition, although
the parties can expressly agree otherwise. A stipulated time for delivery, however, will
be considered to be 'of the essence' of the contract. Similarly, if a date is specified for
shipment of the goods by the seller, this may give the buyer grounds for repudiating
the contract if it is not fulfilled.

> *Rickards* v. *Oppenheim* (1950)
>
> The seller contracted to build a car for the buyer, to be built by March 20th. It was
> not ready by that date. The buyer did not repudiate that contract, but pressed for
> early delivery. When it was still not finished by the end of June, the buyer informed
> the seller that if it was not ready in another four weeks, he would regard the
> contract as repudiated. At the end of four weeks, the car was still not ready.
>
> **Held:** The buyer had acted within his rights. He lost the right to regard the contract
> as repudiated on March 20th by his waiver, but it was a condition of that waiver,
> under those circumstances, that delivery should take place as soon as possible. The
> buyer could therefore revive his right to repudiate the contract, by giving
> reasonable notice. The buyer was under no obligation, after the four weeks, to buy
> the car.

21.2   Remedies for breach of contract

It is important to consider the remedies that are avaiable to the seller, or to the buyer,
in the event of a breach of contract. The contract will not always be completely
avoided by doing so, and it may be in the interests of the other party to accept
damages and continue the legal relationship.

21.2.1   Seller's remedies

If things go wrong for the seller of goods, he has two types of remedy available to him.
The first type of remedy is concerned with the money or the price of the goods, and
the other type with the goods themselves.

The seller has two possible actions to seek in Court to recover the price of the goods if things go wrong.

1 Action for the price of the goods

The seller can bring an action for the price of the goods in either of the following circumstances:

(a) the buyer has wrongfully refused or neglected to pay for the goods according to the terms of the contract; or

(b) the property has passed to the buyer, or 'the price is payable on a day certain irrespective of delivery'.

This does not include the circumstances in which the buyer has rightfully rejected the goods for breach of condition.

The seller cannot, in fact, sue, unless he was ready and willing to deliver at the time of refusal to pay. If the seller has granted the buyer credit, then he cannot sue until the end of the credit period. If there is no certain, agreed date, then the action will only succeed when the property has passed to the buyer.

2 Damages for non-acceptance of the goods

If the seller cannot maintain an action for the price, he may still have a claim for damages for non-acceptance, but usually such damages will be much less than the price, and the seller has the inconvenience of trying to find another buyer.

The second type of remedy is concerned with the goods themselves and is available in four forms:

1 lien;

2 stoppage in transit;

3 the Romalpa clause;

4 resale.

1 Lien

This concerns the right of the seller to retain possession of the goods, even though the property has passed to the buyer. The Sale of Goods Act assumes that delivery and payment are normally concurrent events, except where sales are on credit. The lien, or right to keep the goods, is based on possession of the goods, and is only available for the price of the goods and not for other damages, such as storage charges. It may be a useful remedy in times of economic stress when there are rumours of bankruptcies and liquidations. The unpaid seller may well be financially better off with the goods in his possession than if he had simply become a creditor in the bankruptcy.

Delivery of part of the goods will not destroy the unpaid seller's lien, unless the circumstances show an intention to waive the lien. The unpaid seller will lose his lien if he delivers the goods for carriage to the buyer, and does not reserve the rights of disposal over them, or if the buyer lawfully obtains possession of the goods.

2 Stoppage in transit

If the buyer becomes insolvent and the goods are still in transit, the unpaid seller is given the right of stoppage in transit (stoppage *in transitu* in the Act), and he can recover the goods from the carrier. The cost of redelivery must be borne by the seller in this case.

3 The Romalpa clause

This arose from a case in 1976, *Aluminium Industrie Vassen B.V.* v. *Romalpa Aluminium Ltd*. The case established that the manufacturer or supplier of goods had rights to retain some proprietary interest over the goods until he was paid, even when the goods supplied had been processed or sold. Furthermore, proprietary rights could be maintained even after a subsale of the goods (sale by buyer to another party) so that debts owed to the buyer could be transferred to the manufacturer or supplier, if an appropriate Romalpa clause had been inserted.

4 Right of resale

An unpaid seller can pass a good title to the goods to a second buyer after exercising his right of lien, or stoppage in transit. In these cases the contract with the first buyer is automatically rescinded, so that the property in the goods reverts to the seller, who can keep any further profit made from the resale and any deposit put down by the buyer. If he makes a loss on the resale, then he can claim damages from the original buyer. There is no requirement that the second purchaser takes delivery, or buys in good faith (i.e. without knowledge of the first sale).

> *Ward (R.V.) Ltd* v. *Bignall* (1967)
>
> Two cars were being sold for £850. After paying a deposit of £25, the buyer refused to pay the rest. The seller informed the buyer in writing that if he did not pay the balance by a given date, he would resell the cars. The buyer did not pay. The seller sold one car at £350 but failed to find a purchaser for the other. He bought a claim against the purchaser for the balance of the price and advertising expenses.
>
> **Held:** The seller could not recover any of the price, since the ownership had reverted back to him, but he could recover damages. The remaining car was worth £450, so that his total loss on resale would be £50, minus the £25 deposit originally paid. He was entitled to this £25 plus advertising expenses.

21.2.2 Buyer's remedies

1 Action for specific performance

The Court can make an order of specific performance against the seller in the case of a contract to deliver specific or ascertained goods. This order cannot be made for unascertained or future goods. The seller is required to deliver the goods and he is not given the option of paying damages instead. The Courts will not make the order for such a remedy unless damages for non-delivery would not be adequate. Damages will be adequate except where the goods are in some way unique, or extremely rare.

2 Rejection of the goods

If there is a breach of condition by the seller, the buyer has a right to reject the goods, and may also have a claim for damages. The buyer can exercise this right by refusing to take delivery and informing the seller that he has rejected the goods. He is under no duty, in such circumstances, to return them to the seller who may have to collect them. Under Section 35, the seller will have a right of action against the buyer if the buyer's rejection means repudiation of the contract, or if the buyer has kept the goods for an unreasonable length of time. The buyer does not have a lien over the rejected goods and must hand them back even if his purchase money has not been returned. He can bring an action against the seller to recover the price on the grounds of failure of consideration. It is important to consider the meaning of 'acceptance' of the goods in this context, because it is usually at this point that the contract is made and the risk associated with ownership of the goods is transferred.

Acceptance is made in one of the following ways:

(a) the buyer informs the seller that he has accepted the goods;

(b) the buyer has had reasonable opportunity to examine the goods and he does some act inconsistent with the seller being owner of those goods;

(c) the buyer retains the goods for a reasonable length of time without informing the seller that he has rejected the goods.

3 Action for damages

The buyer can claim damages for non-delivery or for breach of condition or warranty (breach of warranty is the breach of a less serious term of the contract). The buyer may also be trying to recover the purchase price and/or reject the goods.

Section 11(4) of the Sale of Goods Act states that: 'where a contract of sale is not severable and the buyer has accepted the goods or part of them', the buyer cannot reject the goods, but can only claim damages for breach of condition. This is an important limitation on the buyer's right of rejection.

4 Recovery of purchase price

The buyer can recover all payments made if consideration has failed. This may apply to cases of non-delivery, but also where there had been a breach of condition of the sale. If the contract is severable (e.g. separate delivery times and instalments for different parts of the goods) the buyer can accept part and reject part of the goods and recover the price paid on the rejected goods.

21.3 Other legislation for consumer protection

The basic legislation for protecting the consumer in his contract of sale is the Sale of Goods Act, 1979. Other legislation has also been passed to protect the consumer, however. The most important statutes are probably the Trade Descriptions Act, 1968, the Fair Trading Act, 1973, and the Consumer Protection Act, 1987.

21.3.1 The Trade Descriptions Act, 1968

This statute was very different from previous consumer legislation because it provided **criminal** sanctions for offences relating to the sale of goods. It also provides facilities for the judge or magistrate to make a compensation order for the consumer who has suffered loss.

Under this Act it is a criminal offence to apply in the course of a trade or business, a false description to goods, or to sell goods where such a description is applied. 'False' means 'false to a material degree' which means that the deviation from the description must be significant. Misleading trade descriptions under the Trade Descriptions Act, 1968 have included misleading indications as to quantity, method of manufacture, composition and testing of goods.

> *Robertson* v. *Dicicco* (1972)
>
> A car dealer advertised a vehicle as a 'beautiful car'. The car was attractive to look at, but unfit for use.
>
> Held: 'Beautiful' is likely to be regarded as a description of performance as well as appearance. It was a misleading description and an offence was committed.

Although Section 1 of the Trade Descriptions Act involves strict liability, there are two potential defences to a charge, i.e. having exercised due diligence, or innocent publication of material (this latter used by such parties as publishers and advertising agents). It is also possible to issue a disclaimer, and probably advisable. An example of such a disclaimer is the case of car dealers disclaiming responsibility for mileometer readings on cars. To be effective such disclaimers must be as prominent as the trade description on the goods and not just 'small print'.

There were, until recently, important sections in the Trade Descriptions Act 1968 relating to misleading indications about prices. These sections have now been superceded by Section 20 of the Consumer Protection Act, 1987. This Act extends the protection against misleading statements on prices to services or facilities as well as goods. Section 21 of the Consumer Protection Act gives some indication about the nature of the deception, e.g. the method of determining the price is not in fact the one that is really used, or that price comparisons are not valid when all the facts are known.

Under the Trade Descriptions Act, 1968, the Secretary of State for Trade has powers to make orders requiring certain information to be given with goods. The Act is enforced by the local Trading Standards Office. The officers involved have enforcement powers to make test purchases for example, or inspect or test goods. Wilful obstruction of such an officer during his investigation is an offence.

21.3.2 The Fair Trading Act, 1973

This was the Act which created the post of Director General of Fair Trading, to review all commercial activities in the United Kingdom which relate to the supply and production of consumer goods and services. He is bound to be particularly vigilant about practices which affect the economic interests of the consumer. The Director General can make recommendations to the Secretary of State that statutory orders are needed to curb certain practices. An example of such an order is the order made in 1976 to make it a criminal offence to display a notice misleading the consumer about his rights, such as 'no goods exchanged or money refunded' (Consumer Transactions (Restrictions on Statements) Order 1976).

The Director can arrange for publication of information and advice for consumers. He is also charged with encouraging trade associations to prepare codes of practice, in which members voluntarily agree to abide by certain standards. Such codes have been negotiated and approved to cover electrical appliances and shoes for example.

The Office of Fair Trading has influence at a local level through the Trading

Standards Departments, who carry out the director's duties in regard to everyday transactions.

21.3.3 The Consumer Protection Act, 1987

This Act renders the 'producer' of a defective product strictly liable (i.e. without proof of any negligence on the producer's part) for damage caused by his defective product. The producer is liable for such damage for up to 10 years from the time of supply of the product. It makes no difference if the producer argues that he took reasonable care to maintain the quality of his products.

The producer includes the manufacturer of the finished products, the supplier of any raw materials or components of the finished product which were defective, and any person putting his trademark on the product to represent himself as the producer. It also includes any person who imports a product from outside the European Community. It is obvious that for many products, there will be more than one 'producer'. This legislation will mean that those identified as producers will have to take out increased insurance to cover themselves against the cost of large claims. Consumers can sue for death or injury, and damage to personal property over a minimum amount. There is no top limit to some of these claims. Suppliers will have to keep good records of sales and purchases, and are often recommended to offer very specific advice on the use of their products. This will perhaps enable them to avoid an action for damages, if they can prove that they did not in fact supply certain goods, for example, or that the fault could be traced back to their own suppliers. It will also enable the supplier to claim, wherever possible, that the customer ignored warnings printed on the goods, or failed to follow the advice given on the goods. Clearly such precautions might actually save a great deal of money if damages are denied or reduced in an action against that supplier.

This legislation is similar in many ways to the product liability legislation in the United States. It has been brought about by pressure from the European Community, which seeks to extend such protection to all countries in Europe.

21.4 Services

Recently an attempt has been made to bring consumer protection for the provision of services, such as meals in restaurants, house repairs, etc., into line with the sale of goods. The legislation is moving rapidly in this direction, and now the rights of the consumer are virtually the same for both goods and services. Such moves have been achieved by the Supply of Goods and Services Act, 1982 and the Consumer Protection Act, 1987.

Sample questions

1 (a) What remedies has the buyer of goods against the seller, where the latter has been guilty of a breach of contract?

(b) Some months before the Investiture of the Prince of Wales, W, a Welsh shopkeeper, orders from M, a manufacturer, a large quantity of commemorative drinking mugs for delivery one week before the Investiture. In fact the mugs are delivered to him one week after the Investiture. State, with reasons, whether W will be legally entitled:

(i) to refuse to accept delivery of the mugs;

(ii) to claim damages from M.

CIS

Suggested answer

The following points should be considered:

(a) The buyer has various options available to him, depending on the nature of the breach of contract.

If there is a breach of condition by the seller, the buyer has a right to reject the goods, and can have a claim for damages. The buyer can exercise this right by refusing to take delivery of the goods, and informing the seller that he has rejected them. He can bring an action against the seller for the price of the goods on the grounds of failure of consideration.

If the goods are irreplaceable, the buyer can bring an action for specific performance of the contract, which requires the seller to deliver the goods. The Courts rarely issue these, however, and will certainly not if damages would suffice. The buyer can also bring an action for damages for non-delivery, if that is appropriate, or for breach of condition.

Under Section 11(4) of the Sale of Goods Act, 1979, once the buyer has accepted the goods, he can only claim damages for a breach of condition, assuming that the buyer had reasonable opportunity to examine the goods. The seller may have a right of action against the buyer if he rejects the goods after a reasonable length of time. If the goods are deficient in some minor respect, the buyer may claim damages for breach of warranty.

(b) (i) It would be wise for W to refuse to accept delivery of the mugs, since if he accepts them, he cannot repudiate the contract. A buyer who accepts delivery late loses the right to reject the goods, but can claim damages.

(ii) Damages, in this instance, might be quite hard to quantify since it would be difficult to say how many people might have bought mugs at a national event. W would certainly be entitled to damages for non-delivery if he had emphasised the time of delivery, but the amount is hard to determine. The late delivery amounts to a breach of contract in such a case and that alone would be grounds for damages to be awarded.

2 A agreed in writing to sell a dinghy to B for £2000. The dinghy has been altered to B's specifications, and B takes delivery of the dinghy but will not pay for it, even though the terms clearly state 'cash on delivery'. Advise A.

Suggested answer

The following points should be considered:

The seller has two types of remedy, an action for the price, and remedies concerning the goods themselves. Unfortunately, since the buyer has taken delivery of the goods, the seller cannot use any of the latter remedies, but since the buyer has wrongfully neglected to pay for the goods according to the terms of the contract, and provided there is no agreement for credit, the seller can bring an action in the County Court for the price of the goods. Since Court proceedings are lengthy and expensive, it would be wise for A to warn B about the course of action he intends to pursue, and use letters from his lawyer and any other means of persuasion. It would be also be useful for A to use a Romalpa clause in all future sales.

3 What remedy has the customer against the manufacturer if the goods prove faulty, and the mail order firm he bought the goods from has gone into liquidation?

Suggested answer

The following points should be considered:

The customer may have an action in negligence against the manufacturer, if the fault in the goods is a result of negligence in the production. Negligence can, however, be difficult to prove when a fault could have been caused in several ways.

Under the Consumer Protection Act, 1987, the new product liability laws will make the manufacturer strictly liable if injury or damage is caused to person or property as a result of his product. This remedy is obviously dependent on the amount of damage caused, if any, by the faulty goods. The customer has no remedies under the Sale of Goods Act, 1979, because this refers only to contracts between buyers and sellers. The customer may well have access to remedies which do not depend upon the force of law. He should perhaps be advised to contact the manufacturers themselves who may wish to make recompense to avoid adverse publicity and to benefit their public image.

4 You are working for a firm manufacturing perfume (Rochlan perfumes). Rochlan have decided to offer franchises to various shops throughout the country so that the perfume can be marketed nationally, but the product image can be maintained. Packages of materials are to be sent out to managers of shops authorised to sell the perfume, and these packages include a guide to consumer law prepared by your department.

You are asked to prepare the leaflet on the law relating to trade descriptions to be included in the above package. Make it concise, interesting and informative and assume the reader knows very little about the law or the legal process.

BTEC HND, Staffordshire Polytechnic

Suggested answer

The leaflet should explain the following points and be clear and attractively presented.

Explain briefly the Director General of Fair Trading and his remit, the national Office of Fair Trading, and the local Trading Standards Office.

It is a Criminal offence under the Trade Descriptions Act, 1968 to apply a false trade description to goods. The trading standards officers can initiate prosecutions at a local level, as a result of complaints, or of their own investigations. The Courts have been empowered to compensate the victims, as well as ensure that the offenders are prosecuted.

There are various defences available to the accused, e.g. store managers. These are:

(a) reliance on information supplied by another;

(b) mistake;

(c) accident;

(d) act or default of another person;

(e) it was an act beyond the control of the accused.

It is important to show that employees took all reasonable precautions, and exercised due diligence to avoid the offence being committed (e.g. it might be difficult to show that if a similar incident had happened before and nothing had been done about it). An example would help, such as an exclusive and expensive perfume having the same name as a cheaper special offer which has been extensively advertised. If one customer has been misled it would be hard to justify using the same advertisement again, without committing an offence.

Section 13 of the Sale of Goods Act, 1979 protects the customer against a faulty description of the goods, and would enable the consumer to claim damages for loss or inconvenience caused. If there is a misleading indication about the price of the goods, the seller will have committed an offence under the Consumer Protection Act, 1987. This includes such cases as misleading statements about comparative prices, determination of price or future intentions (e.g. a statement that the price is expected to increase in the near future).

Further reading

Harvey, Brian W. *The Law of Consumer Protection and Fair Trading* (Butterworths)
Marsh and Soulsby *Business Law* (McGraw-Hill)

22 Consumer credit

The Consumer Credit Act, 1974 had wide-ranging implications for a society in which consumers are increasingly dependent on credit. It replaced the Hire Purchase Acts, but it also dealt with credit sales, credit cards and all the different types of credit agreement.

The most common forms of agreement are the hire-purchase agreement, credit sales (increasingly popular) and the use of the credit card. The most common questions in this area relate to hire purchase agreements. Hire purchase is a particular form of agreement, in which the customer does not own the goods until the last instalment is paid. This can cause problems if the customer sells the goods before he has paid for them, since he has no good title to the goods to pass on to the other party. Originally, one of the functions of hire purchase was to offer protection to the seller, who did not lose his rights over the goods until the money was paid. However, it also allowed the seller to misuse his advantage by reclaiming the goods at the slightest excuse, and selling them again to make extra profits. The consumer was given protection from this sort of behaviour by the Hire Purchase Acts, and this protection has been incorporated into the Consumer Credit Act. Typical questions surround the formation of regulated agreements, protected goods, and rights of cancellation and termination.

22.1 The formation of regulated agreements

A regulated agreement is an agreement for hire or credit made by a consumer for goods worth less than £5000. It can therefore be a regulated consumer hire agreement or a regulated consumer credit agreement. Certain agreements, such as most mortgage loans, are exempt from this definition.

22.1.1 Licences

Businesses which provide facilities for regulated agreements must be licensed by the Office of Fair Trading. If the licence is refused, then an appeal may be made to the Secretary of State for Trade and Industry. Unlicensed trading is an offence under the 1974 Act, and the unlicensed trader will have no legal means of enforcing his agreement.

Specific offences have also been created concerning canvassing these agreements off trade premises. This is now illegal unless the creditor has a licence to trade in this manner. The canvasser should only respond to written requests to visit a person. (Canvassing involves making oral representations about the agreements, i.e. trying to verbally persuade people to enter into the agreement by making comments about it.)

22.1.2 Form of the regulated agreement

There are certain rules affecting regulated agreements:

1 They must be in writing.

2 The cash price of the goods must be stated in the agreement.

3 It must provide for payment of equal instalments at equal intervals, and must include reference to the method of payment.

4 It must include a description of the goods sufficient to identify them.

5 The agreement must contain certain statutory notices, e.g. about right to terminate, or cancel the agreement where that is applicable. Another notice concerns the customer's rights over 'protected goods'.

6 There are certain regulations about the written format of the agreement, e.g. that the agreement must be typewritten, and the hirer must sign it in a red outlined box which has a printed warning that the hirer must only sign this if he intends to be legally bound by it. Contravention of these provisions results in an agreement becoming unenforceable.

The hirer is entitled to certain copies of his agreement. If the creditor, or finance company, signs at the same time as the hirer/debtor, then the hirer is entitled to a copy of the agreement concluded, on the spot. If, however, there is a time lag and the dealer/supplier has to send the forms off to a finance company for agreement, then the hirer must receive:

1 a copy of his offer, on the spot (called the first statutory copy);

2 a subsequent copy of the concluded agreement within seven days (called the second statutory copy).

All copies must comply with the regulations about form and content. If the agreement is signed off trade premises, (e.g. on the front doorstep of a house or at home), it is cancellable, and there must be a notice in the agreement about the right of cancellation and how it can be exercised, including the names and addresses of persons to whom cancellation can be sent.

22.1.3   Breach of regulations of formation

Breach of any regulations concerning form and content renders the agreement improperly executed. This means that it is unenforceable, except through a Court order. The Courts can grant an 'enforcement order', and in doing so can vary the terms of the original agreement. However, the Courts tend not to do this if the agreement does not comply with the regulations, or the correct notices were not served, or copies given. The correct copies must be given to the hirer or debtor before the Court proceedings. If the agreement did not give notice of cancellation rights where they are appropriate, the Courts will not issue an enforcement order.

22.2   Protected goods

When there is a hire-purchase agreement, the hirer or debtor is protected from repossession of the goods after he has paid one third of the price of the goods or more. Section 90 of the Consumer Credit Act specifies three requirements for the goods to become protected goods:

1 a debtor is in breach of a regulated hire-purchase or conditional sale agreement relating to the goods;

2 the debtor has paid to the creditor one third or more of the total price of the goods;

3 the property in the goods remains in the creditor.

Under Section 90, the owner of the goods which are protected (normally the finance company) cannot enforce his right to repossess the goods, other than by action in the Courts. This normally means getting a County Court order, even though the creditor may wish to terminate the agreement because of the hirer's default.

This section does not apply if the hirer wishes to terminate the agreement himself, and probably does not apply if the hirer has 'disposed of' or abandoned the goods.

> *Bentinck v. Cromwell Engineering* (1971)
>
> A car was the subject of a hire-purchase agreement, and it was involved in an accident. The hirer took the car to a garage for repair, then he failed to pay any more hire purchase instalments or collect the car. The company traced the car and repossessed it. They sold the car and sought to recover depreciation costs from the hirer. He claimed that they had repossessed the car without consent.
>
> **Held:** When a hirer has abandoned goods, and his rights to them show that he no longer has any interest in them, then the owner has a right to repossess, even if the goods had been 'protected' goods. The defendants were held liable for damages, and indemnity.

22.2.1 Effect of repossession without Court order

If the owner does try to repossess the goods without a Court order, in normal circumstances, after the goods have become protected, that action will result in various consequences (see Section 91):

1 The hire-purchase agreement is terminated.

2 The hirer's responsibility is at an end, and he can claim back anything he has paid under the agreement.

3 Any guarantor/indemnifier is released from liability and entitled to recover any security given.

NB A guarantor is someone who guarantees that the creditor will receive payment due to him from the hirer/debtor. It is a secondary responsibility, based solely on the responsibility of the hirer to pay. An indemnity is a promise to pay the creditor for any loss suffered on this contract, and is a primary responsibility to indemnify loss suffered by the creditor as a result of his contract with the hirer. Thus an indemnity may have to be paid when the hirer could avoid responsibility, whereas a guarantor can only be asked to pay where the hirer should have paid.

22.2.2 Action to recover possession of protected goods

The Consumer Credit Act gives the County Court exclusive jurisdiction over all actions relating to hire-purchase contracts within the Act (i.e. personal credit agreements under £15 000). All parties concerned, including any guarantor or indemnifier, must be made party to the Court action, and the Court can make various orders:

1 return order;

2 return order suspended or time order;

3 transfer order.

1 Return order

The hirer is asked to return the goods to the owner/creditor. If the hirer fails to return the goods, the only fall-back position is to send in the bailiffs.

2 Suspended order

This is awarded when the hirer has a reasonable excuse for default, e.g. redundancy or ill health. The Court can vary the terms of the original agreement to enable the hirer to meet his obligations. It can reduce the amount of each instalment, and extend the period of time to pay if this is deemed necessary. These are known as time orders. The effect of a suspended order can therefore be summarized as:

(a) the agreement continues, but with the terms varied;

(b) the owner cannot claim extra interest for the longer period of time;

(c) if the hirer breaks any terms as specified in the agreement, it is possible for the Court to make an order that the creditor can repossess without going back to Court, i.e. implement the suspended order;

(d) the Court can vary the time order upon application from the hirer or the owner, if the hirer's financial circumstances get worse or better;

(e) the hirer may avoid the suspended order by paying off the unpaid balance and becoming the owner of the goods.

3 Transfer order

This order gives part of the goods back to the owner, and allows the hirer to retain part of the goods and become the owner of them. The hire purchase agreement is at an end.

22.2.3 Notice of default

Whenever the owner repossesses the goods, he must serve a 'notice of default'. The notice must give the hirer seven days to pay, or remedy the default, and tell him the total amount due, and the consequences of non-payment, i.e. termination. If the hirer pays in time, the contract will continue as if there had been no default. Notices of default must be issued whenever the debtor is in breach of any term of the agreement, before the agreement can be terminated.

22.3 Rights of cancellation

The debtor may cancel the contract where he has signed it at other than appropriate trade premises, but only where antecedent negotiations included oral representations made in the presence of the debtor by the person negotiating, or on his behalf.

The notion of persuasion is therefore brought into the requirements of this form of protection.

This situation covers doorstep sales, but also the situation where the debtor takes the forms home to sign. The debtor has five days (sometimes known as the 'cooling off' period) from the receipt of the second statutory copy to cancel the agreement, or seven days from the receipt of the notice of cancellation. Notice of such cancellation must be given in writing to the finance company or to the dealer.

From 1st July 1988, the Consumer Protection (Cancellation of Contracts concluded away from Business Premises) Regulations 1987 operate. These cover any agreement by a consumer to buy goods or services from a trader during an unsolicited visit to their home or place of work. The consumer will have a seven-day 'cooling off' period, during which agreements covered by these regulations can be cancelled without any penalty to the consumer.

22.3.1 Effect of cancellation

1 The agreement is wiped out, and there is no liability under it;

2 all sums cease to be payable, and all sums paid out are recoverable;

3 the hirer is not obliged to return the goods, but must hand them over if the owner calls at a reasonable time;

4 the hirer has duty to take care of the goods for 21 days after notice of cancellation;

5 the hirer has a lien on the goods for the repayment of sums paid under the agreement;

6 any part-exchange goods can be recovered within 10 days, or a part-exchange allowance must be given to the hirer.

22.4 The dealer as agent of the finance company

The dealer/supplier is often regarded by statute as the agent of the finance company. He is agent:

1 for notice of cancellation;

2 to receive the goods;

3 to receive notice of withdrawal of offer;

4 to receive notice of rescission of contract;

5 to receive notice of termination.

22.5 Termination of regulated agreement

The debtor can terminate at any time, provided he gives notice to the finance company, or an agent. He may be required to pay up to 50 per cent of the price of the goods (or less if specified in the contract) as well as all sums due. The hirer will be liable for any damage caused by failure to take reasonable care of the goods.

The creditor cannot terminate for any breach of contract without serving a seven day notice of default (see above).

A consumer credit agreement may contain an acceleration clause providing for immediate payment of the whole outstanding balance on default of payment. This is valid, provided it is not capable of being interpreted as a penalty clause. (NB this can be achieved by providing for an appropriate rebate on early repayment.) Such an acceleration clause cannot be operated without at least seven days' notice in writing.

22.6 Extortionate credit bargains

The Consumer Credit Act gives the Court power to reopen a credit agreement, and take action if it finds that a credit agreement is extortionate. A bargain is defined as extortionate when payments imposed on the debtor are grossly exhorbitant, or grossly contravene the ordinary principles of fair dealing. The Court will take into account the prevailing interest rates, and the capacity, age and experience of the hirer/debtor. The Court can rewrite the agreement, or set aside the contract. They can, however, seem to be reluctant to intervene on some occasions.

> *Ketley* v. *Scott* (1981)
>
> Mr Scott had negotiated a loan, and he was paying 48 per cent per annum for it. He had an overdraft at the bank, and the loan was negotiated in a hurry without full enquiries. He defaulted on his loan and the plaintiffs sued him. Mr Scott claimed the interest was extortionate.
>
> **Held:** There was a high degree of risk involved and therefore the interest charged was not disproportionately high.

Lawyers have speculated that the Courts would be reluctant to intervene using this section of the Act. Perhaps the *caveat emptor* ('let the buyer beware') principle has left its mark on the judiciary.

Sample questions

1 What rights of cancellation and termination are given by the Consumer Credit Act, 1974 to a person who enters into a regulated agreement under that Act?

Suggested answer

The issues to be addressed are the circumstances in which the consumer has rights of cancellation, i.e. if he has signed the agreement off trade premises and there were verbal representations made to him about the transaction, and the debtor's rights in these circumstances. In such a case the consumer gets a five-day 'cooling off' period after the receipt of the second statutory copy of the agreement, or seven days from the notice of cancellation. If he does cancel, no further liability exists and the financial position is restored to what it was before the contract.

Further issues surround the rights of termination. The hirer can terminate at any time by giving written notice to the creditor. He may be required to pay as much as 50 per cent of the price of the goods, and he may also have to pay depreciation for any damage to the goods caused by negligence.

The creditor can terminate if the hirer is in breach of his contract by issuing a notice of default. This notice gives the hirer seven days to pay.

2 James, a client of yours, wishes to introduce hire-purchase facilities in his shop. Explain to him what a hire-purchase contract is, and what formalities are necessary for the creation of a valid hire-purchase contract under the Consumer Credit Act, 1974. Also explain to him the legal consequences of failing to comply with these formalities.

(b) Joseph bought a car on hire purchase for £1000 (total hire-purchase price). He paid £350, but then fell into arrears. Bright Motors Ltd, the owners, took possession of the car without his consent. Realising the 'irregularity' of their action, they took the car back, and left it outside Joseph's house. Bright Motors Ltd regard the contract as being still in force and wish to sue Joseph for the outstanding instalments and the return of the car. Advise Joseph as to his legal position.

ACCA

Suggested answer

A hire-purchase contract is an agreement to hire goods with an option to purchase those goods on the final instalment. The retailer may offer finance for the hire-purchase agreement himself, but normally he sells the goods to a finance company, who in turn bail the goods out on hire-purchase terms to the consumer. The creditor/finance company must be licensed to offer loans, and the retailer must also be licensed under Section 145 of the Consumer Credit Act.

Hire purchase can be seen as a form of sale, but the title only passes to the 'hirer' if he agrees to purchase the goods on payment of the last instalment.

The agreements for hire purchase must have various characteristics, e.g. must be typewritten, mention the cash price, the instalments, certain statutory notices, a description of the goods and must have a red box for the signature of the hirer which warns him that if he signs he will be legally bound. The hirer must receive the correct number of copies of the agreement.

If the agreement is 'improperly executed' then it is unenforceable. The dealer can be regarded as agent of the finance company for certain purposes if he receives instalments.

(b) The car comes under the definition of 'protected goods'. The owner cannot therefore repossess the car without a Court order. Hence the Court will not enforce the agreement. Quote *Capital Finance Co Ltd* v. *Bray*.

3 Your company are cutting back on staff and a close friend of yours, Billy Smith, has been made redundant. You chat to him on the phone, and discover that one of his major worries is the amount owed on his hire-purchase agreements. He has agreements on the sofa, the dining table and even a new fitted kitchen. Billy is worried about making payments, which were initially calculated on the basis of a fairly good salary. Write a letter to Billy explaining the options available to him, and any relief from his anxiety that the Courts may be able to offer.

BTEC HND, Staffordshire Polytechnic

Suggested answer

(Laid down in letter form.) Note that, for the immediate future, the goods are safe in Billy's possession if he has paid over one-third of the price, because then the goods are 'protected', i.e. they cannot be claimed back except with the hirer's permission, without a Court order. The letter should also state that, as a result of the telephone call you are drawing his attention to the following options:

(a) pay for the goods now, if you get any redundancy money, or any payments;

(b) contact the finance company and explain the situation, to ask if terms can be changed;

(c) if they are not sympathetic the Court may substitute a 'time order' which has lower payments and more weeks to pay. This would be attached to a suspended order to return the goods, but the Court will review the time order if requested, if there are problems. The Court also has the power to order the return of some of the goods, and to authorize retention of part of the goods according to the amount paid.

4 What are the rules concerning termination of a regulated consumer credit agreement?

Suggested answer

The rules are that a contract may be terminated if the agreement is improperly executed, or the creditor tries to reposses 'protected goods' without a Court order.

Otherwise the debtor may terminate the agreement at any time, but may have to pay up to 50 per cent value of the goods, and for any damage caused by negligence. The creditor can terminate only if there is a breach of contract by issuing a notice of default. This should include certain information, and give the hirer seven days to pay.

It is possible for the hirer/debtor to terminate the contract early, or to speed up the payments.

Further reading

Harvey, Brian W. *The Law of Consumer Protection and Fair Trading* (Butterworths) Marsh and Soulsby *Business Law* (McGraw-Hill)

23 Negotiable instruments

23.1 What is a negotiable instrument?

A negotiable instrument is a document which represents the right to a sum of money, and by definition, the right to sue for that money can be negotiated to another. It is negotiated by delivery of that document to another, or, in some cases, delivering the document and endorsing it to another with a signature. The person liable to be sued need not be notified that it has been transferred. The person who holds the document can sue the person who is liable to pay. Examples of such negotiable instruments are bills of exchange, cheques and bankers' commercial letters of credit.

The practice of using negotiable instruments arose through 19th century merchants, who developed the bill of exchange in order to solve some problems associated with paying for goods abroad. In these cases, the buyer could not pay for the goods easily until he had received them and resold them.

Questions on negotiable instruments typically concern the definition of a negotiable instrument, or the rights of a holder in due course in respect of theft or fraud relating to the document.

23.2 Bills of exchange

The bill of exchange is like the modern cheque, except that it is made out by the seller who is owed the money, and not by the person who owes the money.

For example, if the seller is named John Sellar, and the buyer is called Paul Byer:

£5000	London June 1st 1988

Three months after the date pay John Sellar £5000 for value received.

To: Paul Byer

The advantage of this arrangement is that the seller can shop around for someone to discount the bill (which means buy it from him). This means that the seller gets his money, and the buyer gets times to pay. NB The person who discounts the bill usually makes his profit by paying slightly less for the bill than the agreed sum on the bill. The buyer will normally pay a little over the price for his goods so that the seller receives the correct money when the bill is discounted.

Bills of exchange are the earliest examples of negotiable instruments. The Bills of Exchange Act, 1882, Section 3(1) gives a definition:

> A bill of exchange is an unconditional order in writing addressed by one person to another, signed by the person giving it, requiring the person to whom it is addressed to pay on demand, or at a fixed or determinable future time, a sum certain in money to, or to the order of, a specified person, or to bearer.

This definition needs to be split up into parts and examined. It is an important definition for the subject of negotiable instruments and it must be known and understood.

'An unconditional order in writing' – This means that payment is not dependent on any conditions, such as 'when the goods arrive', and that the order must be written down. It does not say where it is to be written, e.g. a man once wrote his cheque to the tax office on the back of his shirt, and this was considered a legitimate negotiable instrument.

'To pay on demand, or at a fixed or determinable future time' – This means that it must either be payable on presentation, or it is payable on the date specified or the nearest working date. It is possible to specify the date by reference to a particular event, as long as that event is certain to occur, e.g. someone's marriage could not be used as a way of determining the date, as it might never occur!

... 'A sum certain in money' – This means that a specific sum must be stated. It can be payable by instalments or with interest attached, but it must be a fixed price e.g. 'pay however much is owed' would not be acceptable as a bill of exchange.

If a bill of exchange is made out to a non-existent person, then it is payable to the bearer (i.e. the person who holds the bill at that time).

23.2.1   Parties to the bill

There are various terms used to describe the parties to the bill of exchange as follows:

Drawer: The person who draws up the bill, and gives the order to pay is the drawer of the bill. In the first example, he would be the seller of the goods.

Payee: The person who is going to be paid on the bill is the payee. In the example, this is John Sellar who is also the drawer of the bill.

Drawee: The person to whom the bill is drawn up is the drawee of the bill. In the first example, this is the buyer. Once he has accepted it, by writing 'accepted' and signing it, he is also the 'acceptor' of the bill.

It is useful to remember that words ending in -ee usually denote the receiver of something, e.g. payee receives payment; and words ending in -er usually denote the person who does something, e.g. the payer does the paying.

Once the bill has been accepted and has changed hands and been negotiated, the rights of the holder of that bill can vary.

23.2.2   The rights and duties of the holder of a bill of exchange

A holder of a bill can be:

1 a mere holder;

2 a holder for value;

3 a holder in due course.

1 A mere holder is a person who is in possession of a bill, but cannot enforce it, even though they can pass on a good title to the bill to others. Textbooks often use the examples of a spouse or a thief as possible 'holders'; as either of these might have got possession of the bill without actually having given value for it themselves.

NB This is unfortunately not the only instance of legal academics drawing comparisons between wives and people of lowly or questionable status!

2 A holder for value is the holder of a bill for which value has at some time been paid. He can enforce the bill against anyone who signed it prior to the giving of value, but he is not protected if any defects in title have arisen, e.g. if there has been theft or fraud. What this means, in effect, is that a holder for value has exactly the same rights as the person who negotiated the bill to him.

Value could have been given for the bill in the past, in contrast to the rules in contract, where 'past consideration' is not sufficient.

3 A holder in due course has the strongest rights of any holder, and it is the holder who takes the bill in good faith, i.e. without suspicion of anything irregular, and has paid good value for the bill. He can sue any parties who have signed the bill.

A payee cannot become a holder in due course.

23.3   Presentation for payment

In order to obtain payment on the bill, the payee must be a holder for value, or a holder in due course. If the bill is not presented in good time, which is usually within a few days of the fixed date, then the drawer and endorsers are discharged from their responsibilities under the bill. If the bill is payable on demand then it must be paid within a reasonable time after the bill is issued and that reasonable time is determined by the nature of the bill and the facts of the case.

23.4 Negotiation

It has already been stated that negotiation can take place by delivery, or by delivery and endorsement. Endorsements are usually found on the back of the bill and can consist of a signature only, in which case the bill becomes payable to the bearer, or an instruction and a signature, e.g. 'pay Peter', signed by Paul.

A bearer bill is negotiated simply by delivery. It is either expressly made payable to the bearer on the front of the bill, or it has an endorsement which is just a signature, but it could also be a bill made payable to a non-existent payee.

> *Clutton v. Attenborough & Son* (1897)
>
> A clerk employed by Attenborough made out a cheque to George Brett, which Mr Attenborough signed. George Brett did not exist.
>
> **Held:** The cheque was payable to the bearer.

In another case, *Bank of England* v. *Vagliano Bros* (1890), a clerk forged bills payable to the name of a real person, but as he was not to be paid, the Court regarded the payee as fictitious and declared the bills to be bearer bills!

It is possible that, for various reasons, a 'bill' may be delivered signed but incomplete. This is known as an inchoate bill. It can be filled up for any amount within the authority granted, within a reasonable time.

One of the problems associated with negotiation is the forged, or unauthorized, endorsement, which may well happen in cases of fraud or theft. In the case of a bearer bill, then the title to the bill does not rest on the forgery and the transferee will receive a defective title, rather than none at all. A defective title gives the holder the right to sue anyone who endorsed the bill subsequent to the theft or fraud. If he can show that he is a holder in due course, then the defect in title is cured.

If the bill is not a bearer bill and an endorsement is forged then the holder cannot sue on the bill itself, but can sue the person who transferred it to him, for breach of warranty of genuineness, and similarly he can sue anyone who has endorsed the bill subsequent to the forgery.

> *Kreditbank Cassel v. Schenkers Ltd* (1927)
>
> Schenkers had a business in London and a branch in Manchester. The manager of the Manchester branch drew up seven bills, purportedly on behalf of Schenkers, and signed them as Manchester manager. The bills were dishonoured and Kreditbank sued Schenkers as drawers.
>
> **Held:** The bills were forgeries and Schenkers were not liable to pay.

23.5 Dishonour

A bill is dishonoured if it is not paid, when presented for payment at the correct time, or remains unpaid after the due date where presentment for payment is excused.

If the bill is dishonoured for non-payment, then notice of dishonour must be given to anyone who the holder intends to make liable. This is often the last endorser, but could of course be the drawer or any endorser liable on the bill. Notice of dishonour need not take any particular form, written or verbal, provided that the people who might be sued are made aware that the bill is dishonoured. The rules about notice of dishonour are laid out in the Bills of Exchange Act, 1882, Sections 49 and 50. The holder can formally note or 'protest' the bill by giving formal notice to a notary of the time of dishonour. Without this notice, it is possible that the drawer of the bill or endorsers may be discharged from liability. 'Noting' or 'protesting' is particularly important when the bill is a foreign bill.

Damages are available in the event of dishonour and these can be not only for the amount of the bill, but also for the interest which should have accumulated from the point at which the bill reached maturity, and the expenses associated with noting and protesting.

23.6 Discharge of a bill

It is important for anyone who may be affected by the bill to know how and when the bill can be considered discharged, because at that point all obligations cease. There are a variety of ways in which this might happen and the most common of these are:

1 by payment in due course;

2 when a bill is cancelled intentionally;

3 when a bill is altered.

Payment in due course is payment to the holder of the bill after the bill has reached maturity, without notice that the title is defective. The bill is not generally discharged and the acceptor could still find that he is liable to pay the bill. The bill is not discharged unless the acceptor has paid back his loan to the true owner. If a bill has been altered in some material way, the bill is discharged except against the person who authorized the alteration and all subsequent endorsers.

The Limitation Act, 1939 bars a remedy in Court, after the passage of time. This period of time is normally six years when it is associated with a contractual agreement, as in the case of payment for goods. Under this Act, the obligations still exist of the acceptor and endorser, but the right to take action in the Court to recover sums due is barred.

Sample questions

1 (a) What commercial advantages are there in bills of exchange?

(b) Consider the liability of the parties where Norman draws a bill of exchange payable to Olive on Peter. Olive specially endorses the bill to Quentin. Richard steals it from Quentin and forges his signature in a special endorsement to Stella. Stella specially endorses the bill to Thomas.

IPS

Suggested answer

The following points should be considered:

(a) The bill of exchange saves time (e.g. whilst goods are at sea), and offers more convenience than cash.

The buyer is given time to pay by this method, and the seller receives his income straight away if he negotiates the bill.

(b) Peter must have accepted the bill.

Norman is liable, as a party to the bill, to Olive and Quentin, as holders in due course, if Olive and Quentin gave value for the bill.

Richard has no title to the bill and can be sued in conversion by Quentin. Stella's title rests upon a forgery, and she can sue Richard for breach of warranty if she thought the bill was genuine. Thomas can sue Stella for breach of warranty, and may become a holder in due course if he takes the bill in good faith and pays value for it. Thomas would, in this case, have rights against everyone who signed the bill. If Stella had no notice of the defect in title and gave good value for the bill, she too would have become a holder in due course.

2 (a) Define a bill of exchange.

(b) An exporter, E, is sent a bill of exchange from an importer I, relating to certain cases of electronic components shipped from Liverpool on 14th March. The document reads:

'to be paid to E, the sum of fourteen hundred pounds, on the date of the arrival of the ship Penross in the above mentioned port'.

The bank have informed E that this is not a valid bill of exchange. Explain this statement to E.

Suggested answer

The following points should be considered:

(a) The statutory definition of a bill of exchange, i.e. an unconditional order in writing, addressed by one person to another, signed by the person giving it, requiring the person to whom it is addressed to pay on demand or at a fixed or determinable future time a sum certain in money to, or to the order of a specified person or to bearer. It must, therefore be in writing and paid on a date which can be determined exactly. It must be paid out to someone other than the drawer, but it is possible to make the bill out to 'bearer' rather than name a particular recipient. In this case, the bill is negotiated by endorsement and delivery.

There have been cases in which conditions have been attached to the document such as 'to be paid when the ship arrives in port'. Such a document is not an 'unconditional order' and therefore it is not a bill of exchange.

(b) It is not a valid bill of exchange because payment is conditional on the ship arriving in port. If the event referred to is certain to occur, e.g. someone's death, then the instrument could be valid, but it is possible that the ship will not arrive in port.

3 (a) How is a bill of exchange negotiated?

(b) What is the difference between the rights of a holder in due course and those of a holder for value?

Suggested answer

The following points should be considered:

(a) A bearer bill is negotiated by delivery.

An order bill is negotiated by endorsement and delivery. The endorsement can be open, to make the bill a bearer bill, or special if it is made out to a particular person.

(b) A holder in due course is the person who takes the bill, complete and regular on the face of it, before it is overdue and without notice of dishonour, and he takes it in good faith and for value. A holder for value, on the other hand, is a holder of the bill, possibly the payee or an endorsee or the bearer of a bearer bill, who has legal possession of the bill on which value has, at some time, been given. The holder for value can claim on the bill if it is not defective.

Should the bill be defective, the holder in due course, who did not know of any defect in title of the person negotiating the bill to him, can remedy the defect and sue on the bill.

Further reading

Kobrin D. and Stott V. *Negotiable Instruments* (Anderson Keenan)
Redmond, P. W. D. *Mercantile Law* (M & E Handbooks)

24 Cheques

24.1 A cheque as a bill of exchange

A cheque is a bill of exchange which is drawn on a banker and payable on demand. Cheques came into use when merchants were finding increasing difficulties in discounting bills of exchange. The banks could offer this service, provided they secured some protection for themselves against the possibilities of economic loss. The rules relating to bills of exchange payable on demand apply to cheques.

'Banker' is defined as a body of persons who carry on the business of banking as their main business. A banker must:

1 take current accounts;

2 pay cheques drawn on itself;

3 collect cheques drawn on its customers.

The most important rules relating to cheques are in the Bills of Exchange Act, 1882, and the Cheques Act, 1957.

A cheque is payable by the drawer (person who draws up the cheque). The payee (person to be paid) has six years from the date of the cheque to enforce the order, under the Statute of Limitations 1939. Many banks reduce this time in practice by only paying, without question, cheques drawn up to six months previously, but this does not negate the payee's rights to sue, as long as the six years have not elapsed.

Typical questions about cheques surround fraud, and the rights of the paying and collecting banker. There may also be a short question on the difference between cheques and other bills of exchange.

24.2 The differences beween cheques and other bills of exchange

1 A cheque is not 'accepted'. The drawee is always the banker, and the bank is not liable to the holder of the cheque, only to the customer. In contrast, in the case of a bill of exchange the drawee, who is also the 'acceptor', is liable to the holder of the bill.

2 A cheque is always drawn on a banker, and payable on demand. A bill may be drawn on anyone, and may be payable on demand, or at a fixed or determinable future time.

3 A cheque can be crossed in several ways, whereas bills of exchange cannot be crossed.

4 If a cheque is returned to a banker, no notice of dishonour is necessary in order to claim against the drawer, in contrast to a bill of exchange which would require such a notice.

5 A banker who pays out for a cheque with a forged or unauthorized endorsement in good faith and in the ordinary course of business is not liable to the holder or to his customer. If however, the drawee of a bill of exchange pays the bill with a forged endorsement he is still liable to the true owner.

6 Delay in presentment of a cheque does not discharge the drawer of a cheque, unless he suffers actual loss from that delay. A bill of exchange payable on demand, however, must be presented within a reasonable time, or the drawer of the bill will be discharged from liability, i.e. he will not have to pay!

24.3 Crossings

A cheque can be crossed in various ways, but the types of crossings generally recognized are as follows:

1 A general crossing – this is simply when parallel lines are drawn across a cheque, or parallel lines with '& Co' or '& Company' written between them. Such a cheque can only be paid through a bank and not over the counter.

2 A special crossing – this is when the name of a particular bank is written between the parallel lines, and then only that bank can accept payment.

3 'Not negotiable' – this can be written between the lines, with or without the name of a bank. This phrase, strangely enough, does not acutally stop the cheque being negotiated, but, because the person receiving the cheque has notice that it should not be negotiable, that person acquires no better title than the person who negotiated it to him (transferor). This means, in practice, that he accepts a risk since he accepts the cheque with any defects in title. It is therefore unlikely that anyone would accept a cheque with this crossing.

4 'Account payee' – when this is written across a cheque, it is a direction to the collecting bank that the proceeds are only to be credited to the account of the named payee. The cheque is still negotiable, in theory (it would not be if the phrase read 'account payee only') but the bank will be liable to the owner if it credits an account of a person who holds the cheque without justification. In practice, this means that the bank would be unlikely to accept the cheque for anyone other than the named payee, because of the risk involved. Many service industries such as gas and electricity boards specify to the consumer that they would prefer this type of crossing, as it is least likely to be open to fraud.

> *House Property Co* v. *London County & Westminster Bank* (1915)
>
> A cheque, which was crossed 'Account Payee' was made payable to 'F.S.H. or bearer'. The customer of the bank had possession, but no right to the cheque. The bank collected payment and credited his account.
>
> **Held:** The bank was liable in conversion to the true owner, because it was negligent, as the customer was neither F.S.H. nor the proper bearer.

NB The tort of conversion protects title to personal property. It usually renders the defendant liable for the full value of that personal property, because he has denied the owner's rights.

24.4 Relationship between banker and customer

The basic relationship of banker and customer is that between debtor and creditor. It is a contractual relationship.

The customer has certain duties towards the bank:

1 A customer has a duty of care to his bank not to draw up cheques carelessly.

> *London Joint Stock Bank* v. *MacMillan & Arthur* (1918)
>
> A clerk employed by M & A used to prepare cheques for signature. He prepared a cheque payable to the bearer, saying that it was for petty cash, with the amount of two pounds written in figures but not in words. The space for words was left blank. After the cheque was signed, the clerk altered the figures to £120, and filled in the space for words with that amount. He cashed the cheque and M & A brought an action against the bank to recover £118.
>
> **Held:** The customer owes a duty to the bank to take reasonable care to draw up cheques so that the amount cannot be altered. This does not extend to filling in the space between the payee's name and 'or order'.

2 A customer owes a duty to his banker to inform him if he knows of a person forging his signature. He may, otherwise be estopped from denying the validity of that signature.

> *Greenwood* v. *Martins Bank Ltd* (1933)
>
> A wife had been forging her husband's signature. The husband was aware that this had been happening, and he failed to inform the bank. In this particular case, she obtained £410 by using the forgery.

There is a general duty for the customer to do what he can to protect the banker. The bank also has certain duties towards the customer:

1 To pay money out of the customer's account whenever the customer writes an order to do so. The banker must honour cheques provided he has funds belonging to the customer, or it is within an agreed overdraft limit. If the banker fails to do this he may be liable in an action by the customer for wrongful dishonour of the cheque. If the customer is only a private person, however, and not a trader or professional person, he will receive only nominal damages.

2 To keep the affairs of his customer secret. There are some exceptions to this duty of secrecy, however, e.g. where disclosure is compulsory by law, or where there is a public duty to disclose; or if at the customer's request for information is released.

3 There is a duty to keep customers correctly informed about their financial position.

24.5 Protection of the banker

24.5.1 Paying bank

The ordinary principles of common law provide that if a paying bank pays a customer's cheque to a person not entitled to it, he will be liable to the owner in conversion, and he cannot debit the customer's account. Under statute law the paying bank has four defences in this situation as follows:

1 Section 59 of the Bills of Exchange Act provides that payment of a bill at the correct time, to the holder in good faith, and without notice of any defect in the holder's title discharges the drawee. It therefore discharges the banker in these conditions when he has paid to the bearer of a 'pay bearer' cheque. It does not protect the banker in the case of an order cheque (made out to a specific payee), however, because the person will not be a 'holder' of the cheque in law if he has no title to it.

2 Section 60 of the Bills of Exchange Act protects the banker 'if when there is a forged endorsement, the banker pays the cheque drawn on him, payable on demand to order, in good faith and in the ordinary course of business, he is deemed to have paid the cheque in due course' (i.e. it will be treated as if the cheque had been properly paid). In this case the drawer of the cheque is treated as having discharged his liability, and, as stated, the bank can debit the customer's account and is not liable in conversion.

Charles v. *Blackwell* (1877)
X drew a cheque in favour of Y's order. Z stole it and forged Y's signature as an endorsement. X's bank paid Z in good faith and in the ordinary course of business.
Held: The bank could debit X's account.

3 Section 1 of the Cheques Act, 1957. Where a banker pays a cheque drawn on himself in good faith and in the ordinary course of business he is protected, in the absence of an irregular endorsement or a missing endorsement. This section made it clear that endorsement was not necessary when presenting a cheque for payment.

4 Section 80 of the Bills of Exchange Act. This section states that if a banker pays out on a cheque that has been crossed to another banker, then he is protected from liability. Similarly, if the cheque has been crossed specially, then the banker is protected if he paid out to the bank specified on the crossing.

24.5.2 Collecting bank

1 Section 2 of the Cheques Act
This enables the collecting bank to have the same rights to hold the cheque as a 'holder in due course', even without the cheque being endorsed to it. The collecting bank also has a lien on any cheque validly presented to it if the customer's balance is insufficient to meet the unpaid debt.

2 Section 4 of the Cheques Act, 1957

This section protects the bank from being sued in the tort of conversion. If the bank receives payment for the customer in good faith and without negligence, the bank does not incur any liability.

The collecting bank is also bound, by law, to fulfil certain duties. These are:

1 Not to let a customer open an account without proper references and enquiry into his identity and circumstances, the nature of his employment and the name of his employer.

2 To be alert to the obvious forms of misappropriation, e.g. to check up on a cheque drawn in favour of the customer's employer.

Underwood Ltd v. *Bank of Liverpool & Marins Ltd* (1924)

Underwood was the sole director and major shareholder of Underwood Ltd. His private bank was L bank, but the company's account was at another bank. Cheques drawn in favour of Underwood Ltd were paid into Underwood's personal account, and payment was collected by L bank. Underwood Ltd sued L bank for conversion.

Held: They succeeded, because L bank was negligent in not enquiring whether Underwood Ltd had a separate account, and if so, why the cheques were not paid into it.

Sample questions

1 L drew a cheque for £100 in favour of X, and gave the cheque to Y (L's secretary) to remit to X. Y endorsed the cheque, by forging X's signature and negotiated it to M in return for goods. Advise L as to his rights.

Suggested answer

The following points should be considered:

Draw attention to the virtues of drawing up a cheque carefully, and using a crossing on the cheque. The banker will be protected if a cheque is carelessly drawn.

L can sue Y in conversion. L will have to pay and the collecting bank is protected. If he discovers the whereabouts of the cheque in time, L can stop the cheque, preferably by written instructions to his bank. The paying bank is otherwise protected by the Cheques Act, 1957.

2 (a) Explain the rights and duties of a paying banker and a collecting banker in relation to cheques.

(b) How is a banker's authority to pay a cheque drawn on him by his customer terminated?

ACCA

Suggested answer

(a) The following points should be considered:

Paying bank: rights are that the customer has a duty not to draw up cheques carelessly, and must do what he can to protect the banker. It also has certain statutory protections when paying out on cheques. The bank has a duty to pay money out of the customer's account on order. It also has a duty to keep the affairs of the customer secret, and keep the customer correctly informed of his financial position.
The collecting bank: rights are the same as those of a holder in due course. It has a lien on the cheque, and cannot be sued in the tort of conversion.

The duties of the collecting bank are that it must not let a customer open an account without proper references and without discovering the name of his employer. It must also be alert to obvious forms of misappropriation, e.g. banking a cheque made payable to his employer.

(b) A banker's authority to pay a cheque is terminated by notice from the customer, which it is safer for the customer to deliver in written form.

The authority can also be terminated under Section 59 of the Bills of Exchange Act where the bank has already paid out on that cheque at the correct time to the holder in good faith without notice of any defect in the holder's title: i.e. where a banker has paid out on a 'pay bearer' cheque.

The other ways in which authority is terminated are through the ordinary rules of termination of contract.

i.e. customer's mental incapacity

customer's bankruptcy

Court order

cheque drawn for unlawful purpose

customer's death

3 (a) Explain and illustrate the endorsement that can appear on a bill of exchange.

(b) K draws a cheque for £500 in favour of L as payment for goods received. L endorses the cheque and negotiates it to M. M does not endorse the cheque, but negotiates it to P in good faith. K is dissatisfied with the goods and stops the cheque.

(i) Can P recover his £500?

(ii) Would it make any difference if M knew that K had stopped the cheque?

Suggested answer

The following points should be considered:

(a) An endorsement in blank turns the bill into a bearer bill. A special endorsement is made out to a named person. There is also a conditional endorsement, e.g. 'Pay A only', but this effectively stops the bill being negotiable and so it ceases to be a cheque.

(b) (i) P has given goods value for the cheque, and received it in good faith. He can therefore sue anyone liable to the cheque. This includes K or L, who has endorsed the cheque. M has not endorsed the cheque but could be liable to P for breach of contract if the cheque was given as consideration.

(ii) If M knew that K had stopped the cheque, he would have responsibilities to P for breach of warranty, for representing to P that the cheque was valid.

Further reading

Kobrin, D. and Stott, V. *Negotiable Instruments* (Anderson Keenan)
Redmond, P. W. D. *Mercantile Law* (M & E Handbooks)

Glossary of
legal terms

Glossary of legal terms

Ab initio	This means from the beginning. Some contracts, e.g. illegal contracts, are said to be void *ab initio*.
Accord and satisfaction	This is the procedure whereby a person provides consideration in order to be released from a contractual agreement. In other words the person does some action in order to escape having to do another.
Account stated	This is a written acknowledgement of a debt.
Act of God	An occurrence which is independent of human intervention, e.g. storm, earthquake.
Administrator/ Administratrix	A person appointed by the Court to manage the property of another. A person interested in the estate of a deceased person may be appointed as administrator where the deceased has not appointed any executors.
Agent	A person employed to act on behalf of another, known as the principal.
Appellant	The person who appeals to a higher Court against the judgment of a lower Court.
Arbitration	Determination of a dispute by arbitrators.
Bailee	A person to whom the possession of goods is entrusted by the owner.
Caveat emptor	Let the buyer beware.
Consensus ad idem	This literally means 'agreement as to the same thing' and is the underlying meeting of minds that is said to be necessary before the making of a contract.
Contra proferentum	The effect of this doctrine is that the least favourable interpretation of an exclusion clause to the interest of the person seeking to rely on it will be adopted by the Court.
Court order	A command or direction from the Court.
Credit sale	Agreement for the sale of goods, payment for which is by five or more credit instalments.
Debenture	This is the term used to describe both the debts, and the document creating them, given by companies.
Defendant	The person against whom an action is brought.
Delegatus non potest delegare	A delegate cannot himself delegate.

Equity	A body of rules created alongside the original common law, which claimed moral superiority.
Expressio unius est exclusio alterius	Express mention of one thing excludes all others.
Fiduciary	A relationship between two people akin to that of a trustee and beneficiary. The person in such a position has to use any powers in good faith in the interest of the other.
Gazette or *The London Gazette*	Government publication in which legal notices are published.
Gratuitous	Unpaid.
Habeas corpus	Right to be produced before a Court.
Hansard	Specific Parliamentary reports.
Hire purchase	An agreement for the hire of goods under which the hirer has an option to purchase.
Imperitia culpae adnumeratur	Inexperience is taken into account when assessing the standard of care in negligence.
Inter alia	Among other (things).
Interests	Rights and duties in respect of that thing.
Joint tortfeasors	Those who are jointly and severally (independently) liable for the damage caused.
Judgment creditor	This is a person who has been awarded a judgment against another person for a particular sum of money.
Justinian	Roman emperor and lawyer.
Laches	This is an unreasonable delay in taking legal action to enforce rights. The rights are lost as a consequence of the delay. As an example the right to rescind a contract for misrepresentation may be lost due to delay.
Lien	The right to hold the property of another as security for a debt owed.
Litigation	A case before the Court.
Mortgage	The transfer of an interest in land to secure a debt.
Nemo dat quod non habet	No one can pass on a good title to that which he does not own (the law identifies exceptions to this rule).
Non est factum	This literally means 'not his deed' and arises where a person signs a document without knowing its true nature. The document may not be enforced if this defence is successful.
Notary	A person who can attest deeds and legal documents (usually also a solicitor).
Notice of default	Notice bringing the fault to the attention of the debtor.

Novation	In effect this is an agreement whereby a third party replaces an existing party to a contract. In fact a new contract between the original party and the third party replaces the contract between the original parties. The agreement of all of the parties concerned is required.
Novus actus interveniens	A new intervening act which breaks the chain of causation in negligence.
Nudum pactum	This simply means a 'naked agreement', in other words an agreement without consideration; and as such it is unenforceable.
Obiter dicta	Other declarations made by the judge, which are not fundamentals to the case in hand.
Pari passu	Where debentures are issued *pari passu*, it means that they are to be treated equally without preference as regards repayment.
Parol	This means by word of mouth, and applies to contracts which are created otherwise than in writing or under seal.
Parties	People suing or being sued.
Per incuriam	With inaccuracy through oversight.
Per se	By itself.
Plaintiff	One who brings an action in Court.
Poll	This is a procedure for voting at company meetings other than by a show of hands. Usually each share has one vote and a person can vote to the extent of his shareholdings.
Prima facie	This literally means 'at first appearance' and it relates to cases where some presumption will be applied unless the contrary is proved. For example contracts in restraint of trade are *prima facie* void, unless shown to be valid.
Proxy	This is a person deputed to vote for another.
Quantum meruit	This literally means 'as much as he has earned' and it applies, either where no rate of payment has been established under a contract, or where a party has only performed part of their contractual undertaking. In the latter case the party cannot claim under contract for the simple reason that they have not performed their part of the agreement fully, but they may still be able to claim as much as they deserve for what they have actually done.
Quasi-contract	The major difference between this source of action and contract is that this action is not based on agreement. The law simply enforces a right to payment under particular circumstances.
Quorum	The minimum number of persons required to constitute a valid meeting.
Ratification	Adoption of a contract by a person not originally bound by that agreement.

Ratio decidendi	The reason for a decision based on the material facts of the case.
Re	In the matter of.
Res ipsa loquitur	The thing speaks for itself; this applies wherever it is improbable that the accident would have occurred in the absence of negligence.
Respondent	The party against whom an appeal is brought.
Statute	An Act of Parliament.
Statutory copy	Copy of a document which is required by statute.
Strict liability	Liability without proof of fault.
Sub-agent	Agent of an agent for purposes connected with the original agency contract.
Tort	A civil wrong.
Ultra vires	Outside the authority of.
Volenti non fit injuria	Where a person expressly or impliedly consents to the act causing the damage, there can be no actionable tort.
Waiver	To renounce the benefit of something.

Index
of cases

Index of cases

Index of Statutes

Subject index